Making Ends Meet: Congressional Budgeting in the Age of Deficits

Making Ends Meet: Congressional Budgeting in the Age of Deficits

Daniel P. Franklin
Georgia State University

A Division of Congressional Quarterly Inc.
Washington, D.C.

Cover design: Dan C. Royer

1414 22nd Street, N.W., Washington, D.C. 20037

Printed in the United States of America

Library of Congress Cataloging-in-Publication Data

Franklin, Daniel P.
Making ends meet : congressional budgeting in the age of deficits / Daniel P. Franklin.
p. cm.
Includes bibliographical references and index.
ISBN 0-87187-717-1 -- ISBN 0-87187-656-6 (pbk.)
1. Budget--United States. 2. Budget deficits--United States.
I. Title.
HJ2051.F73 1992
353.0072'2--dc20 92-33123
CIP

Contents

TABLES

FIGURES

Preface

Ever since I began teaching courses on Congress, I have considered it important to give students a sense of not only the structure but also the flow of the legislative process. At the same time, I have felt the need to respond to the astonishing amount of misinformation about the budget process that appears in the popular press. With these two goals in mind I decided to write this book, a story of the budget process for one fiscal cycle that culminated in the final 1992 federal budget.

Most of the work of Congress is associated in one way or another with the budget. Congress marches to the rhythm of the fiscal year and the budget process follows its imperative. Representing this process in a way meaningful to students presents quite a challenge. Instead of the standard textbook approach, I decided that the budget process would be best understood if introduced in chronological and narrative form.

With this in mind, *Making Ends Meet: Congressional Budgeting in the Age of Deficits* is divided into three parts. The introduction and first two chapters offer short descriptions of the legislative and budget processes in Congress as they stood prior to the 1990 budget agreement. This basic information on the congressional process, as well as the context in which decisions were made in 1990-1991, prepares the reader to understand the narrative that is to come. The next eight chapters, or Part II, make up the heart of the book, telling a story that is both simple and complex. Opening in September 1990 with the start of Congress's budgetary work and closing in November 1991 when the final bill was passed, Chapters 3-10 trace the authorizations, appropriations, budget resolution, mandatory deficit reduction, and reconciliation of the fiscal 1992 budget. As much as teach about the budget process, these chapters provide a flavor of the legislative process, institutional roles and influences, and the politics behind the budget. Finally, in Part III—the last chapter and epilogue—I evaluate the success of procedural reforms and also proposals for future change.

In telling this story, I have made a number of decisions concerning scope and coverage. My rule of thumb for these editorial choices has been to include all the details that are essential and some of the minutiae that are interesting. My intent has been to focus on Congress through the prism of the budget process, rather than the reverse. Many of the highs and lows of legislative policy making are outlined, including some of the less-than-pleasant foibles of the modern Congress. Nevertheless, this is also the story of what I am convinced is an institution in which the vast majority of members are devoted public servants. The legislative process is not pristine, but then neither is the human heart.

This book was conceived in the classroom, made possible by the American Political Science Association Congressional Fellowship Program, and born on Capitol Hill. There are many people and organizations to whom I feel indebted in the preparation of this book. In particular, I would like to recognize the vital contribution made by the American Political Science Association through its annual Congressional Fellowship Program. As an APSA congressional fellow, I had access to events in the congressional budget process that are rarely observed by outsiders. Kay Sterling, director of the fellowship program, and its corporate sponsor, MCI, deserve kudos for providing this unique opportunity to a small group of relatively junior scholars every year. I would like to convey my special greetings and best wishes to the other members of my congressional fellowship "class."

I would like give special thanks to Rep. Larry Smith and Sen. Tom Harkin and their staffs. In particular, I appreciated the opportunity to tap the legislative expertise of Representative Smith's legislative director, Bob Dobek, whose patience and good humor were unfailing. Marc Pearl, Representative Smith's administrative assistant, also provided valuable guidance and help. Others on Representative Smith's staff who assisted me were Lucy Herman, Karin Walser, Miamah Braddox, and Jane Blair. Matt Littman's advice and experience were inspirational.

On Sen. Tom Harkin's staff I would like to thank Kay Casstevens and Ed Long, the senator's administrative assistant and legislative director, respectively, as well as legislative assistants Phil Buchan and Jim Sweeney. Shelley Seddon, also of Senator Harkin's staff, was willing to lend a hand at crucial moments in the preparation of this text.

I would like to reserve a separate paragraph to recognize the contribution to this book of two of the most dedicated civil servants on Capitol Hill. Tom Pines, formerly of Representative Smith's staff, was always willing to let me tag along on projects related to the budget process that were in his area of responsibility. We are lucky as taxpayers to have Tom Pines, who is currently working for Rep. Mel Levine, on our team. Rich Bender, on Senator Harkin's staff, was an invaluable resource for me. There is simply no one else on Capitol Hill who knows as much about the budget process as he does.

I often relied on Julie Dwyer and Nancy Kirshner of the Democratic National Committee, whose keen political insights were extremely helpful.

At Colgate University, I would like to thank Dean Charles Trout and President Neil Grabois for their assistance in financing this project. I would further like to thank the administration at Georgia State University for giving me leave to complete the manuscript.

The editorial suggestions and comments of Professors Lawrence Dodd, Ross Baker, and Leroy Rieselbach were useful and instructive and have ultimately become part of this book. Finally, last but certainly not least, I would like to thank Brenda Carter, Ann O'Malley, and the editorial staff at CQ Press. Brenda has all the attributes of a great editor. She knows the topic as well as the market, she recognized the value of this project, and she has the patience and good humor to guide a project to a timely and successful conclusion. Ann was skillful and pleasant in guiding the book through the editorial process.

PART I

Evolution of the Budgetary Process

INTRODUCTION

Running on Empty: The Search for Deficit Control

"Lord, What Fools These Mortals be!" *A Midsummer-Night's Dream*
(Inscribed below a statue of Puck facing the U.S. Capitol)

On Thursday evening, March 7, 1991, Rep. Jim Slattery (D-Kan.) rose on the floor of the House of Representatives to offer an amendment that in many ways captures in microcosm the pitfalls and pratfalls of the modern budget process. It was the end of a hard legislative week. The attention of the House had been focused on a bill that would provide the funding necessary to finance Operation Desert Storm. Slattery's amendment took the House from the gravest decisions to the ridiculous. In doing so, he and his Republican cosponsor from Ohio, John Kasich, were trying to make a point that was far from a joke. Something needed to be done, they argued, to plug the multitude of leaks that were draining the nation's coffers. Slattery and Kasich were going to start by eliminating what they saw as one of the most symptomatic examples of waste in the budget. As Representative Slattery put it,

> We are talking about deleting $500,000 that was included in the Agriculture, rural development, and related agencies appropriations bill that was passed last year. This money, as the Members may recall, was included in a conference committee report in the late hours of the session. It did not receive any review by the House committee, by a subcommittee, or by a Senate committee or subcommittee meeting by itself.[1]

The $500,000 appropriation to which Slattery referred was intended to fund a German-Russian Interpretive Center, a museum at the birthplace of bandleader Lawrence Welk in North Dakota.

But what may seem to be just plain common-sense fiscal responsibility may not be so clear when viewed in the context of the congressional budget process. Rep. Jamie Whitten (D-Miss.), chair of the powerful House Appropriations Committee, chair of the Agriculture subcommittee that had jurisdiction over the Lawrence Welk grant, and senior member of the House, rose in opposition to the Slattery amendment. Whitten reminded Slattery and his young cosponsor from Ohio about some of the facts of life in the congressional budget process:

> May I say that we have a national program in which we have tried to help communities throughout the country. I have some mighty good friends from North Dakota, folks that I have served with, Mr. Dorgan (D-N.D.) and others. They are the best ones to decide how they wish to do those things.[2]

Whitten went on to issue a not so subtle threat:

> I know that my friend, the gentleman from Kansas [Mr. Slattery], means well. Now, this committee received this letter on March 5, from the gentleman. He wants us to add $5 million for a project in Kansas for—What is it? What is the word here? Oh, this is for the hall of fame in Kansas. But he is against this rural development project in North Dakota. I just cannot understand his position.[3]

The project Chairman Whitten was referring to was Slattery's request for $5 million in funding for a National Agricultural Hall of Fame at Bonner Springs, Kansas. Representative Kasich was not immune either. He was the cosponsor of a $516,000 appropriation for the restoration of President William McKinley's family home in Ohio.

The House ultimately approved Representative Slattery's amendment, but that is not the end of the story. In the Senate version of the bill the Slattery amendment was included. Nevertheless, the money for the Interpretive Center was eventually appropriated (as the Senate interpreted the Slattery amendment, it did not apply to all aspects of the North Dakota project). When application was made to the Department of Agriculture for the release of the funds, however, the application was rejected on the recommendation of the president's Office of Management and Budget. Ultimately the funds, although appropriated, were not spent on that particular project. Parenthetically, probably in retaliation for Rep. Slattery's amendment, the Appropriations Committee cut $3.7 million slated for a Plant Science Center at Kansas State University in his congressional district.

In this story resides almost every twist and turn of the congressional budget process writ large. The money was never spent, but only because the administration blocked the project. Nevertheless, it is likely that just as the German-Russian Interpretive Center was blocked, other similar requests were quietly approved. Representative Slattery managed to succeed in this consciousness-raising exercise, but at the expense of an appropriation that was slated for his own district. Was this act of congressional "theater" worth the price? Probably not for Slattery. He and other members similarly inclined will probably think twice before resorting to the same tactics again. The congressional pork barrel rests on much too precarious a foundation to be jostled by junior members.

In order to understand the delicate balance that makes it so difficult to delete funding for such a seemingly superfluous project in North Dakota, it is necessary to examine the budget process from beginning to end. These kinds of appropriations do not appear out of the blue, nor do they survive because the congressional system is corrupt or beset by special interests. The appropriation for the German-Russian Interpretive Center in North Dakota is the product of a complex pattern of compromise that annually produces the federal budget.

This book is a case study of one budget cycle. As such it attempts to examine the context from which emerge such projects as the Agricultural Hall of Fame in Kansas. More to the point, the book documents the rhythm of congressional life. Congress is an institution driven by three different calendars: the biennial electoral cycle, the calendar year, and the fiscal year. The quest for reelection drives much of the members' constituent activities and "homestyle." The calendar year marks the beginning and end of the congressional session. But the heart of the legislative process is the fiscal year. Because a significant percentage of legislation has some kind of connection with the federal budget, much of the scheduling and politics of the legislative process is directly tied to the rhythm of the fiscal year.

There is always a danger in making generalizations based on an individual case. The adoption of the fiscal year 1992 budget was in many ways unique. In constructing this budget, Congress was operating for the first time under the strictures of a new process imposed by the 1990 budget agreement. A discussion of "fire walls," "spending caps," or "pay-as-you-go" budgeting—cornerstones of the 1990 budget accord—may or may not have enormous significance in comparing 1992 with 1996. But one commonality that will almost certainly exist from one budget cycle to the next for the foreseeable future is the rhythm of the fiscal year. The winter will always signal the State of the Union address and presentation of the president's budget. The spring will always bring authorizations, committee "marks," and the budget resolution. The summer will be the season of appropriation bills and compromises in conference. The fall will signify the rush to finish before the September 30 end of the fiscal year.

For the student of congressional process, this book is not only a lesson in timing but also a practical examination of how things get done in Congress. It is a frank, nonjudgmental examination of how the goods of the institution are distributed. One hopes that the reader will come away from this book with a better understanding of the legislative process as well as a more subtle appreciation of just how closely the budget process is linked to the lives of ordinary citizens.

FIGURE I-1 Budgetary Cycle, Fiscal Year 1991

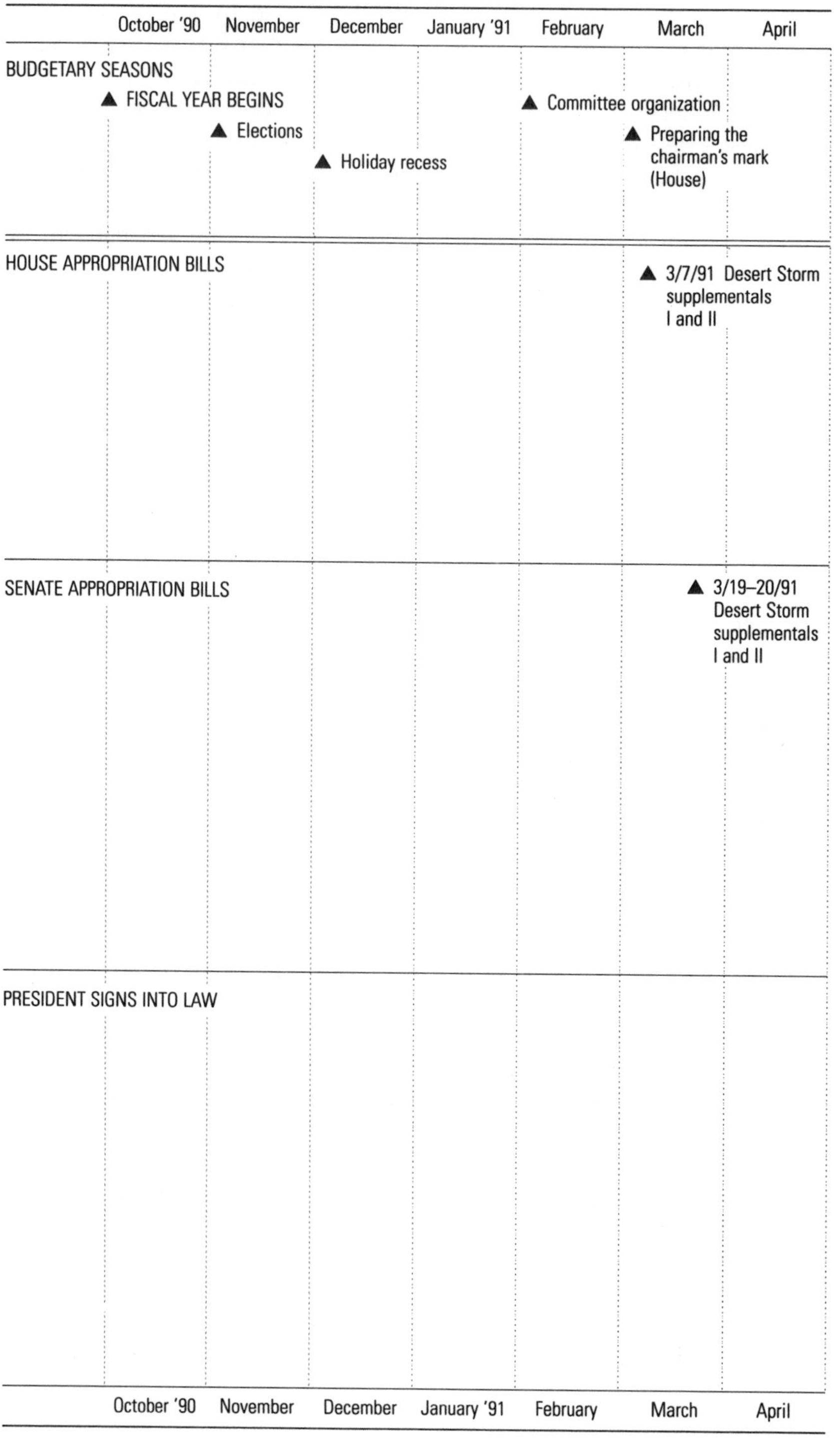

	October '90	November	December	January '91	February	March	April
BUDGETARY SEASONS	▲ FISCAL YEAR BEGINS	▲ Elections	▲ Holiday recess		▲ Committee organization	▲ Preparing the chairman's mark (House)	
HOUSE APPROPRIATION BILLS						▲ 3/7/91 Desert Storm supplementals I and II	
SENATE APPROPRIATION BILLS						▲ 3/19–20/91 Desert Storm supplementals I and II	
PRESIDENT SIGNS INTO LAW							
	October '90	November	December	January '91	February	March	April

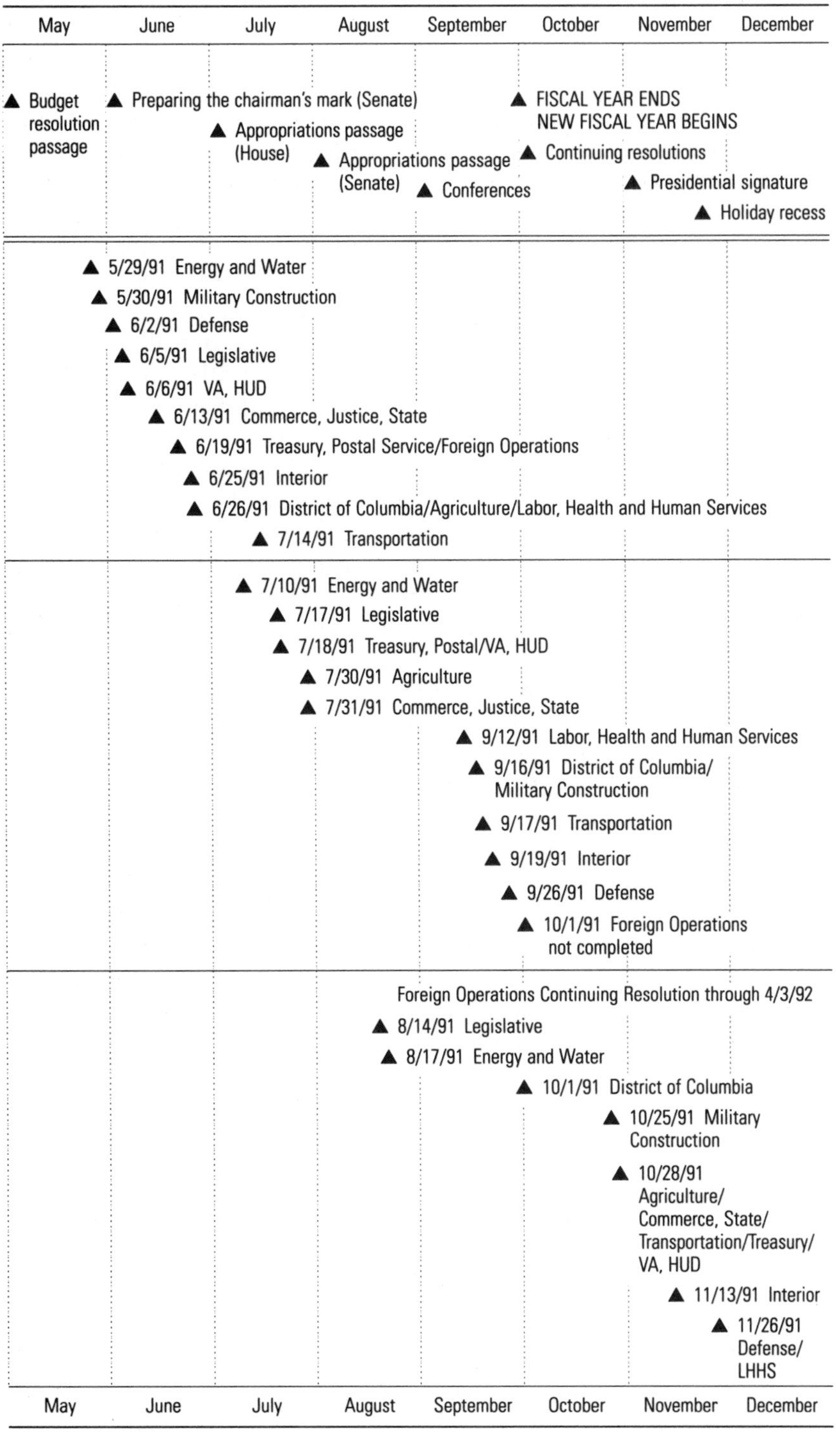

May | June | July | August | September | October | November | December

▲ Budget resolution passage
▲ Preparing the chairman's mark (Senate)
▲ Appropriations passage (House)
▲ Appropriations passage (Senate)
▲ Conferences
▲ FISCAL YEAR ENDS
NEW FISCAL YEAR BEGINS
▲ Continuing resolutions
▲ Presidential signature
▲ Holiday recess

▲ 5/29/91 Energy and Water
▲ 5/30/91 Military Construction
▲ 6/2/91 Defense
▲ 6/5/91 Legislative
▲ 6/6/91 VA, HUD
▲ 6/13/91 Commerce, Justice, State
▲ 6/19/91 Treasury, Postal Service/Foreign Operations
▲ 6/25/91 Interior
▲ 6/26/91 District of Columbia/Agriculture/Labor, Health and Human Services
▲ 7/14/91 Transportation

▲ 7/10/91 Energy and Water
▲ 7/17/91 Legislative
▲ 7/18/91 Treasury, Postal/VA, HUD
▲ 7/30/91 Agriculture
▲ 7/31/91 Commerce, Justice, State
▲ 9/12/91 Labor, Health and Human Services
▲ 9/16/91 District of Columbia/
Military Construction
▲ 9/17/91 Transportation
▲ 9/19/91 Interior
▲ 9/26/91 Defense
▲ 10/1/91 Foreign Operations
not completed

Foreign Operations Continuing Resolution through 4/3/92
▲ 8/14/91 Legislative
▲ 8/17/91 Energy and Water
▲ 10/1/91 District of Columbia
▲ 10/25/91 Military
Construction
▲ 10/28/91
Agriculture/
Commerce, State/
Transportation/Treasury/
VA, HUD
▲ 11/13/91 Interior
▲ 11/26/91
Defense/
LHHS

May | June | July | August | September | October | November | December

The story of the budget is not just about the appropriation of money. If that were the case, the design of the federal budget could be left to accountants. The budget is the structure of policy that has a very real effect on people's lives. All too often, especially in this age of deficits, we tend to forget that the government was not created to save or spend dollars but rather to better the lives of its citizens.

In that sense, the title of this book, *Making Ends Meet,* is both an accurate and a misleading reflection of what goes on in adopting the federal budget. Budget balancing is only one of the ends Congress strives to meet. In fact, many of the ends Congress tries to meet in adopting the budget are irreconcilable. For example, there is no limit to the number of worthy projects that deserve federal funding. However, *Not Making Ends Meet* would make a less effective title (and would not be entirely accurate anyhow), so the reader will have to plumb the depths of this rather cryptic but descriptive title.

The reader should be cautioned that what follows is not a textbook, civics-class description of the legislative process. Because members of Congress are only human, the politics of Congress is rife with examples of unbridled ambition, thoughtlessness, compromised morals, and the incumbent cynicism that come from the frustrations of the legislative process. At the same time, however, I hope to demonstrate that there exists on Capitol Hill a kind of rough justice in which the hopes, demands, and dreams of citizens are generally served.

This volume is divided into three parts. Chapters 1 and 2 in Part I are a brief introduction to the history of the U.S. budget, the legislative process in Congress, and the context in which the budget for fiscal year 1991 was forged. Figure I-1 on pages 6 and 7 is a rough schematic of the fiscal year. Part II is devoted to a month-by-month description of the budget process for one year. While the process does not always conform exactly to the calendar, a rough relationship always exists between the budgetary cycle and the stage of the legislative process. Finally, in Part III, the last chapter is a brief summary of some of the effects of the 1990 budget reform and an examination of some proposals for reform, most prominently the balanced-budget amendment and line-item veto.

NOTES

1. *Congressional Record,* March 7, 1991, H1538.
2. Ibid.
3. Ibid.

CHAPTER 1

The Budget Process: The Crucible in Which Policy Is Forged

So much is written about the various components of the federal budget process that we often miss the forest for the trees. The federal budget is the monetary manifestation, or a sort of skeletal structure of our political system and public philosophy. In fact, the budget is more reflective of our political philosophy than are the many issues that so often capture the public's attention when debated in Congress. The flag-burning issue, prayer in school, and the ever-present abortion controversy are primarily attempts by members of Congress to gain political advantage. In the main, however, most of the issues about which important decisions are made and important compromises reached are related to the budget. A member of Congress who brings to the floor a constitutional amendment to ban abortion, knowing full well that the resolution doesn't have a chance, wouldn't dream of playing the same game with an appropriation bill that is dear to his district or near to his heart. The budget process is a deadly serious game in which the hopes of members and their constituencies can be rewarded or dashed on the rocks of stalwart opposition or bungled tactics. In the congressional budget process timing, strategy, institutional position, and legislative skill become crucial elements in the dispensing of the country's favors.

Some of what an examination of the budget process reveals will come as a surprise to even the well-informed observer of national politics. For example, it shows that *there are remarkable levels of consensus in American politics.* Since the end of World War II, Congress has never changed the president's aggregate budget request by more than 2 percent. We shouldn't be surprised by this. The perception has been fostered in the media and by our electoral, partisan politics that there are tremendous ideological, deep-seated disagreements in Congress over matters of policy. However, the budget process and its outcomes reflect the most profound levels of concord in American society and some of the most important trends in this century and the last. The budgetary outcomes tell us that we almost universally support a special type of free market liberalism. A study of the history of the budget process tells us that in the last two centuries, at first slowly and rapidly accelerating in the twentieth century, there has been a relative shift in power and resources from the states to the federal government, and within the national government itself a shift in control over policy from Congress to the president and the executive branch.

Our examination of the adoption of one budget during one fiscal year will tell us something about how the budget process works in Congress, and just as importantly, it will provide a snapshot of how Congress works in the last decade of the twentieth century. The budget process is in microcosm (if this can be said about a budget that authorizes expenditures of a trillion and a half dollars) representative of the politics of Congress and the political philosophy of the United States frozen for a moment of time in terms of dollars and cents.

POLITICAL PHILOSOPHY

The United States is a liberal nation, not necessarily driven by the liberalism of the left (although that is part of it) but by the liberalism of Adam Smith and John Locke. It is no historical accident that Smith's *Wealth of Nations* was published in the same year the Declaration of Independence was issued. In the eighteenth century the United States became the quintessential expression of the liberal ethic. In everything from the nature of its free economy to the structure of its government, the United States served as an example of the possibilities of a liberal, democratic, republican state.

From the beginning, however, it was apparent that monumental problems were being caused by the original design of the American government. Under the Articles of Confederation the federal government had no independent taxing authority nor little to do with the regulation of trade. This lack of revenue and influence led to chaos, as largely independent state legislatures began to adopt regulations that resulted in restraint of trade on a national scale. This was particularly devastating at a time when the departure of the British forced American manufacturers to look inward for markets and raw materials. The territorial ambitions of European colonial powers and domestic political unrest strained to the limit the ability of the central government to provide for domestic tranquillity and national defense.

When a group of prominent citizens met in 1787 in Philadelphia to reform the Articles of Confederation they took into account their liberal precepts leavened by having experienced life under colonial rule and the rule of state legislatures. What they came up with was a Constitution that represents a revolution in balance. In exchange for creating a federal government fully empowered to levy taxes and enforce its demands, the Framers created a political system that was so fragmented as to negate some of the effect of centralization of power. This institutional design is reflected to this day in the legislative process. Bills in Congress reflect not only programmatic concerns but also the multiple layers of representation that were built into the original Constitution. For example, rural concerns are more heavily represented in the Senate, while large state, urban interests are more likely to be represented in the House. This bias is played out in budgetary negotiations, so that the Interior Department, with its responsibilities for public lands (located primarily in the lightly populated West), is more likely to do well financially in the Senate than in the House—for the fiscal year 1990, $5.7 billion as opposed to $5.3 billion. There is, of course, a lot more to this process. Also at work are dynamics that make the Senate in some ways more liberal and in other ways less liberal than the House of Representatives, all of which has something to do with the institutional design of the houses of Congress under the Constitution. Election cycles, term lengths, special constitutional grants of power, and the internal design of the institution all contribute to and are reflected in the outlines of the budget.

The liberal philosophy in respect to government is best summed up by Jefferson's oft-quoted remark that "the government that governs best governs least." Indeed, throughout the late eighteenth and nineteenth centuries, the budget reflected this general philosophy. In fact, until the New Deal, which represented a revolution in the role of government, the federal budget was a relatively small percentage of the gross national product.[1] For example, in 1929 the federal budget was about 3 percent of the GNP, while by 1990 that figure was closer to 24 percent. The first federal budget in 1790 allocated the expenditure of about $7 million, or a little over $1 billion in current dollars, while the budget for 1993 is projected to commit about $1.5 trillion in outlays.[2]

What changed in the interim, between the founding of the Republic and the founding of the welfare state, was a transformation in our basic political philosophy.[3] Although in the margins of the American body politic one can still find those who prefer an unfettered economic market or, at the opposite end of the spectrum, a planned economy, the opinions of the public and their representatives largely fall somewhere in between. While, for the most part, we accept the outcomes associated with and the advantages of a free market system, we are willing to sacrifice some of the benefits of an unrestricted economy in order to ensure that the poor and the sick are taken care of, that certain pursuits in the areas of national defense or scientific and artistic endeavor are funded, and that monopoly pricing or unsafe products are eliminated from the market.

There is almost universal agreement on the overriding value of most of these goals. Even the most conservative politicians, for example, Ronald Reagan, will come to admit the need for a "safety net" in society for those who have fallen on hard times or who are working to overcome disabilities not of their own making. What constitutes a disability, however, or a project worthy of funding is a matter of great dispute. The budget process is an annual debate about national priorities, most of which we agree about, a few of which we do not. The budget reflects and balances this enormous set of complex and conflicting values. It should again be noted that although disagreements over the budget reflect the parameters of debate in American society, the budget process also represents a high degree of consensus over things political in our society as a whole. The fact is that the vast majority of expenditures are adopted in an atmosphere of near unanimity.

GENERAL TRENDS IN BUDGETING

Article I, Section 8 of the Constitution directs that "the Congress shall have the power to lay and collect Taxes, Duties, Imports and Excises, to pay the Debts and provide for the common Defence and general Welfare of the United States." Furthermore, the Constitution requires that "All Bills for raising revenue shall originate in the House of Representatives; but the Senate may propose or concur with Amendments as on other Bills" (Article I, Section 7), and that "No money shall be drawn from the Treasury but in consequence of Appropriations made by law" (Article I, Section 9). Over time, the de facto alteration of this construct has come to reflect the changing realities of the American political system. Specifically, the transformation of the budget process has demonstrated the rising status and influence of the presidency in American politics.

The history of the federal government in the nineteenth century was the story of its adaptation to dramatically changing conditions. The 1800s spanned the transformation of the United States from an agricultural backwater to an industrial giant and world class military power. With this transformation came the growth and evolution of the federal government. When most of the economy was localized, when the United States did not clash with distant powers, the federal government was relatively unimportant. Aspiring politicians sought to build their careers in the state capitals where the truly important decisions of government were being made. This fact was reflected during the first half of the nineteenth century in the high rate of turnover (mainly through voluntary retirement) of members of Congress.[4]

The Civil War catapulted the federal government into the forefront of the American economy. The war not only established, once and for all, the federal government's supremacy over the states but also had the effect of kicking off the industrial revolution in the northern states. The result was a tremendous growth in responsibilities and complexities of the tasks confronting the federal government. For example, the power of Congress "to regulate Commerce with foreign Nations, and among the several States" (Article I, Section 8) was relatively unimportant when most of the trade was intrastate. However, the rise of the modernized industrial state meant that Congress was increasingly responsible for regulating trade and managing the economy. In an attempt to smooth over the effects of inevitable fluctuations in the free market economy and to protect so-called infant industries within the United States from foreign competition, Congress used fiscal policy and its taxing authority to manage the economy. It was quickly recognized that the federal government was a major player in managing the performance of the economy.

In the early 1800s, when the federal budget was small and of little consequence to the economy, Congress had little trouble managing the budgetary process. However, the centrifugal forces of an institution based on local representation made it difficult for Congress to coordinate fiscal policy. In addition, the expansion of governmental activities and an increase in the sheer scale of the federal government after the Civil War made it difficult for Congress to play a coordinating role in drawing up a budget. In order to deal with the complexity of the budgetary process, prior to the Civil War, Congress began to divide its annual appropriation bill into a number of separate pieces of legislation. For example, in 1856 Congress passed separate appropriation measures for the three branches of government and also for a number of special projects such as roads and waterway construction. In addition, the responsibility for budgeting began to be parceled out to a number of different committees. For example, immediately after the Civil War the Ways and Means Committee was stripped of everything but its taxing and tariff authorities. At the same time, a separate Appropriations Committee was established to take up the slack. It, too, was slowly stripped of its responsibilities by other committees of Congress that were to make appropriations on their own. The problem with this fragmentation—one that has yet to be overcome even to this day—was that in order to get a majority in Congress to pass an appropriation bill, it was a relatively uncomplicated task to guarantee a majority simply by ensuring that at least half the membership, preferably two-thirds (in anticipation of a presidential veto), had a direct incentive to vote for the measure. In order to enlist this widespread support, as many members as were necessary for safe passage were guaranteed a portion of the goods the bill had to offer. Members and their committees traded support in the form of "logrolling," which remains characteristic of the modern Congress. Fiscal responsibility in such an environment of fragmentation and vote trading was all but impossible. As President Chester Arthur observed in vetoing a public works bill in 1882, it appeared that "as the bill becomes more objectionable, it secures more support." [5]

Particularly exorbitant in the second half of the nineteenth century were spending bills intended to provide pensions for war veterans. Members of Congress viewed the awarding of veterans' benefits as a simple and seemingly patriotic way to reward constituents. From the national budgetary perspective, however, veterans' pensions (many of which were undeserved) represented a substantial, long-term financial commitment. For example, so generous was the nineteenth-century Congress in granting these pensions that the last Revolutionary War benefit was paid out in 1906! [6] In his first term in office, President Grover Cleveland vetoed 241 special pension bills passed by Congress to provide benefits for individuals (another 42 were pocket vetoed).[7]

By the end of the century, the president was popularly regarded as the protector of the national treasury. Nevertheless, Congress was still reluctant to share its budgetary prerogatives with the president, who only gradually came to play a substantial role in the budgetary process. Several times in the late nineteenth century, in an attempt to smooth over the effects of a series of economic downturns, the president began to take it upon himself to coordinate and oversee budgetary requests made to Congress by executive agencies.[8] In 1873, in the midst of an economic depression, the chairman of the House Appropriations Committee sponsored a bill that would have given full responsibility to President Ulysses Grant for revising downward the estimates of requests for appropriations submitted by the executive departments. Congress, however, was still predisposed to bypass the president in assigning budgetary responsibilities to the executive branch. In fact, it was much more likely that Congress would grant authority to oversee the formulation of budget proposals to the Treasury Department, whose secretary was beholden to the Senate that confirmed him.

In the latter half of the nineteenth century various attempts were made to centralize and transfer control of budget proposals to the executive branch. These proposals were inevitably blocked by a Congress that saw such moves as a raid on its constitutional authority. In 1909, however, the situation began to change. After running a budgetary surplus for twenty-eight uninterrupted years (before 1903), the federal government encountered a series of peacetime deficits (six, to be exact). Investigations were initiated to learn the cause of the shortfalls.

In addition to declining customs revenues and the cost of the Panama Canal, which contributed significantly to the debt, it was discovered that executive departments were operating at a high level of inefficiency. Congress ordered the secretary of the treasury to estimate revenue shortfalls and, if deficits seemed likely to occur, recommend ways to reduce appropriations. In 1911, as the budget crisis deepened, President William Howard Taft issued Executive Order 1142, prohibiting lower-level division heads from directly applying to Congress for funding without first clearing requests with their department secretaries. In addition, President Taft took it upon himself to review departmental requests for budgeting. In 1912 a special Commission on Economy and Efficiency recommended that the executive branch assume sole responsibility for presenting a comprehensive budget to the legislature. Nevertheless, that same year, events conspired against adoption of the commission's recommendations. A dramatic increase in revenues that created a surplus and the likelihood that Taft would not be reelected obviated the need and the incentive to transfer budgetary powers to the executive. In fact, when Taft attempted to implement the commission's recommendations, Congress acted by requiring department heads to submit budget estimates directly to Congress.

In our modern era of presidential budgets, it may be difficult to understand Congress's reluctance at the turn of the century to allow the president to make mere proposals for expenditures, even though it retained the right to pass appropriation bills. This reluctance on the part of Congress was, to some extent, a function of the politics of the day, but it was also a function of constitutional design. To allow the president to draw up the budget would allow him to set a budgetary agenda. Congress feared that it would lose control over the character and priorities of executive-branch agencies. These fears, as we shall see, were not entirely unfounded. In ceding authority to draw up budgets, as it eventually did, Congress ceded much of its budgetary and thus its policy primacy that is guaranteed under the Constitution.

In just three years, U.S. involvement in World War I increased the size of the federal budget from about $700 million in 1916 to $20 billion in 1919. The corresponding budget deficits were unprecedented. Proposals again began to surface to centralize the process for budget initiation. At first President Woodrow Wilson opposed a plan for allowing the president to draw up a national budget (his Democratic party platform opposed any budget proposal that would erode the power of the Democratic majority in Congress). However, in 1919 a select House Committee on the Budget in Congress recommended the establishment of a Budget Bureau in the Office of the President to coordinate the formulation of a national budget. That same year Wilson finally announced his support for the presidential submission of a national budget. In 1920 Congress adopted a bill that authorized the establishment of a Bureau of the Budget, but Wilson vetoed the legislation because it permitted Congress alone to remove certain budgetary officers (the comptroller general and assistant comptroller general). Wilson viewed this as a violation of the president's appointment powers under the Constitution. Congress could not muster enough votes to override the veto.[9]

In 1921, with a Republican majority in Congress and a new Republican president, Congress passed, and Warren Harding signed, the Budget and Accounting Act of 1921, which provided for the establishment of a Bureau of the Budget within the Department of the Treasury. The budget director was to be appointed by the president and serve under close presidential supervision. The bureau was granted the authority to "assemble, correlate, revise, reduce, or increase the estimates" and thus present to Congress the budget proposals of all the agencies of the federal government except for the Supreme Court and the legislative branch (whose estimates were to be submitted to Congress unadulterated). The workings and traditions of the Bureau of the Budget were very much the reflection of the bureau's first director, Charles G. Dawes, who believed that his role was to safeguard the Treasury by effecting savings. Almost immediately Dawes issued directives outlining procedures for cutting expenditures in the agencies. He made it clear that he would regard the appropriations of Congress as only ceilings on spending. Consequently, any measure that could be implemented to deliver government services below those budget ceilings would be carried out under the supervision of the Budget Bureau.

Dawes believed, perhaps naively, that the administration of the budget could be conducted in a nonpartisan manner and that his bureau's operations could be likened to those of a private enterprise. In government, however, the administration of public institutions requires making choices that affect public policy. Deciding to fund a program or establish priorities through funding one agency at the expense of another, or even to cut seemingly wasteful programs, involves decisions that are not made on the basis of cost efficiency (as guided by the invisible hand of the market) but rather on the basis of deciding what kind of public justice to deliver. It should not come as a surprise, therefore, that the history of the Budget Bureau—the Office of Management and Budget (OMB), as it came to be known in 1970—is in part a history of the increasing *power* of the bureau and in part a history of the increasing *partisanship* of what has become the modern president's OMB.[10]

In 1933 the bureau was given the authority "to make, waive, and modify the apportionments of appropriations."[11] This authority to decide how appropriated funds were to be apportioned at the subdepartmental level had previously been vested in the heads of the various departments and agencies. In 1939 the Budget Bureau itself was transferred from the Department of the Treasury to the newly created Executive Office of the President. This move directly associated the bureau with the policies of the president and also formalized the relationship between the president and the budget director by eliminating the intercession of the treasury secretary. It was the culmination of an almost hundred-year process that transferred to the president the power to propose the budget. Later the bureau gained even more authority over budget submissions as well as the actual execution of the budget. In 1950 the bureau was given formal authority to make sure that agencies, when spending their allocation, conformed to the "intent" of the law.[12]

By the early 1980s, the OMB not only controlled most agency requests for funding and oversaw the expenditure of appropriated funds, but it was also empowered to oversee and reject agency regulations (rules promulgated by agencies to interpret congressional intent, which are published in the *Federal Register*) for being cost-ineffective.[13] The OMB now has more than 500 permanent employees and an annual budget of about $50 million. As we shall see, the budget director has become a prime actor and partisan player in the budget process.[14]

Congress is still responsible for enacting appropriation legislation. However, the impetus and starting point for that legislation now resides, after a two-hundred-year process of transformation, in the Executive Office of the President. This is not an altogether inappropriate change. The transformation from a localized economy to an integrated welfare state has been reflected in the dramatically increased size of the federal budget (as a percentage of the gross national product) and a different set of priorities. Expenditures for national defense even in the aftermath of the cold war constitute about 25 percent of the budget, while entitlement programs or payments to individuals account for 45 percent. Increases in defense expenditures mirror the expansion of the president's power as commander-in-chief and the rise of the United States to superpower status. Expenditures for entitlements and regulatory purposes reflect the nationalization of the American economy and the imposition of national standards for environmental safety and personal well-being. Finally, as a legacy of deficit spending, roughly 15 percent of the budget is devoted to paying interest on the national debt. This, too, reflects a transformation. The increase in the debt over the last two decades reflects a natural inclination of voters to demand more services than they are willing to pay for and the electoral politics that are designed to service those demands. Clearly, the character of the federal budget tells us a lot about the philosophy and current condition of the American polity.

FIGURE 1-1 Budget Expenditures, Fiscal Year 1992

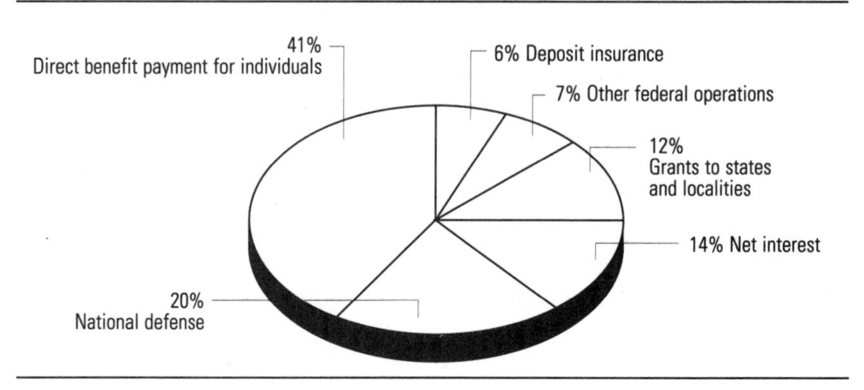

Source: OMB estimates cited in *Congressional Quarterly Weekly Report,* February 9, 1991, 333.

SPENDING IN THE FEDERAL BUDGET

The federal government spends money in a number of different ways. (See Figure 1-1.) The commonly accepted model of Congress appropriating money to each agency and program on a yearly basis, accounting for much of the expenditure side of the budget, is inaccurate. In the modern federal budget only 25 percent of the budget is considered "controllable" through the budget process. This means that the 75 percent of the budget that represents "uncontrollable" expenditures has to be reduced, increased, extended, or authorized through another mechanism. About 77 percent of uncontrollable expenditures are open-ended government commitments that exist in current law.[15] (See Figure 1-2.) For example, the Social Security Act establishes the conditions under which individuals are entitled to have access to the Social Security Trust Fund. It is impossible to make appropriations in advance for this entitlement because the size of expenditures does not depend on levels of appropriation but on how many people in a given year qualify for and claim Social Security benefits. While these payments are fairly predictable—the government has a fairly good idea of how many people are going to qualify on the basis of their age—a number of other entitlement payment levels are almost impossible to predict. For example, levels of unemployment assistance are a function of the performance of the economy. When a recession causes unemployment to rise, so do government obligations to pay for unemployment assistance. Another form of uncontrollable expenditure—about 23 percent of all uncontrollables—is the obligation undertaken by the government when entering into multiyear contracts. For example, the lead time for production of most military hardware extends well beyond the fiscal year.

FIGURE 1-2 Total Spending, Fiscal Year 1992 (in billions of dollars)

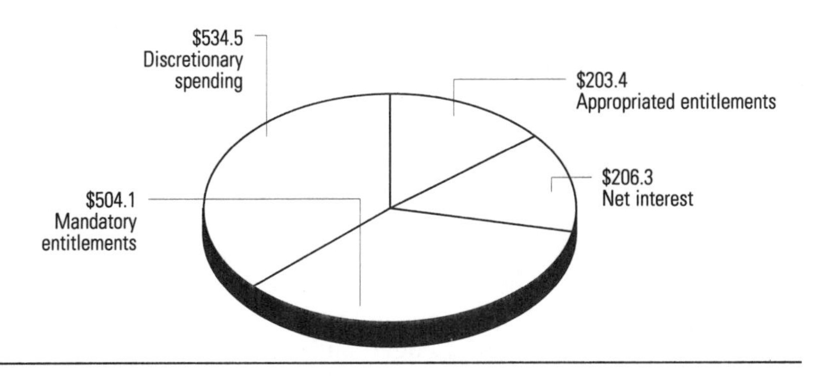

Source: OMB estimates cited in *Congressional Quarterly Weekly Report,* Special Report, December 7, 1991, 17.

The fact that entitlements and contract authorities are labeled uncontrollable is a misnomer and somewhat misleading. While Congress cannot control levels of eligibility in the population, it can control such levels under the law. For example, in the early 1980s the decision was made to delay a cost-of-living adjustment (COLA) for Social Security recipients, which led to immediate savings in outlays from the Social Security Trust Fund. The only way to control entitlement expenditures, therefore, is through a modification of eligibility requirements or a decision by Congress and the president to alter the government's obligations under the law. By the same token, the only way to reduce multiyear obligations is to cancel ongoing contracts.

It would be more accurate to say that, *politically,* entitlements are relatively uncontrollable. To restrict an existing entitlement is to take back from some segment of the population a benefit for which there was a previous government commitment. Voters do not look kindly on a reduction in government benefits and respond in a predictably hostile fashion to such suggestions. In the early 1980s the Reagan administration learned this lesson when it floated a trial balloon suggesting a freeze in Social Security cost-of-living increases. Republican candidates took a beating on this issue in the 1982 congressional elections, losing twenty-six seats in the House. Subsequently the administration sought "cover" for cost-of-living reductions by citing the recommendations of a bipartisan presidential commission appointed to study the Social Security program.

Of the rest of the expenditure side of the budget, the 25 percent labeled controllable, until lately roughly two-thirds was appropriated for national defense, with the rest devoted to civilian discretionary programs.[16] The fact that these programs are termed controllable is also something of a misnomer. While they are subject to the appropriations process, certain levels of national consensus exist with regard to defense spending and provision of society's safety net. Consequently, even controllable expenditures are relatively resistant to change through the political process.

There is another dimension to spending. Each year Congress approves expenditures in the form of budget "outlays" and "authorities." These outlays are disbursements from the federal Treasury in the form of checks or cash. For the purposes of determining the size of the deficit or surplus, budget outlays are balanced against government receipts. Outlays are in part a consequence of authority granted for the year in which they are spent and in part a consequence of authority granted in previous years. Budget authorities, therefore, are legal obligations that will result in outlays during the year in which they were adopted and/or in future years. Budget authorities may be in the form of contract authorities that obligate the government to pay for the completion of a specific project or multiyear authorities that commit the government to pay for a program for a specified period of time. Most but not all budget authority is approved as part of the appropriations process.

Recently, however, controversy has arisen over a number of bills passed by Congress that are not associated with the appropriations process but still obligate the government to make some kind of financial commitment. Altering benefit levels in entitlement programs or approving costly program changes are examples of backdoor spending. This tendency has created quite a bit of tension between the Appropriations Committee and other congressional committees that use nonbudget authorities as a way to bypass the appropriations process.

The fact that most federal programs represent a multiyear or even a permanent commitment creates a dilemma for Congress. Since the vast bulk of government expenditures is disbursed pursuant to long-term authorizations, there is some question about the democratic accountability of the budget process. On the one hand, in order to pursue certain goals, the government must make a multiyear commitment, but, on the other hand, multiyear or permanent authorities reduce the ability of current members of Congress to break the bonds placed on them in previous years. The fact is that multiyear budgeting limits Congress's ability to maneuver in adopting the budget, not only in terms of making cuts but also in terms of taking on new commitments responsive to changing conditions.

This last point also highlights one of the ways in which the budget reflects political philosophy and developments of the twentieth century. As the government has taken on wider and more complex commitments associated with a superpower foreign policy and the rise of the welfare state, Congress has increasingly lost control of the budget. Some of this control, as noted earlier, has been surrendered to the executive, but that is only part of the story. The growth in scale and complexity of the government's tasks has led to a general derogation of democratic control. Much of the responsibility for making policy now rests with the bureaucracy of the administrative state. One of the next great challenges for American democracy will be to reconcile the growth of the welfare state with the demands of democracy. Rationalizing the spending side of the budgetary process will be a crucial component of that task.

TAXING FOR THE BUDGET

All too often discussions of the budget implicitly or explicitly exclude considerations of the revenue side of budgeting. Yet issues of taxation constitute at least half of the equation in determining the size of the federal deficit (or surplus). With the personal income-tax rate at somewhere between 17 and 28 percent (even so, personal income taxes generate only 37 percent of all federal revenues), the taxation side of budgeting has a tremendous effect on the income as well as the behavior of individuals. The budget, therefore, is also a reflection of national attitudes toward issues of taxation. Perhaps the fact that we tend to focus on the expenditure (as opposed to the revenue) side of the budget is related to our having, as a nation, experienced budget deficits in thirty-one out of the last thirty-two years. The modern era of budgetary politics will probably come to be viewed, in retrospect, as the era in which the revenue side of the equation was integrated into the budget process as a whole. We will examine this new trend in budgeting as manifested in the increasingly common pay-as-you-go approach to appropriating.

Taxation is traditionally one of the most sensitive and controversial issues in American history. True to form, the sensitivity with which we view this issue is a reflection of our liberal precepts. One of the primary values of the liberal state is its regard for the protection of private property, which is enshrined in the Fifth Amendment to the Constitution proscribing the taking of "private property . . . for public use without just compensation." However, the fact that the state needs to generate revenues in order to operate and must violate absolute property rights to obtain those revenues engenders a national dilemma.

The Constitution also sanctions the levying of taxes. In its original form the Constitution imposed some unusual but—from the perspective of the Constitutional Convention—understandable restrictions on Congress's power to impose taxes. Article I, Section 8 provides "that Congress shall have power to lay and collect taxes, duties, imposts and excises, to pay the debts and provide for the common defense and general welfare of the United States." This broad grant of authority is later modified in the same section by the phrase "all duties, imposts and excises shall be uniform throughout the United States." This national standard is further modified in Article I, Section 9, which states that "no tax or duty shall be laid on articles exported from any state" [17] and that "no capitation, or other direct tax shall be laid, unless in proportion to the Census." This last restriction was a concession to the slave states at the Constitutional Convention. As these states were relatively sparsely populated (not counting slaves), in the imposition of taxes they would be at the mercy of larger state delegations in the House of Representatives, which was to be selected by proportional representation. (Please see note 18 for a further explanation of a "direct tax.")[18]

Throughout most of the nineteenth century the vast majority of revenues raised by the federal government was derived from customs charges and tariffs. In general, these sources of revenue were more than enough. From 1789 to 1894 the budget was in surplus with major exceptions recorded in times of war and economic recession. During the Civil War, when large deficits began to appear, the government looked to personal income taxes as a source of revenue. Individuals with annual incomes between $600 and $5000 paid a 5 percent income tax or 10 percent on incomes above that amount. The personal income tax was abolished in 1872, but not before its constitutionality was challenged in court. In the case of *Springer v. United States,* the Supreme Court was unanimously of the opinion that inasmuch as the income tax was not a direct tax, it thus was constitutional.[19] This seemed to settle the question of the legality of taxes until 1895 when the tax was again challenged in court.

In 1894 the Cleveland administration moved to lower tariffs in order to encourage trade. To make up for the corresponding shortfall in revenues, President Cleveland proposed a federal income tax that would levy a flat 2 percent tax on all annual incomes above $4000. Almost all forms of income were to be subject to this tax. In the case of *Pollock v. The Farmers' Loan and Trust Company,* the Supreme Court held that taxes on wages and salaries were constitutional.[20] However, because the Court also found that the tax on incomes derived from stocks and bonds was direct and therefore subject to apportionment, the entire tax law was ruled unconstitutional. The Court's decision was so unpopular—it was perceived as a sop to the rich since only a small percentage of the population had incomes in excess of $4000—that a few years later a constitutional amendment was proposed. Ratified in 1913, the 16th Amendment permitted the federal government to "lay and collect taxes on incomes, from whatever source derived, without apportionment among the several States and without regard to any census or enumeration."

In these days of "read my lips" antitaxation pledges, it is hard to imagine that there was a time when the public clamored for income taxes. Here again is an example of a situation in which budgetary policy reflected the national political ethos. At the turn of the century the income tax was perceived as a more equitable way to share the burden of government. We will see that tax policy continues to be more or less responsive to public demands (if not in the public "interest").

In the twentieth century the structure of the national tax system has sometimes demonstrated conflicting trends. Most studies indicate that taxes are getting less and less progressive (the burden of taxation shifting to those who are better able to pay). For example, since about 1950 there has been a dramatic shift in the source of government revenue. In 1954, 44 percent of the federal government's revenues were obtained from personal income taxes, 30 percent from corporate income taxes, and 11 percent from payroll taxes.[21] Payroll taxes, such as payments for Social Security, are deducted from employee salaries to provide for disability, retirement, and medical care. Because wage laborers derive almost all of their income from salaries and because the Social Security tax has a flat rate with a "ceiling" (above a certain income level, payments do not continue to rise), payroll taxes are tremendously regressive.[22] On the other hand, income derived from interest or investments is largely exempt from payroll taxes (although not from most income taxes). Since wealthier individuals generally obtain at least part of their income from investments, payroll taxes do not affect them as heavily. In 1990, while the portion of federal revenues derived from personal income taxes remained at about 41 percent of the total, corporate tax rates had dropped to about 14 percent and payroll taxes had risen to 37 percent of the total.[23] According to some estimates, it may now be the case that 50 percent or more of all U.S. households pay more in Social Security taxes than they do in income taxes.[24] (See Figure 1-3.)

While the consequences of the modern tax structure are subject to debate on the basis of equity issues, taxes are also the focus of debate over issues of policy. The fact is that taxes are important policy tools because they not only provide revenue but also serve to sanction or encourage certain types of behavior. For example, tax breaks (generally termed tax "expenditures" because they represent a net loss for the Treasury) in the form of tax-payment deferrals for money invested in individual retirement accounts have been given to individuals to encourage savings. Home ownership is encouraged through a home mortgage interest deduction. Other forms of investment have also been encouraged. In addition, marriage, childbearing and rearing are social goals encouraged through the tax system.

Tax expenditures are, in some ways, an excellent approach to delivering benefits, enabling the government to encourage certain types of individual behavior (such as marriage) without paying any of the administrative costs of government transfer programs. The problem is

FIGURE 1-3 Budget Revenues, Fiscal Year 1992

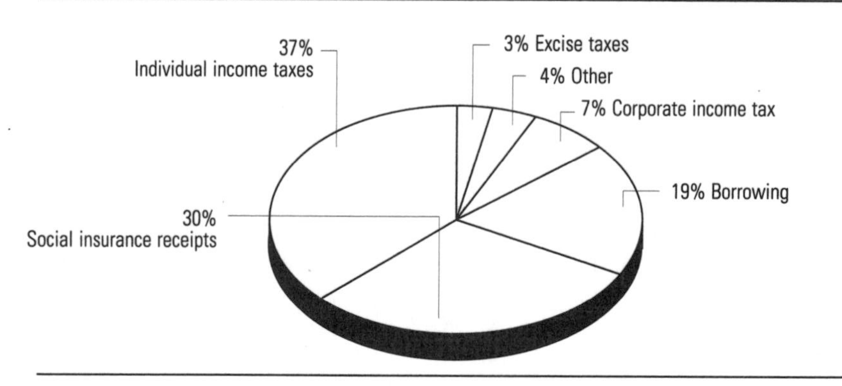

Source: OMB estimates cited in *Congressional Quarterly Weekly Report,* February 9, 1991, 333.

that tax breaks (often called loopholes) have unintended consequences and also mainly benefit those with extra income to invest and large enough incomes to itemize deductions on their tax returns. In addition, many lucrative tax expenditures remain relatively hidden from public scrutiny because they do not require a special appropriation measure even as they extract funds from the Treasury. Before the passage of the 1986 Tax Reform Act, which cut or eliminated a number of these loopholes, tax expenditures sheltered roughly half of all revenues that were eligible to be collected under the federal income tax system. Even so, in 1990 the home mortgage interest deduction alone cost the federal Treasury about $35 billion.[25]

While the expenditure side of the budget process has undergone some centralizing reform, there have been problems in coordinating the construction of the tax system. As we shall see, the budget committees in Congress have encountered some of their greatest difficulties in reining in and rationalizing the American tax structure. The basic reality remains that revenues do not remotely reach levels of expenditures, resulting in large and chronic deficits. Clearly the next great step in eliminating the deficit shortfall is going to be the balancing of the federal tax structure with the rest of the budgetary process. This step, however, will not be easy. Taxes are often the most sensitive issues in the American political process.

THE DEFICIT

Probably for the foreseeable future an enormous volume of material is going to be written about the national debt. Some of what is said about the debt, but certainly not all, is unnecessarily alarmist. The debt and, more accurately, our inability to balance the budget present a serious problem, to be sure, but it is not as serious as we have been led to believe. If expenditures as a percentage of GNP (the measure used earlier) are the comparative indicator across time, then the deficit as a percentage of GNP is probably a good relative measure as well. By that standard, in the largest deficit year in the 1980s, 1983, the deficit stood at about 6.3 percent of the gross national product. In that year the budget deficit was close to $208 billion. By the same measure, when the deficit was $220 billion three years later, the deficit was only 5.3 percent of GNP. The downturn continued until 1991, when the economy was gripped by recession. Until 1991 there was a relative reduction in deficit spending because while the deficit level remained basically the same in dollar amounts (or less in some years), the economy grew at a steady albeit unspectacular rate (about 4 percent per year between 1982 and 1990), and inflation has eroded the relative value of the dollar.

Another good measure of the size of the deficit is accumulated debt as a percentage of the gross national product. In 1977 the total federal debt was $709 billion, or 36 percent of the GNP. In 1990 the debt topped the $3 *trillion* mark, or about 54 percent of GNP. This is a sort of "good news, bad news" story. As a percentage of GNP, the federal debt is actually lower now than it was in 1955 when the accumulated debt was running at close to 60 percent of GNP.

A lot of people feel more comfortable and can better comprehend problems of debt when those issues are stated in terms of personal finance. For example, we are often told that the average individual could not sustain spending 15 percent more than his or her annual income (as did the federal government in running a deficit in 1990). In fact, this is not necessarily true. For example, a first-time home buyer (even with no appreciable assets and a small down payment) could borrow money from a bank to purchase a $50,000 home if he or she had an annual income of $30,000. For that year, the individual would have authorized expenditures of almost 60 percent more than his or her annual income. By the same token, when this individual's annual income increased to $60,000, he or she would probably want to move into a larger house that would, again, result in debt well in excess of his or her annual income and even assets. This does not even mention the debt individuals accrue associated with car loans, student loans, credit cards, and much more. By that standard, the federal debt is really not that large. Annually the government purchases more services, but at the same time its revenues increase. In addition, the government holds enormously valuable assets (such as public lands) that almost certainly exceed in value the accumulated national debt. Viewed from that standpoint, the government is better off than many home owners and businesses.

Now for the bad news. The fact is that because in the early 1980s the federal deficit grew at a much faster rate than GNP, the annual interest the government has to pay to service the debt increased by about 60 percent during that decade. In other words, in 1980 about 10 percent of the federal budget was devoted to servicing the debt. In 1990 the debt-service requirement was about 16 percent of the budget, or about $190 billion for the fiscal year, and by the end of 1991, the problem only seemed to be getting worse. This money goes to pay for an obligation that delivers no goods and services.

Also of concern is the fact that, with no end in sight, the federal government has run a deficit in twenty-six of the last twenty-seven years. It is not necessarily bad for the government to experience an occasional deficit. In times of war or economic recession it may be necessary for the government to spend in excess of its revenues in order to provide for national defense or compensate for the effects of economic displacement. This is a so-called cyclical deficit that responds to environmental conditions. The current deficit, however, is a chronic or structural deficit that the government (and taxpayers) tends to generate regardless of the economy's performance. There is no way, short of permanently increasing revenues or decreasing expenditures, that a structural deficit can be overcome. That fact creates the kind of political difficulties that will characterize the adoption of the federal budget for the foreseeable future.

Finally, according to some economists, because deficit spending has to be covered by borrowing and because Americans are not very good savers, chronic deficits may contribute to a recession that will make it impossible for the government to balance the budget.[26] In order to borrow money to cover its annual revenue shortfall, the federal government must go into the financial market for loans. If the deficit is large enough, the government has the potential of borrowing enough money to crowd out or at least compete against other borrowers who are attempting to obtain credit to expand their businesses or finance construction. If available funds for lending dry up or interest rates are driven up by government competition in the credit market, a recession may result as buyers withdraw from the market for big-ticket items such as homes or automobiles that require institutional financing.

CONCLUSIONS

Several conclusions can be drawn from this very brief examination of the budgetary system. First, it is apparent that the budget process and its outcomes very much reflect the American political psyche. We, as a people, are willing to provide a safety net for those who are less fortunate, but not to the extent of subverting the core of a free market economy. There are disagreements about the appropriate levels of assistance to the disadvantaged or adequate provision of national defense, but few dispute the underlying principles and assumptions that drive our economic and political system. The outcomes of the budget process and the institutions and procedures utilized to achieve that outcome are very much a reflection of the American consensus and the types of compromises we arrive at in settling our differences.

Second, when examined in an historical context, the size of the budget deficit and the national debt, in particular, do not appear to constitute quite as grave a problem as we have been led to believe. The government is in a position to sustain a certain level of debt. In fact, at times it is important that the government commit to deficit spending. However, when that deficit is chronic and appears to be a function not of context but of the structure of our political system, then there is cause for concern. Presumably at some point (yet to be determined), a structural deficit will have some serious, injurious effects on the performance of the economy and the living standards of our citizens. It is because of that uncertain future that an examination of the structural causes of the deficit is important.

This study of the budget process for one fiscal year should be viewed with the understanding that each year is different and that American politics are always evolving. There are, however, some general lessons to be learned from this one case study. It will become apparent that Congress is not the whole problem and, therefore, is not the entire solution to problems of the budget process. Congress is a remarkably representative institution. We may bristle at the suggestion that it is a reflection of a broad range of America and its values, but that happens to be the case. If Congress does indeed well represent the nation, then solutions to the budget question lie not so much in the structure of the institution nor in its procedures nor in the political courage (or lack thereof) of its principals, but in the public's willingness to sacrifice and play an active role in seeking a system of balance and fairness.

NOTES

1. For a discussion of this fundamental shift in American politics, see Theodore Lowi, *The End of Liberalism: Ideology, Policy, and the Crisis of Public Authority* (New York: Norton, 1969).
2. See Howard E. Shuman, *Politics and the Budget: The Struggle between the President and the Congress,* 2d ed. (Englewood Cliffs, N.J.: Prentice-Hall, 1988), 151-152; and Office of Management and Budget, *Budget of the United States Government, Fiscal Year 1990* (Washington, D.C.: U.S. Government Printing

Office, 1989), Part 10, 9.

3. Lowi, *The End of Liberalism.*
4. See Morris P. Fiorina et al., "Historical Change in House Turnover," in Norman J. Ornstein, ed., *Congress in Change: Evolution and Reform* (New York: Praeger, 1975), 24-57; and James Sterling Young, *The Washington Community: 1800-1823* (New York: Harcourt Brace Jovanovich, 1966).
5. Quoted in Louis Fisher, *Presidential Spending Power* (Princeton, N.J.: Princeton University Press, 1975), 25. For an expanded version of this entire argument, see the first two chapters of Fisher's book.
6. See Fisher, *Presidential Spending Power,* 25.
7. All but one of these vetoes were sustained. By comparison, Cleveland vetoed only thirty private bills during his second term several years later. See Robert J. Spitzer, *The Presidential Veto: Touchstone of the American Presidency* (Albany: State University of New York Press, 1988), 75.
8. Economic recession was understood to make government taxation and thus commitments to expenditures a drag on the economy. The federal government's natural reaction at the time was to cut spending during recessions.
9. At the same time, in order to recentralize authority over budget proposals, the House returned to its Appropriations Committee original jurisdiction over all supply bills. In 1922 jurisdiction over spending was centralized in the Senate as well.
10. For an excellent historical examination of the development of the Bureau of the Budget, see Larry Berman, *The Office of Management and Budget and the Presidency, 1921-1979* (Princeton, N.J.: Princeton University Press, 1979).
11. Executive Order 6166.
12. Agencies in the late 1940s had a disturbing tendency to spend all their appropriations before the end of the fiscal year and then go to Congress to request supplemental appropriations or else have to suspend service. In 1950, pursuant to the Anti-Deficiency Act (31 U.S.C. 665 [c] [2]), the Bureau of the Budget was authorized to supervise agency expenditures over the course of the fiscal year in order to ensure that surplus funds were available "to provide for contingencies, or to effect savings whenever savings are made possible."
13. Executive Order 12291, February 17, 1981.
14. For an excellent account of the modern role of the budget director, see William Greider, "The Education of David Stockman," *Atlantic Monthly* 248 (December 1981): 51.
15. Office of Management and Budget, *Budget of the United States Government, Fiscal Year 1990,* 10-26.
16. Ibid.
17. This modification refers to the regulation of interstate trade.
18. This last provision was later to become a barrier to the development of a personal income tax mainly because of substantial disagreement over what constituted a direct tax in the meaning of Article I.

    A direct tax is a tax on property or an activity that cannot be passed on to another segment of the market. For example, property taxes are borne directly by the landowner (although it could be argued that renters pay property taxes), while tariffs on imported goods are passed on to the consumer. As early as 1798, Congress voted to impose a direct tax on property in order to raise $2 million, the costs of which were to be apportioned equally by population among the states. The collection of this tax, given the limited resources of the national government, was slow and difficult, so that direct taxes did not become a major source of the federal government's revenue until much later in the nation's history.

19. See *Springer v. United States,* 102 U.S. 586 (1881) and also an earlier decision, *Hylton v. United States,* 3 Dallas 171 (1796), in which the Supreme Court ruled that only taxes on property were to be considered direct taxes.
20. 157 U.S. 429 (1895).
21. Secretary of the Treasury, *Annual Report* (Washington, D.C.: U.S. Government Printing Office, 1980), 11.
22. There is some question about the progressivity of corporate income taxes, which in part are passed on to consumers as a sort of indirect sales tax. Sales taxes are also considered to be regressive.
23. *Budget of the United States Government, Fiscal Year 1990,* pt. 4, 2.
24. Social Security Administration, *Social Security Bulletin* (December 1982): 12-18, cited in Shuman, *Politics and the Budget,* 96.
25. Office of Management and Budget, *Special Analyses: Budget of the United States Government, Fiscal Year 1990* (Washington, D.C.: U.S. Government Printing Office, 1989), G-41.
26. See Shuman, *Politics and the Budget,* 154-156.

CHAPTER 2

The Congressional Budget Process in Practice and Theory

Congress is an institution in flux, and that constant change has its effects on the structure and outcomes of the congressional budget process. As dynamic as the institution is, however, there are two constants in congressional life. First and foremost, *Congress is an institution that makes its own rules.* This means that for every set procedure, for every requirement codified in statute or as a rule of the House or the Senate, there is an exception. The fact is that with the assent of a majority, the rules of procedure can be changed in either house, and the process can take off in a totally new, unexpected direction. This principle makes it very difficult to follow something as complicated as the budget process, and this complexity works to the advantage of politicians who would prefer to duck the responsibility for making tough political decisions.

The other verity of congressional life is the fact that *what is good for the individual member of Congress is not necessarily good for the institution.* A corollary of this principle is that *what is good for an individual congressional district is not necessarily good for the nation as a whole.* Members who seek to enhance their own authority within the institution in order to better serve their districts will, if successful, simultaneously contribute to the derogation of centralized leadership within the institution and to disjointed policy making.[1] This verity has been built into the structure and procedures of both the House and the Senate throughout the twentieth century. Congress has well served the needs of its members but, at the same time, has lost some of its ability to legislate as a unified entity.[2]

The budget process in Congress and its outcomes reflect this second congressional fact of life. Individual members have extensive access to the budget process and thus to the national Treasury. As a result, the budget process, as it is now organized, serves well the interests of individual members but not the institution as a whole. Appropriations legislation tends to distribute the benefits of government spending as widely as possible even if, through such a distribution, a deficit results. The only way to effectively reverse this tendency would be to adopt reforms that involve some type of derogation of the authority of individual members—in other words, a recentralization of power within the institution. Members are understandably reluctant to surrender authority to their leaders, and because Congress makes its own rules, many rules and the structure of Congress reflect the reluctance of members to surrender authority to their leaders.

The story of the budget process in Congress since 1974 concerns the leadership's attempts to impose some kind of overall intelligence and control over the adoption of the budget. A number of reforms have been implemented, designed to improve the quality and amount of overall control. The results have been mixed at best. The Gramm-Rudman-Hollings Emergency Deficit Control Act (GRH) has enjoyed some limited success. However, GRH is only the tip of the iceberg insofar as efforts at budget reform are concerned. Also central to the new congressional budget process are the institutions and procedures established by Congress when it passed the Budget and Impoundment Control Act of 1974.

THE "OLD" NEW BUDGET PROCESS (1974)

Prior to 1974, the budget was adopted in thirteen separate appropriations bills (there were often supplemental appropriations measures as well). Coordination, much less control, was impossible in a system in which thirteen separate spending bills were produced every year. While the Appropriations Committee had a certain coordinating influence, the budget process began to escape control in the early 1970s. This happened, in part, because of the adoption of a number of major entitlement programs associated with President Lyndon Johnson's Great Society and, in part, because of the expenses associated with the Vietnam War. Entitlement programs are relatively uncontrollable because individuals qualify (or are "entitled") for benefits under these programs, depending on their personal circumstances. It is impossible, therefore, to plan in advance for expenditures under such programs through the regular appropriations process. Spending under entitlement programs is a function of the condition of the economy and the demographics of the population.

By 1970 the federal government began to run the series of deficits that continue to this day. As it had done in the past when faced with chronic deficits, Congress began to search for ways to cut the deficit that primarily involved the delegation of power to the executive. There is a certain logic to delegating authority to cut the budget to the president. In doing so, members of Congress sacrifice some of their constitutional authority, but they also manage to duck the blame for making the tough political decisions associated with budget reductions.

There are limits, however, to how much power members of Congress are willing to delegate to the executive branch. This was particularly true in the early 1970s when Congress was controlled by the Democrats and the president was a Republican, Richard Nixon. President Nixon was more than happy to use budget-cutting authority to put his own philosophical stamp on public policy in the name of "fiscal responsibility." In 1971 and 1972, for example, he opted to withhold from expenditure, or impound, monies for particular programs he did not like. He argued that the impoundments were necessary and legitimate pursuant to the president's statutory authority to protect against inflation and high levels of unemployment.[3] In one particularly egregious instance in 1972, while Congress was in its Christmas recess, the president decided to cut off funding for four farm programs (Rural Environmental Assistance Program, Water Bank Program, Farmers Home Administration, and the Rural Electrification Administration). Farm-state members of Congress were enraged by the president's actions, and legislation was introduced in Congress to limit the president's impoundment authority.

In addition to proposed limits on the impoundment authority and in response to mounting deficits, it was hoped that a way could be found to better enable Congress to adopt balanced budgets on its own. These two positions—the anti-impoundment sentiment and the desire for congressional budget reform—tended to break down along party lines. Democrats were primarily concerned with the president's impoundments. Republicans were unwilling to restrict the president's authority to impound appropriated funds unless Congress was willing to reform its own budget process in order to produce a balanced budget. This division had the makings of a grand compromise, and indeed in 1973 a conference committee comprised of members from both houses of Congress reported H.R. 7130, a bill that basically grafted budget reform onto anti-impoundment provisions. This conference report, later approved overwhelmingly by both houses, came to be known as the Congressional Budget and Impoundment Control Act of 1974.[4]

Among other things, the act reformed the budget process by creating three new congressional institutions and an entirely new budget procedure. The Congressional Budget Office (CBO) was to provide Congress with analyses and estimates of the budget, independent of those provided by the executive branch, particularly the OMB. It was believed in Congress, not totally without justification, that the OMB (an agency in the Executive Office of the President) was politically biased in its estimates of the administration's budgetary proposals. The CBO, which is now considered to be one of the most accurate sources of economic forecasting in the government, was intended to be a bipartisan institution, responsive to requests from members of Congress from both sides of the aisle.

Also created by the act were two new budget committees, one for each house of Congress. Under the law, these committees were to be responsible for drawing up budget proposals separate and distinct from the budget submissions presented by the president. Using this congressional budget plan, the budget committees were to guide the deliberations of the authorization, taxation, and appropriations committees of Congress in their consideration of the budget. If the House Appropriations Committee was unable to stay under spending ceilings established by the House Budget Committee, the Budget Committee would then have the authority to order that appropriations bills exceeding their targets be "reconciled" with the congressional budget guidelines. The work of the budget committees was intended to impose congressional priorities on spending measures and, at the same time, force the timely adoption of the budget before the beginning of the new fiscal year.

In practice, however, the reformed budget process has been less than successful. First, inasmuch as most of the federal budget is uncontrollable through the budget process, it was and is probably unrealistic to expect a reformed process to halt deficit spending. While the Budget and Impoundment Control Act does place controls on the adoption of *new* entitlement programs, these controls are too little, too late. Most current entitlement authority was established in the 1960s and was essentially "grandfathered" by the Budget Reform Act of 1974. (Under this act, only new entitlement programs are subject to budget discipline.) Since it was unlikely, in any event, that Congress would adopt new entitlement authorities in the context of high levels of deficit spending, the Budget Reform Act's controls on the adoption of new entitlements would likely have little impact. Without being able to roll back existing entitlements, the budget committees' hands were tied.

In addition, simply reforming the system did not magically create a consensus on spending priorities in Congress. The budget committees can impose a "congressional" approach to budgeting only if there exists within Congress a consensus on priorities in spending. Such a consensus does not exist, nor would it be realistic to expect it to develop. There will always be disagreements in Congress about the relative importance of different national priorities. Furthermore, regardless of mandated procedural reforms, the fact that Congress makes its own rules means that the requirements of the reformed process can be (and frequently are) waived at the convenience of the institution. This is particularly true inasmuch as the standing committees, particularly in the House, tend to be more powerful and influential than the House Budget Committee. As a result, the budget process in the House is much more likely to conform to the wishes of the Appropriations Committee or the authorizing committees than it is to the desires of the Budget Committee. In other words, in terms of spending control, the Budget Reform Act of 1974, on its own, has had little effect.

GRAMM-RUDMAN-HOLLINGS

Eleven years later, with deficits still mounting, Congress imposed on itself a statutory balanced-budget requirement in the form of the Gramm-Rudman-Hollings Emergency Deficit Control Act. In a kind of "dress rehearsal" for a balanced-budget amendment, Congress was to balance the budget under the law by fiscal year 1991. In each year prior to 1991, Congress was to adopt budgets with increasingly smaller budget shortfalls. These so-called deficit reduction targets were to be gradually introduced in order to reduce the negative economic effects of cutting the federal budget too quickly. If Congress was unable to meet its requirements pursuant to the act, the law required that funds be *sequestered* in the amount exceeding the deficit target. (When funds are sequestered, they are withheld from expenditures until the deficit reduction targets are met.) The requirements of GRH were to be waived in case of war or economic recession.

Gramm-Rudman-Hollings was both a success and a failure. By setting targets for deficit reduction, the act has provided legislators with an annual budgetary goal. Although it is difficult to know how Congress would have performed had the Emergency Deficit Control Act not been in effect, the fact is that the annual budget deficit has probably declined in real terms since 1985. I say "probably" because the act has highlighted some of the serious problems associated with deficit reduction. One of the negative effects of Gramm-Rudman is that it has become very difficult to know what actually constitutes the budget that is to be kept in balance for the purposes of the act. For example, Social Security receipts that are in surplus when compared with expenditures are counted for the purpose of offsetting the deficit. These receipts, however, are not earmarked for anything other than the Social Security Trust Fund, which by law cannot be used for general expenditures. A number of members of Congress have argued that because the Social Security system is a separate entity, its revenues have no impact on the budget and, therefore, cannot be counted for the purposes of deficit reduction. This same basic argument is repeated in a number of similar cases. The president's ability, with the full complicity of Congress, to hide "off budget" net budgetary losers (such as a portion of the savings and loan bailout) and include as "on budget" accounts in surplus (including the Social Security Trust Fund) means that for the purposes of deficit reduction, what constitutes the "budget" is probably not an accurate reflection of government expenditures.

In addition, economic forecasting plays a very important part in the maneuvering that goes into deciding what constitutes the "true" budget deficit. Economic forecasts tell budget planners how much revenue the government can expect to receive from taxation and how much the government will have to pay out in entitlement benefits. Since neither the president nor Congress wants massive unplanned cuts in spending (and benefits), unduly optimistic economic forecasts can be used to magically reduce the deficit. For example, the OMB is widely known to fudge its economic forecasts (which then become part of the GRH process) for the benefit of the president's political position. The president is particularly concerned about the effects of large sequestrations for two reasons. First, if a large sequestration were to touch off an economic recession, the president and his party would probably take the blame. Second, in the event of sequestration, approximately 50 percent of the funds withheld would be taken from the Defense Department's budget, which constitutes less than a quarter of the total budget. In other words, sequestration affects the Defense Department at least twice as heavily as it does any other program. The president as commander-in-chief and chief diplomat simply cannot allow massive unplanned cuts in military expenditures to occur, as those cuts would undermine American military and diplomatic commitments abroad.

Finally, the fact that the Deficit Control Act exists in statute rather than as a constitutional provision has proved to be in some ways a liability and in other ways an advantage. In 1987, when it became obvious that Congress was not going to be able to meet its deficit reduction targets, it amended the law to raise these targets and put off into the future the possibility of a balanced budget. This incident highlights both the advantages and disadvantages of adopting a balanced-budget requirement in statutory form. On the one hand, since statutes are open to adjustment, the requirements of the GRH process are sensitive to environmental conditions. On the other hand, this flexibility allows Congress and the president to put off painful budgetary decisions until later, perhaps after the next election. Nevertheless, congressional reaction to the Gramm-Rudman-Hollings Emergency Deficit Control Act was best summed up by Sen. William Armstrong (R-Colo.) when he said that the law "is not worse than doing nothing. But I am not very confident of my opinion."[5]

THE BUDGET TIMETABLE

The Budget Reform Act of 1974 established a schedule for budgeting that, while rarely followed to the letter, captures the rhythm of the budget process throughout the fiscal year.

OCTOBER 1—This is the beginning of the new fiscal year (October 1, 1990, marked the beginning of the 1991 fiscal year and consideration of the fiscal year 1992 budget). All action concerning the budget for this fiscal year is to be completed by this date. Although Congress has completed its budget work on time only once since the Budget Reform Act was passed, October 1 is a target date in more ways than one. Any agency or activity for which budgetary decisions have not been made by October 1 will generally run out of funds by this date. In that event, Congress must pass a temporary, stop-gap appropriations bill (a continuing resolution) that will fund programs until Congress finishes its budget work for the year.

On average, Congress will pass two or three continuing resolutions at the beginning of any given fiscal year. These resolutions are designed to fund a program temporarily at its current level until a regular appropriations bill can be passed. In the event of unforeseen circumstances or simply because Congress failed to appropriate sufficient funds, certain programs may require a supplemental appropriation. For example, the eruption of Mount St. Helens in 1980 occasioned an emergency supplemental appropriation of $1 billion. Congress generally adopts at least one supplemental every year, and in some years (1978) as many as nine.

NOVEMBER 10—By this date, the president is required to submit the current services budget, which is an estimate of the cost of maintaining the current level of government services if existing programs and policies remain unchanged for the next fiscal year. For the purpose of drawing up this budget, all expenditures are adjusted for inflation. Thus the current services budget gives Congress and the president a standard by which to measure the increase or decrease in the delivery of services. This budget is often called the "baseline." While the baseline budget is almost always higher than it was the previous year, "cuts below the baseline," in the confusing lexicon of the budget process, are generally touted as reductions in spending.

MID-JANUARY (fifteen days after the beginning of the congressional session)—The president submits his budget pursuant to the Budget and Accounting Act of 1921. This is an occasion for both serious policy making and political maneuvering. To the extent that most of the president's budget is a fairly accurate assessment of the amount of money that will be spent in the next fiscal year, it is the opening salvo of the year's budgetary debate. The president's figures will portend (albeit not always accurately) the size of the upcoming budget deficit as well as the areas (signified by budget reductions or increments) in which he intends to take a stand.

As a rule, Congress tends to cut the president's requests for appropriations. Between 1968 and 1988, Congress cut aggregate presidential requests in seventeen out of twenty-one years.[6] Just as important is the fact that Congress, in its adoption of the budget, will juggle the priorities of the president's budget. Members of Congress often claim that it is the more fiscally responsible institution because it generally cuts the president's budget. Those representatives who make this claim fail to mention, however, that Congress has not yet significantly reduced entitlement programs, which constitute almost half of all government spending. These entitlement cuts (which require changes in legislation, not appropriations) are largely beyond the control of the president in making his budget submission to Congress.

APRIL 15—On or before this date, Congress is required to pass its budget resolution. This resolution, which is supposed to be binding, is a unified statement of congressional budgeting priorities. The budget committees develop and report these resolutions to their respective chambers on the basis of the reports made to them by the other standing committees of Congress, economic forecasts made by the CBO, and pursuant to the budget deficit reduction targets established by the Gramm-Rudman-Hollings Deficit Control Act.

Drawing up this resolution is not a simple task. For one thing, the various standing committees, anticipating that their requests will be reduced, will inevitably make budgetary requests that exceed deficit reduction targets. In addition, it is very difficult for the Budget Committee to project six months to a year in advance what the performance of the economy will mean in terms of entitlement payments. Finally, the taxation committees (the Senate Finance and House Ways and Means committees) are very poorly integrated into this system. Not only is it difficult to forecast expected tax receipts based on existing law, it is almost impossible to forecast revenues given the likelihood of changes in the tax laws during the next few months. Nevertheless, the committees produce a resolution that is debated, amended, and passed by both houses. The differences between the two versions of the resolution produced by the House and Senate are merged in a conference committee and then voted on by both houses. The budget resolution is *not* signed by the president and, therefore, does not become law. It is, instead, more or less internally binding (remember rule number one of congressional life: Congress makes its own rules).

On or about the time Congress passes its budget resolution, the Budget Committee may begin to prepare a reconciliation bill. This is a process mandated by the Budget Reform Act that authorizes the budget committees to order the reconciliation of all pending budget legislation with the budget resolution. The budget committees can identify authorization and appropriations bills (most, if not all, of which have yet to be passed) that exceed the dictates of the budget resolution and order that the spending levels be reconciled. In other words, the Budget Committee leaves to the discretion of the appropriate committee decisions about how appropriations are to be cut in order to meet the demands of reconciliation. The resultant cuts are either placed in a spending bill before it is reported to the floor for consideration, passed in the form of a budget reconciliation resolution, or even passed in the form of legislation to be signed by the president if the appropriations in question have already been signed into law.

It should be noted that the Budget Committee is not always successful at getting the Appropriations Committee to reconcile its legislation with the dictates of the budget resolution. The Budget Committee has been known to revise the resolution to conform to the demands of the appropriations committees. By a three-fifths vote in the Senate, it may also be possible to waive budget resolution requirements as they apply to individual pieces of legislation.

JUNE 30—By this date all thirteen appropriations bills should have been passed by the House. This never happens, which makes the rest of the process that much more difficult to follow.

SEPTEMBER 1—On this date the president, on the advice of the OMB, issues a sequester order if necessary. This order requires that the amount of outlays in excess of the deficit reduction targets mandated by Gramm-Rudman-Hollings be withheld (or sequestered). The president has little discretion over the distribution of these cuts to the extent that GRH requires that all accounts subject to sequestration (a number of programs are exempt) be cut at the same percentage rate across the board. This sequestration order does not go into effect until September 30 (or the end of the fiscal year), so that Congress still has time to cut the budget on its own.

SEPTEMBER 30—Congress is supposed to have finished its budget work for the fiscal year that is about to start. It rarely does. As a consequence, the next few months, before Congress adjourns at the end of the session, are a period of high drama as Congress seeks to meet its obligations to finish the appropriations process, pass stop-gap funding measures, and conform to the requirements of GRH or face the prospect of across-the-board cuts. The drama of the moment is enhanced by an awareness that should Congress fail to complete its work, all or selected parts of the government will simply cease being funded and thus discontinue operations. It is this realization that drives congressional sessions late into the night. It is this tension that sparks some of the sharpest and most colorful debates on the floor.

THE CAST OF CHARACTERS

Literally every member of Congress is involved in the budget process in one way or another. Depending on their organizational affiliations and seniority, some members are more influential than others. In this section we will examine some of the organizational structures within the houses of Congress that participate in the budget process.

THE BUDGET COMMITTEES

It is obvious that the budget committees in both houses have been assigned a daunting if not impossible task. Because what these committees do infringes on the jurisdiction of almost every other committee, they have met resistance at every turn. In one sense, however, the size and persistence of recent budget deficits have conferred a certain legitimacy on the power and authority of the budget committees. The reconciliation process has been integrated into the overall consideration of the budget and coordinated with the GRH deficit reduction requirements. The appropriations committees, if only grudgingly, have begun to coordinate their activities with the budget committees. In the end, the reform of the budget process that began in 1974 (and is ongoing) may succeed for no other reason than the fact that it is the only game in town.

There are subtle differences in composition and effectiveness between the House and Senate Budget Committees. The Senate Budget Committee is a regular standing committee, meaning that members appointed to the committee serve for as long as they remain in the Senate or until they decide to transfer. This is not the case in the House committee, whose members are permitted to serve for a total of only four years for every ten they are in Congress. This creates a rotation of membership and leadership, resulting in a relative lack of cohesion and professionalism. Moreover, since all of the members of the House Budget Committee are permanent members of other standing committees, including Appropriations and Ways and Means (the exclusiveness requirement of the Appropriations Committee is waived for the purposes of service on the Budget Committee), they tend to be more loyal to their other committees. As a consequence, the House Budget Committee has been less successful at imposing the controls of a reformed budget process on the institution. The Senate Budget Committee, by contrast, has standing on a par with any other committee in the institution, the result being more centralized budget control in the Senate.

Authorization Committees

The rules of the House read, "No appropriation shall be reported in any general appropriation bill ... for any expenditure not previously authorized by law."[7] This authorization requirement is a reflection of the principle that the government's primary responsibility is to provide services, not to make budgetary decisions. Thus policy decisions come first in the appropriations process. Authorization committees designate services to be provided and establish the legal requirements under which programs must be implemented. Authorization legislation, in some cases, also limits the amount of, or prohibits the expenditure of, funds that can be appropriated for a particular program or task. Roughly 40 percent of all appropriations are approved pursuant to authorizations that set ceilings on the dollar amounts to be spent. Most of the remaining government expenditures are sanctioned pursuant to open-ended legislation that authorizes the spending of "such sums as may be necessary to carry out the provisions of this act." Most entitlement programs are funded pursuant to open-ended authorizations.

Authorization committees and subcommittees, appropriately enough, are organized according to governmental function. By contrast the Appropriations Committee is subdivided along the lines of government budget accounts. For example, not all foreign affairs (authorizing) activities are administered under the State Department account (appropriating). Thus there is not always a complete concurrence of appropriation and authorizing committee jurisdictions.

A total of eighteen House committees share some authorization responsibility. Roughly 45 percent of all authorization responsibility, in dollar amounts, is under the jurisdiction of the Ways and Means Committee. In addition to its responsibilities for taxation and trade regulation, this committee oversees the Social Security program, unemployment compensation, and government health programs such as Medicare. These entitlement programs are, by far, the largest domestic programs in the budget. Another 25 percent of all authorization responsibilities are the purview of the Armed Services Committee. The other sixteen authorization committees share responsibility for the remaining portion of the budget. (See Table 2-1.)

Integrating the authorization committees into the reformed budget process has led to some serious problems, most of which stem from the

TABLE 2-1 House Committees in the Appropriations Process

Authorization	*Appropriation subcommittees*	*Revenue*
Agriculture	Commerce, Justice, State, and Judiciary	Ways and Means
Armed Services	Defense	
Banking, Finance, and Urban Affairs	District of Columbia	
District of Columbia	Energy and Water Development	
Education and Labor	Foreign Operations, Export Financing, and Related Programs	
Energy and Commerce	Interior	
Foreign Affairs	Labor, Health and Human Services, and Education	
Government Operations	Legislative	
House Administration	Military Construction	
Interior and Insular Affairs	Rural Development, Agriculture, and Related Agencies	
Judiciary	Transportation	
Merchant Marine and Fisheries	Treasury, Postal Service, and General Government	
Post Office and Civil Service	Veterans Affairs, Housing and Urban Development, and Independent Agencies	
Public Works and Transportation		
Science, Space, and Technology		
Small Business		
Veterans' Affairs		
Ways and Means		

Note: The House Budget Committee, which acts only as a mechanism of internal control, should also be mentioned.

inherent tension between making policy and providing funds for those policies. Although the government can provide an unlimited number of valuable and useful services for its citizens, only limited funds are available for those services. These limits are particularly conspicuous when the government is running a large deficit and must make large payments to service the debt. Authorization committees want to ensure that the projects they authorize are not only funded but also that the appropriations committees do not indirectly control the policy process by virtue of their budgeting responsibilities. The authorization committees have developed a number of tactics designed to protect their jurisdictions from this sort of intrusion.

Authorization committees prefer to adopt annual as opposed to multiyear or permanent authorizations. Annual authorizations allow the committees to oversee more directly the programs within their jurisdiction. A certain degree of tension has always existed between the appropriations and authorization committees with respect to the use of annual authorizations. Since the appropriations committees cannot finish their work without an authorization establishing the guidelines under which appropriators will operate, they would prefer authorization committees to pass multiyear authorities. This has been particularly true since 1974 when the Budget Reform Act mandated the passage of appropriations bills by June 30. Waiting for passage of annual authorization legislation invariably delays passage of appropriations legislation, making it almost impossible for Congress to complete its budget work by the end of the fiscal year. On the other hand, authorization committees perceive calls for multiyear authorizations as a raid on their authority.

To elude interference from the appropriations committees, authorization committees have used the tactic of adopting measures that approve "borrowing" or "contract" authorities. Borrowing authorities permit agencies to borrow funds in order to finance certain activities. Contract authorities permit agencies to enter into contracts that may commit the federal government to the expenditure of funds. This backdoor spending is a form of authorization that virtually requires the appropriations. The Budget and Impoundment Control Act included controls on backdoor spending that, among other things, subjected contract and borrowing authorities to reconciliation (reduction).

As bad as relations may have been between authorization and appropriations committees, relations are even worse between authorization and budget committees. Not only do the budget committees primarily focus on the budget as a fiscal instrument as opposed to a device for the provision of goods and services, they also have the tools, in the form of reconciliation, to deny funding to programs created and overseen by the authorization committees. In addition, through the reconciliation process, the Budget Committee can select individual portions of legislation to be cut. Thus the Budget Committee can, in effect, make policy choices—decisions that until recently were the responsibility of the authorization committees. Consequently, the reconciliation process helps tip the balance of power within the institution into the hands of the bean counters at the expense of the policy makers.

Appropriations Committees

The appropriations committees in both houses enjoy a special status. No program authorized, no policy goal pursued, can be carried out without funding. While the authorization committees have found ways around the appropriations committees, the fact remains that most discretionary spending has to be approved by the appropriations committees.

The Appropriations Committee, especially in the House, enjoys a special status because it is an institution within an institution. Competition for seats on this committee is intense, and the leadership is very selective about which members it chooses. Within the committee certain norms of behavior are encouraged, so that it becomes an insular, singular organization. This insularity is reinforced by the fact that members of the House Appropriations Committee are not allowed to serve on other committees (most of the other House members serve on two or more committees). The Appropriations Committee, particularly in the House, is traditionally perceived as being more hardworking, more professional, more fiscally conservative, and more unified than any other committee in the House.[8] Consequently, its decisions are more likely to be endorsed by the entire House than are recommendations from any other standing committee. This deference to Appropriations Committee decision making is reinforced by the fact that most appropriations legislation is considered on the floor of the House under a modified closed rule, or a restraint that forbids or restricts amendments. Thus appropriations legislation in the House is, in many ways, privileged.

Within the appropriations committees there are, in both houses, thirteen subcommittees—one for each yearly appropriations bill. Each subcommittee is in many ways its own little world. By tradition, subcommittees tend to defer to one another's expertise. Thus the subcommittees of the full Appropriations Committee for the most part tend to dictate to the House or Senate spending policy on their own particular bill. So powerful are the subcommittees of the full House Appropriations Committee that subcommittee chairs are subject to challenge in the Democratic Party Caucus, as are the chairs of the other standing full committees of the House.

As powerful as the Appropriations Committee is, it would be even more so were it not for the fact that so much spending (in excess of 70 percent) is uncontrollable. While the appropriations committees could have resisted the authority of the budget committees as a raid on their jurisdiction—as did the authorization committees—they have reached an accommodation of sorts within the reformed budget process. There are at least three reasons for the establishment of this close working relationship between the budget and appropriations committees. First, there is an imbalance of power between the Budget Committee and the Appropriations Committee, particularly in the House. The Appropriations Committee controls the resources members need—even members of the budget committees—to deliver the goods to the districts. Thus the House Budget Committee has often been willing to accommodate the demands of the Appropriations Committee. In addition, the Budget Committee and Appropriations Committee share a goal to control spending, whereas the authorization and budget committees tend to work at cross purposes. Finally, the Budget Reform Act also put controls on backdoor spending and new entitlement programs that in the past tended to bypass the authority of the appropriations committees.

TAXATION COMMITTEES

Perhaps the most powerful and certainly among the most sought-after committee assignments are the Ways and Means Committee in the House and the Finance Committee in the Senate. These committees are not only, by far, the most powerful authorization committees but they also have as their primary responsibilities control over taxation (and trade policy as well). The relationship between the budget committees and the taxation committees is probably the shakiest and least coordinated of all. The relationship displays the characteristic animosity that exists between the authorization and budget committees, as well as an imbalance of power characterizing the relationship between the appropriations and budget committees. Tax policy is in every way as important (in some cases more so) to members of Congress as are appropriations. Tax policy can deliver goods to constituents as surely as direct transfers of funds. Consequently, the budget committees have problems imposing their control over the revenue side of the budget. In addition, it is very difficult for the budget committees (and the CBO) to anticipate and plan for revenue receipts. Finally, and most importantly, unlike the restrictive treatment of entitlement programs under the 1974 Budget Reform Act, there are few restrictions on the passage of potentially costly tax-code revisions.

The internal politics of the Ways and Means and Finance

committees bear some resemblance to the internal politics of the appropriations committees. There is a certain emphasis on selecting "responsible" legislators for this exclusive committee assignment. Nevertheless, less coordination and control on the taxation committees are now more evident than in the past. This is, in part, a function of the subcommittee reforms of 1973 that stripped the full committee chair of many of his powers to control the flow and content of legislation. At the same time, the Ways and Means Committee was deprived of its traditional power to make all committee appointments, as well as being expanded from twenty-five to thirty-seven members, with a fifth subcommittee added. All of this reform led to a certain amount of decentralization of power on the committee itself, so that, in an atmosphere of "every man for himself," the committee has been enormously generous in its allocation of tax expenditures.[9] In combination with the fact that the Budget Committee exercises very little control over tax expenditures, the revenue side of the budget process in the House remains largely independent of centralized control. While the Finance Committee in the Senate has been less affected by this process of decentralization, the retirement in 1986 of longtime Finance Committee chair Russell Long (D-La.), who was thought to know more about the tax code than practically anyone else in government, led to a certain amount of decentralization of power within the Senate Finance Committee as well.

PARTY LEADERSHIP

Congress was not always bereft of strong centralized leadership. Only through a rather complex evolution did it become the type of institution it is today. Throughout most of the nineteenth century, Congress, particularly the House, was characterized by strong leadership and a largely supine rank and file.

In 1910, however, there was a "revolt" in the House against a particularly objectionable Speaker, "Uncle" Joe Cannon. The power of the Speaker to make committee appointments was transferred to the party caucus. In addition, the seniority system (the automatic advancement of members on the basis of terms of consecutive service in the House) was institutionalized to guarantee that members could not be denied access to positions of power on committees because of a capricious whim of the Speaker or the party. These reforms had the effect of reinforcing members' desires to serve for the long term in Congress. Only through long and continuous service could they gain power within the institution. The Senate went through the same general process of transformation.

In the absence of a strong speakership, between 1910 and 1970 the House was dominated by the chairs of its standing committees. Each individual chairman ran his committee as a fiefdom, controlling his individual piece of the policy agenda by seeing to it that legislation never reached the floor without his stamp of approval. Overall coordination, much less control, was difficult under this system. Legislation adopted during that period reflected the overwhelming influence of committee chairs who had achieved their positions of authority merely by managing to stay in Congress longer than anyone else. This bias associated with the seniority system had the effect of favoring members who represented relatively homogeneous and thus electorally stable congressional districts. Before the passage of the Voting Rights Act in 1965, the most stable congressional districts tended to be in the South, where minority ethnic groups were effectively denied the vote. Congress tended to be dominated by members from the South until about 1970. This fact was reflected in the relative conservative bias in both houses of Congress for most of that period.

Just as members chafed under the dominance of the Speaker in the nineteenth century, so in the twentieth century members who were relatively junior, or from the North, or from the minority party tended to resent the power of the committee chairs. Before 1970, however, membership turnover in the House was so low that there were simply not enough junior members to challenge the dominance of the committee chairs.

Between 1970 and 1978, not only did turnover in Congress increase, particularly in the Democratic party, but the ideological tilt of the majority party began to change as well. In the congressional election of 1970, thirty-eight freshman Democrats were elected, and although that number represented only a twelve-seat gain for Democrats in the House (twenty-seven incumbent Democrats had retired or been defeated), there was a qualitative difference. The Democratic class of 1970 was significantly more reformist than those members it had replaced.[10] Within the Democratic Party Caucus, this infusion of new blood tipped the balance in favor of reform. In 1971 the Caucus in the House adopted the so-called Hansen Committee reforms limiting members to holding no more than one subcommittee chair, which had the effect of distributing power to a greater number of members. Committee chairmen previously had the power to appoint themselves or their political allies to one or more subcommittee chairs.

The Hansen Committee reforms were reinforced in 1973 by the adoption of a provision in the congressional Democratic party rules that allowed for the challenge (by secret ballot) and replacement of committee chairs in the Democratic Party Caucus. At that time the caucus replaced or passed over for promotion some of the party's more senior members and autocratic committee chairs. As a result, the power of committee chairs was reduced and the effective legislative authority of the institution was extended to the chairs of the 135-odd subcommittees in the House. This so-called subcommittee government represents the extreme in the decentralization of power in Congress. Without the discipline of centralized leadership or someone in the position to say "no" to members' requests for funding, deficit spending can be the only result.

Party leaders are only as strong as the sanctions they can bring to bear. In the British Parliament, where members depend on the leadership for help in getting elected and for appointments to the cabinet, party leaders are almost all powerful and can "whip" members into line. In the U.S. Congress, however, where the party doesn't control large campaign resources and where advancement to positions of authority is based on seniority or presidential largesse rather than leadership approval, the leadership is more in a position to persuade than to command. While the Speaker, as party leader, has some control over legislative scheduling and initial committee appointments, members are ultimately largely independent—primarily reliant on the support of those constituencies that got them elected. In fact, ideological or regional divisions within congressional parties can be just as profound in both houses as divisions between the parties themselves. For example, between 1978 and 1988, a majority of Democrats were aligned in voting against a majority of Republicans on only 49 percent of all recorded votes in the House and 45 percent of all recorded votes in the Senate.[11]

Because neither the majority party leadership nor any other coalition in Congress is dominant, there seems to be no overarching philosophical direction in the deliberations of the body. As a consequence—and this returns to the second principle of congressional life—the budget process serves the needs of the individual and his or her congressional district. Whether the national interest is served at the same time is a difficult question to answer. Would the nation be better off if members of Congress were less capable of serving their constituents? This would be the case if the Budget Committee, the party leadership, or the president were given more power over distribution of the budget and taxes. Whether citizens would be better off in that event is not entirely clear.

RESULTS OF BUDGET REFORM

When members of Congress voted to reform the budget process in 1974, they hoped to balance the budget, change national priorities, or stimulate some combination thereof. The budget clearly has not been brought into balance, although the situation may be improving. Whether the reformed budget process in Congress had anything to do with that improvement is difficult to determine. It is just as likely that Gramm-Rudman-Hollings or the simple consensus recognition of the seriousness of the deficit problem had as much to do with deficit reduction (such as it was) as did budget reform. Whether the reformed budget process had anything to do with the change in national spending priorities is another difficult question to answer. In the early 1980s there was a significant shift in spending from domestic programs to the military. It is just as likely, however, that the popular appeals of Ronald Reagan were as responsible for this shift as any procedural reform in Congress.

There is, however, one clear consequence of the reformed budget process. By adding another layer of legislation to the process, the budget reform of 1974 almost certainly contributed to delay. Between 1974 and 1989, Congress on the average adopted only four of its regular thirteen appropriations bills before the end of the fiscal year.[12] In 1986, 1987, and 1988, Congress adopted *none* of its regular appropriations bills on time.

This failure to adopt appropriations bills in a timely fashion increases the congressional workload and decreases the democratic accountability of Congress in the budget process. Between the end of the fiscal year and the passage of the regular appropriations bill, Congress must pass one and sometimes several continuing resolutions. Congress passed a total of five continuing resolutions in both 1986 and 1988. These resolutions tend to become a grab bag of legislation, bills in which all the loose ends of government are tied up into one ball. For example, in 1986 and 1987, Congress bundled all thirteen regular appropriations bills into one continuing resolution.

These continuing resolutions are so large and unwieldy that members of Congress can create so-called "Christmas tree" bills. This designation illustrates the fact that members can use large, complex, and hurriedly prepared legislation as vehicles for the passage of pet projects. With Congress in a hurry to adopt the legislation before funding for agencies expires, and because the president does not have a line-item veto, omnibus continuing resolutions become "trees" on which members can hang their own special "ornaments" in the form of new budget authority.

On October 17, 1986, both houses of Congress passed H.J. Res. 738 (P.L. 99-491) a $576 *billion* continuing resolution that was to fund the government for the 1987 fiscal year. As of this writing, it is the largest single spending bill ever passed. Although members complained about the size and complexity of the bill (no one person could possibly know all of its provisions), they were so anxious to recess in order to campaign for the 1986 midterm congressional elections that debate on the floor was speedily concluded. Paradoxically, as large as the bill was, it was not sufficient to prevent the necessity for passing a supplemental appropriations bill later on during that fiscal year. The passage of this legislation in 1986 was perhaps the nadir of congressional attempts to reform the budget process.

In an attempt to prevent a recurrence of the 1987 debacle, in 1988 the leaders of Congress from both parties attended a budget summit with President Reagan and his staff in order to negotiate a bipartisan budget agreement before the budget process got under way. The success of this summit was reflected in the fact that, for fiscal year 1989, Congress passed all thirteen of its appropriations bills before the beginning of the fiscal year (for the first time since 1977). Success, however, is by no means guaranteed as the result of such negotiations. The fact is that because there is no such thing as a consensus regarding priorities within the budget in most years, a budget summit is likely to be doomed to failure most of the time.

Finally, in an attempt to salvage something good to say about the 1974 Budget Reform Act and its antecedent fine tuning, it should be observed that the reconciliation process, in particular, seems to serve a useful purpose. In November 1989 Congress passed a reconciliation bill (P.L. 101-239) that did cut some $14.7 billion from the fiscal year 1990 budget and allowed the government (given favorable economic assumptions) to meet its GRH deficit reduction targets. The fact is that there has never been anything quite like the reconciliation process that comprehensively allows Congress to alter its appropriations and authorization strategy after the fact. The reconciliation process and the budget committees exist as resources that can be tapped should a consensus develop in Congress that it is more important to balance the budget than to deliver goods to constituents.

SUMMARY

It should be fairly obvious by now that the congressional budget process is a multifaceted and multilayered operation that exists in a constantly changing environment. The authorization committees set policy; the appropriations committees determine the levels and distribution of discretionary spending; and the taxation committees determine the volume of revenues and distribution of the tax burden. All these activities are supposed to be coordinated by the budget committees so that Congress can meet its policy obligations and budget deficit targets pursuant to the Emergency Deficit Control Act.

A number of obstacles stand in the way of budget control working as it was designed. First and foremost, almost half of all governmental spending obligations exist in the form of entitlements, or uncontrollable spending. Although it is theoretically possible for Congress to change existing statutes and cut entitlements, in the political sense, this is almost impossible. To cut programs such as Social Security, Medicare, and, to a lesser extent, unemployment compensation would require, on the part of members of Congress, a degree of political courage bordering on the suicidal. With regard to the rest of the budget, or the so-called discretionary items, many of those programs are not really controllable in the political sense. In theory, the budget committees, using the tool of reconciliation, should be able to impose some sort of overall intelligence on this process, but they cannot. In reality, the appropriations and taxation committees are much more powerful than the budget committees, making it difficult, if not impossible, for the budget committees to impose their will. Some progress has been made in controlling the spending side of the equation, but taxation remains largely beyond the control of the budget committees. Trying to control the budget process without being able to control the revenue side of the budget is like trying to create a lake by damming a dry riverbed.

As serious as these problems are, they are merely symptomatic of a larger, more intransigent obstacle. The concept of budget control violates the second rule of congressional life: what is good for the member is not necessarily good for the institution. Enacting truly effective budget reform would require members to sacrifice much of their power within the institution. Authorization and appropriations subcommittee chairs would have to defer to the dictates of the budget committees or perhaps the party leadership on budgetary matters. Would voters be understanding if their members of Congress could no longer deliver the benefits of pork-barrel spending or prevent tax increases? I suspect, as do most members of Congress, that they would not. Presumably, at some point, the deleterious economic effects of a structural deficit will outweigh the political advantages of the current system. Even then, meaningful budget reform will likely be difficult to implement. *Distributing the hardships of budget cuts and tax increases is infinitely more problematic in Congress than distributing the benefits of a surplus.* No member of Congress will be willing to suffer in isolation the political costs of budget discipline. Such a reform, to be successful, would require a system of distribution so delicate and a structure of leadership so powerful that it is difficult to envision such a scenario in the modern Congress.[13]

NOTES

1. For an excellent discussion of the causes and effects of this principle of congressional behavior, see Lawrence C. Dodd and Richard L. Schott,

Congress and the Administrative State (New York: John Wiley and Sons, 1979). In particular, see chap. 3, "Congress: The Rise of Committee Government," 58-105.

2. See Nelson Polsby, "The Institutionalization of the U.S. House of Representatives," *American Political Science Review* 62 (March 1968): 144-168.
3. In testimony before the Senate Judiciary Committee in 1971, Caspar Weinberger, deputy director of the OMB, argued that the administration was permitted to impound funds for policy purposes pursuant to: (1) the U.S. Constitution, which makes the president part of the legislative process; (2) the fact that appropriations made by Congress constitute only ceilings under which the president is permitted to operate at his own discretion; (3) the Anti-Deficiency Act of 1950 authorizes the executive to establish reserves for unforeseen contingencies; and (4) inasmuch as Article II of the Constitution requires that the laws be "faithfully executed," the president is enjoined to implement the "spirit" rather than the letter of the law. Cited in Howard E. Shuman, *Politics and the Budget* 2d ed. (Englewood Cliffs, N.J.: Prentice-Hall, 1988), 211-212.

   Eventually, the courts found that the president had no constitutional authority to impound funds that had been appropriated by law for these programs. See, for example, *National Association of State Universities and Land Grant Colleges v. Weinberger,* Civ. Action No. 1014-73 (D.D.C. 1973).
4. P.L. 93-250.
5. "Doubtful Congress Clears Gramm-Rudman Fix," *Congressional Quarterly Weekly Report,* September 26, 1987, 2039.
6. Norman Ornstein, Thomas Mann, and Michael Malbin, *Vital Statistics on Congress: 1989-1990* (Washington, D.C.: Congressional Quarterly Inc., 1990), 179.
7. House Rule XXI, clause 2(a) and Senate Rule XVI.
8. For a dated but still fairly accurate exploration of the politics of the Appropriations Committee in the House, see Richard Fenno, *The Power of the Purse* (Boston: Little, Brown, 1965).
9. The 1986 Tax Reform Act had the effect of reversing some of these tendencies. The act did away with a number of tax loopholes. Nevertheless, the ability of a decentralized committee to resist amending the tax code for the benefit of its constituents will inevitably put enormous pressure on the fragile coalition of support for the 1986 reform.
10. Norman J. Ornstein, "Causes and Consequences of Congressional Change: Subcommittee Reforms in the House of Representatives, 1970-1973," in Ornstein, ed., *Congress in Change: Evolution and Reform,* (New York: Praeger, 1975), 88-114.
11. Ornstein et al., *Vital Statistics on Congress: 1989-1990,* 200.
12. Ornstein, ed., *Congress in Change,* 182.
13. Perhaps the model in this regard should be the 1986 Tax Reform Act. To the surprise of many observers, Congress managed to reform the tax code by repealing a wide range of tax loopholes for special interests in exchange for a reduction of the top rate for income taxes and a simplification of the tax code. Of course, the application of this example can be taken only so far inasmuch as the reform was purported to be revenue neutral. Had the reforms been designed to increase taxes, however, it is not clear that such a deal could have been made so easily. For an excellent discussion of the adoption of the 1986 Tax Reform Act, see Jeffrey H. Birnbaum and Alan S. Murray, *Showdown at Gucci Gulch: Lawmakers, Lobbyists, and the Unlikely Triumph of Tax Reform* (New York: Random House, 1987).

PART II

Seasons of the Budget

CHAPTER 3

September 1990: A Tidal Wave of Debt

Scholars have long observed that one of the most important characteristics of change in the budget is incrementalism.[1] Budget totals are not built from the ground up but are layered on existing law. Any new procedural structure also exists as an artifact of the past. It is impossible, therefore, to discuss in isolation a particular event or set of events in the budget process. In 1990-1991 the budget process was affected by and was in many ways the product of ongoing controversies. Most notably, the story of the creation of the 1990 budget summit agreement is central to any discussion of the budget process that was to follow.

In this chapter I will place in historical context some of the ongoing controversies that were being debated at the beginning of fiscal year 1991. This was in many ways a historic year. For all intents and purposes, Gramm-Rudman-Hollings was reduced to a shell of its former self by the compromises contained in the 1990 budget summit accord. The new emphasis in budgeting, as we shall see, would be spending rather than deficit control, but this fundamental change did not occur easily or overnight. Change in this case was the product of a round of negotiations in September 1990 that was one of the most tumultuous ever to take place.

From a budgetary perspective, 1990 began as a relatively upbeat year. When President Bush proposed his 1991 budget in January 1990, there was optimism that although the president may have fudged his economic projections a bit, the inevitable cuts necessary to meet the Gramm-Rudman-Hollings deficit reduction target ($64 billion) would not be so massive or harmful that politicians or the economy would incur substantial risks in that election year. What happened in the ensuing months, however, quickly dissipated this complacency.

By the beginning of September, a sense of panic and foreboding rarely experienced by even the most seasoned insider swept the Capitol.

What turned the optimism of January into the doom of September was a change in conditions that illustrates a general point. *For every economic projection, for every guideline cast in statute or even in the Constitution, there is a series of events unplanned for—either because they were unexpected or too politically unpalatable to contemplate—that will derail the most thoughtfully conceived plans for governing.* Or, to put it more succinctly, "It's always something." Natural disaster will strike, the economy will cycle downward, or international events will conspire to negate even the most careful planning. In other words, this principle demands that government be somewhat flexible. Such a construct makes the prospect of designing a process to guarantee an annual balanced budget largely impossible (and probably undesirable). What happened to the GRH statute in 1990 is a classic illustration of the pitfalls of inflexible budgetary planning.

THE PRESIDENT'S BUDGET AND ESTIMATION SHORTFALLS

When President Bush presented his 1991 budget, he projected a deficit of about $100 billion. This would require, pursuant to GRH, $36 billion in spending reductions or revenue increases. In fact, because the GRH law allows for a $10 billion margin of error, it was more likely that the president and Congress would have to find only $26 billion in deficit reduction if the OMB's January assumptions about the nation's economic performance were correct. These figures did not seem too troublesome, as $26 billion is only about 2.2 percent of a $1.2 trillion budget. Furthermore, the president had every reason to believe that the windfall of the "peace dividend" and the economy's steady expansion since 1982 would make the GRH targets relatively easy to achieve.

Almost from the beginning, however, there were signs of trouble. In early February the Congressional Budget Office issued a report disputing Bush's economic assumptions. The president's OMB had projected, in drawing up its budget proposal, a growth rate of 2.6 percent. The CBO, on the other hand, projected a growth rate of only 1.8 percent. In terms of dollars and cents, the CBO projected an expansion of the economy of about $40 billion less than the president's projections. This disparity represented a potential shortfall of about $10 billion in revenues below the president's original projections (the federal budget is about a quarter of the gross national product). The CBO also disputed the OMB's projection for lower interest rates. Higher interest rates would increase the government's costs in servicing the debt. In addition, early in the year, administration officials were suggesting that the cost of the savings and loan bailout for the year would be $30 billion more than the government's original estimates. Finally, the CBO suggested that the president's budget overestimated the effect of his proposed "administrative savings" by about $10 billion.[2] The CBO therefore arrived at a deficit estimate of about $131 billion—$31 billion above the OMB's projections and almost $70 billion above the Gramm-Rudman target for fiscal year 1991.

If the CBO was correct and the government was forced to find $70 billion in deficit reduction, through budget cuts, tax increases, or a sequester, the economy would probably suffer devastating effects. Because a great deal of economic activity is dependent on government spending, the effect of sudden, massive cuts in funding at the end of the fiscal year would have a negative effect that would ripple through the economy, resulting in a contraction of economic activity well in excess of $70 billion. Economists call this the multiplier effect. For every dollar spent by the government, collateral economic activity is stimulated equivalent to two or three dollars. This means that for every worker constructing a weapons system, there are other workers in a subsidiary or support role who depend on the health of defense-related industries for their jobs. In addition, because pursuant to GRH interest on the debt and certain programs are exempt from sequestration (mainly domestic entitlement programs such as Social Security), the full weight of a sequester must be borne by a very small part of the budget—roughly half from defense and the rest from domestic discretionary spending (education, law enforcement, housing, transportation, etc.). A $70 billion reduction in spending would therefore profoundly affect the level of government services.

Later in the year, on May 17, the CBO issued a report assessing the effects of a theoretical $75 billion sequester. According to the CBO, it would cut 19 percent from defense and 28.3 percent of nondefense discretionary spending. In more human terms, such a sequester would eliminate, among other things, more than 100,000 children from the Head Start program and 900,000 Pell grants for education. Clearly such a drastic cut in services was politically unacceptable—so much so that as the months passed and the budget projections became even more dismal, the president began to lobby Congress for a budget summit meeting. Such a summit, the White House hoped, would provide the consensus and political "cover" needed for some of the more politically unpalatable budgetary choices that would have to be made. Specifically, any new budget agreement almost certainly would have to include some combination of three politically disastrous prescriptions: tax increases, benefits reductions, and the gutting of Gramm-Rudman-Hollings.

Unfortunately for the president, a number of roadblocks stood in the path of a budget summit for 1990. The one held the previous year had been beset by partisan squabbles. In April 1989 the budget summit had produced a compromise package of spending cuts and $5.3 billion in "unspecified" revenue enhancements that would help the federal government meet its fiscal year 1990 $110 billion GRH deficit reduction target. It was over this unspecified revenue increase that acrimony erupted.

THE 1989 LEGACY

Bush, in his 1988 nomination acceptance speech at the Republican National Convention, had made his famous "read my lips" promise not to support any new tax increases. Furthermore, he consistently clubbed his Democratic opponent, Governor Michael Dukakis, and the Democratic party throughout the 1988 campaign as being the candidate and party supporting high levels of taxation and expenditure. With the 1990 elections in mind, the Democrats were reluctant to recommend any new tax measures lest the president's campaign charges be proved true. Consequently, when the 1989 negotiators arrived at a budget agreement in April, both sides, particularly the Democrats, were reluctant to specify how the new revenues were to be raised. The president, however, had a plan to raise almost all the needed revenues in a way that would not look like a tax increase.

During his presidential campaign, candidate George Bush had proposed a reduction in the capital gains tax rate. This tax imposes a government levy on the profits from sales of most properties or securities. Prior to the passage of the 1986 Tax Reform Act, capital gains had been taxed at a lower rate than regular income. The 1986 tax reform raised the capital gains tax rate by treating capital gains as regular income. The president and a number of economists argued that this revised assessment of capital gains was not only bad for business—because it discouraged investment—but also unfair.[3]

The budgetary effect of such a reduction in the capital gains rate is not entirely clear. However, it seems probable that, in the short run, such a reduction would produce a net gain for the Treasury (as investors sold off their holdings), while in the long term a capital gains tax reduction would produce a net loss as the lower rates shielded profits from the tax collector.[4] In addition, the benefits of a capital gains reduction are mostly realized by the wealthy, who have excess income to invest and the greatest opportunity to utilize the valuable tax advantages available to them through itemizing deductions on their tax returns. Consequently, most congressional Democrats opposed the reduction in the capital gains rate not only because it was potentially a net revenue loser and threatened the delicate compromise reached in the 1986 Tax Reform Act but also because it would create further inequities in the nation's tax structure. In the short run, however, a reduction in capital gains could be politically popular because it would provide a rare opportunity to cut taxes and raise revenues at the same time.

As the fiscal year drew to a close in 1989, the success of the April agreement hinged on how the congressional tax-writing committees were going to raise the $5.3 billion in new revenues. Eventually a sort of standoff developed. No one in Congress or in the administration wanted to be the first to recommend new taxes because to do so would mean taking the heat in the next political campaign for being the party of higher taxation. When Ways and Means Committee chair Dan Rostenkowski finally recommended a package of revenue enhancements (a politician's code word for taxes) that did not include a capital gains reduction, a group of conservative Democrats on the committee led by Ed Jenkins of Georgia rebelled. Jenkins proposed, and over the objections of Rostenkowski managed to pass through the committee, a reduction of the capital gains tax rate that was projected to generate $4.8 billion (almost all the needed revenues) in the first year. The House eventually adopted the Jenkins proposal. At this point, seizing the opportunity presented by renegade Democrats, the White House also began to push for adoption of the capital gains reduction in the Senate.

Congressional Democrats felt betrayed. By supporting the capital gains tax cut, the White House put congressional Democrats in a difficult position. Senate Democrats were particularly discomfited (the House having already passed the measure). By opposing the capital gains tax rate reduction, Senate Democrats would seem to oppose a politically "immaculate conception"—an increase in revenues that, in fact, reduced the taxes of constituents. Senate Democrats were furious. They had entered into the April budget agreement with the understanding that the nonspecified $5.3 billion would be raised without increasing the deficit in future years or contributing further to tax system inequities. In other words, they hoped that the president would be forced to propose new taxes, thus going back on his campaign pledge.

It is not too cynical to suggest that the Democrats would then have had a political club with which to bash the president during the next electoral cycle. Instead, they found themselves outmaneuvered, not necessarily by the White House but by the circumstances and by members of their own party in the House. Senate Democrats refused to budge on the issue. Given the prospect of a political logjam, minority leader Sen. Bob Dole managed to convince the president to drop his insistence on a capital gains reduction for the 1990 fiscal year. Nevertheless, the 1989 experience made congressional Democrats especially cautious going into 1990.[5]

Added to this legacy of conflict was the bad blood that existed between congressional leaders and budget director Richard Darman. Darman had been one of the most partisan budget directors since the

OMB was moved to the Executive Office of the President in 1939. Not only had he been the administration's point man during the 1989 capital gains controversy, but he also had taken the unusual step of including in the printed version of the president's 1991 budget proposals an introduction that scolded Congress for its lack of responsibility in the budget process.

In his "Director's Introduction to the New Budget," Darman made headlines by comparing the federal budget to the "Sesame Street" character, the Cookie Monster. The budget, Darman said, was in itself benign and intended to do good for society but was potentially damaging to the economy because of its tendency to gobble up every available resource destined for investment and production in the private sector.[6] Within the budget, Darman wrote, there were hidden budgetary PACMEN waiting to eat up every available resource in the budget and more. Among these PACMEN were the rising cost of health care passed on to the government through the Medicare and Medicaid programs, expensive obligations to clean up federal nuclear weapons production facilities, and the cost of insuring the accounts of depositors in savings and loan institutions.[7] Finally, and most directly aimed at Congress, was Darman's suggestion that the congressional approach to budgeting was characterized by games that helped members shirk their responsibility to balance the budget.

Congressional profligacy, Darman argued, was shielded from the public by the "spend the Peace Dividend" game, in which members of Congress not only overestimated the size of this dividend but proposed plans that would spend the proceeds of the windfall many times over.[8] Darman also specifically attacked Democratic senator Daniel Patrick Moynihan's plan to cut Social Security taxes. This "cut the social security game," Darman claimed, would not only undermine that program but lead to higher taxes somewhere else.[9] Finally, Darman criticized the "beat the budget game," which he characterized as a cynical, self-serving attempt by members of Congress to avoid, postpone, and eventually find political cover for the shirking of politically difficult budgetary decisions.[10]

CONGRESS TRIES IT ON ITS OWN

Congressional Democrats were so angered by Darman's attacks that they decided to draw up their own budget plan in the spring of 1990 without entering into a budget summit with the president and his budget director. The Democrats were confident that they could write their own budget resolution since they enjoyed a large majority in both the House and the Senate. Furthermore, while individual appropriation measures would be subject to a presidential veto (and thus could be derailed by the Republican minority), the budget resolution, being an entirely intrainstitutional construct, would be the Democrats' province to dictate.[11] As it turned out, however, this was an overly optimistic assumption. The Democrats would still face an enormous obstacle in gaining majority agreement in the House because they could not guarantee unanimity even within their own party. This was very quickly discovered when they tried to pass their budget resolution by April 15.

Congressional Republicans refused to participate in the process of devising a congressional budget resolution, and there was tremendous disagreement within the Democratic party over, among other things, the distribution of the peace dividend. So divided was the party that by the time the Democratic budget resolution (H. Con. Res. 310) came to the floor, it attracted only 218 votes—the absolute minimum number of votes needed to constitute a majority in the House. No Republicans voted for the plan, and thirty-four Democrats defected from the party line.

The greatest fault of the Democratic budget resolution, aside from its shaky political foundation, was that it was obsolete even before being passed. The measure provided for only $36 billion in deficit reduction—a figure that was useful in January when the deficit was projected to be $100 billion (with a deficit target of $64 billion). However, by the time the resolution was passed in the House on May 1, deficit projections had been revised upward to the $120-$170 billion range. Under those conditions, a devastating sequester would still be impossible to avoid.

However obsolete the House measure, it was still better and farther along than similar legislation in the Senate. By May 1 the legislation had yet to leave the Senate Budget Committee, owing to the severe conflicts among Senate Democrats over the character of the budget resolution.

Both President Bush and Congress were now in a quandary. With October 1 quickly approaching, the president faced a massive sequester for which he and his party would take much of the blame. In Congress it was difficult for the appropriations committees to begin work without the targets provided by a completed budget resolution. Authorization measures passed during the late spring and early summer tended to authorize spending well in excess of the president's requests and the confines of reasonable budgetary constraints. Members felt free to authorize this excess spending in the expectation that the actual appropriations for the authorized programs would either be cut or sequestered. For members, authorization measures were thus a "free vote" for excess spending that would never actually be funded.

By early May 1990 the prospect that the budget process could proceed further without some kind of bipartisan budget negotiations was beginning to fade. Up to this point, budget summits had provided compromises necessary to gain majority support in both houses from both sides of the aisle. Just that kind of consensus was needed here. Congressional Democrats, however, were not ready to begin negotiations until the president would state his willingness to consider new taxes as part of any deficit reduction package.

THE 1990 BUDGET SUMMIT

The stalemate was broken on May 9 when the president announced that he would enter into bipartisan budget negotiations with congressional leaders without any preconditions. This meant that a tax increase (of any kind) was open to discussion. Democrats were jubilant at the prospect of making President Bush retreat from his no-new-taxes pledge. Republicans, on the other hand, were devastated and publicly began to desert the president in droves. On the day of the president's announcement, eighteen Republican senators led by Connie Mack of Florida held a press conference to reiterate their opposition to any new tax plan. Soon thereafter, two-thirds of all House Republicans signed a pledge to oppose any new tax measures to reduce the deficit.

Reflecting the dissension even within the White House staff over the president's decision to consider new taxes, a number of stories were leaked to the press (most likely from White House sources) indicating that the president had no intention of supporting any new tax increase. Congressional Democrats, already sensitized by the previous year's experience, reacted by suggesting that they were being led into a trap that would force them to broach the subject of taxes and cause them to take the blame. Only a last-minute phone call from President Bush to House Speaker Thomas Foley was able to assuage the Democrats' concerns and save the summit before it even got started.

The selection of the summit conferees did not augur well for the success of the negotiations. In addition to representatives from the Appropriations, Finance, and Ways and Means committees, some of the more partisan, unyielding members of Congress were selected. From the House came Republican Minority Whip Newt Gingrich of Georgia, who was adamantly opposed to any tax increases. As a devotee of supply-side economics, he supported tax reduction as a way to stimulate the economy and thus generate new revenues. For the Democrats, Majority Leader (and former presidential candidate) Richard Gephardt, who was in the midst of a public feud with President Bush, was appointed to preside over the summit in the president's absence. From the Senate side came Phil Gramm (co-author of GRH) and Bob Packwood, a sponsor of the capital gains reduction plan from the year before. The administration was represented by the conservative, abrasive presidential chief of staff, John Sununu, and the much reviled budget director, Richard Darman (along with Secretary of the Treasury Nicholas Brady). Because of the broad-based composition of the panel, any compromise the summit managed to reach would almost certainly serve the interests of the broadest number of members of the full House and Senate. However, the participants' ideological diversity and personality conflicts would prove to be stumbling blocks that made reaching a compromise quite difficult and, in the end, impossible.

Throughout the summer of 1990, the budget summit met without reaching an agreement. In the meantime, external conditions conspired to aggravate the budget impasse. By the middle of July, projections on the state of the economy continued to worsen. According to the OMB, the projected growth in GNP was reduced from 2.6 percent to 2.2 percent while inflation was projected to increase. Interest rates were also projected to increase—an added cost for the government as it paid higher interest rates on the borrowed money necessary to cover deficit spending. The unemployment rate was also expected to rise. Because OMB projections are, by law, used as a basis for GRH sequesters, the fact that the OMB was projecting a deficit in excess of $148 billion ($48 billion higher than its original projection in January) meant that without a budget agreement reducing the deficit to $74 billion ($64 billion plus the $10 billion "fudge factor" GRH permits) the government would be facing a sequester of as much as $75 billion on October 1. The size of these cuts was so unthinkable, so potentially damaging to the national economy and national security, that the budget summit would have no choice but to cut the deficit and, at the same time, consider the repeal or reform of GRH itself.

Even if the summit were to reach an agreement, the budget cuts and taxes necessary to meet the GRH target as it then stood would be ruinous to the economy. Once before, in 1987, Congress had simply voted to put off its GRH obligations for a year. It was expected that as part of the package for this year the summiteers would again recommend an extension or outright repeal of GRH along with a limited (below the target) package of deficit reductions.

All of this was easier to plan for than to agree on. As it was an election year, members were in no mood to make tough budget decisions that would hurt them on the campaign trail. Incumbents were already under attack for widespread involvement with individuals and political action committees associated with the savings and loan scandal. In late June, Common Cause, a public interest research group, released a report documenting the distribution of more than $11 million in campaign contributions to members of Congress by organizations or individuals representing savings and loan institutions. Members of Congress running scared on this issue were reluctant to go along with painful budget cuts or tax increases. This mood permeated the budget summit. Any agreement adopted would ultimately have to be voted on by both houses of Congress and probably supported by majorities on both sides of the aisle.

The meetings of the summit in July, before the August recess, were permeated with acrimony and a thickening atmosphere of desperation. House Majority Leader Richard Gephardt, who chaired the summit, opened the July 19 meeting by accusing Republican negotiators of blocking the success of the talks with their public refusal to consider new taxes. He was responding to the no-new-taxes resolution adopted in caucus by the 176 GOP House members the day before. The meeting then degenerated into a round of recriminations, with each side accusing the other of failing to negotiate in good faith. In actuality, the summit faced the same problem it had confronted the year before, the only difference being that the stakes were higher and getting higher all the time. On July 27 the Commerce Department revised its GNP growth rate estimates downward. Such a decline was likely to lead to an increase in unemployment and a corresponding decline in revenue receipts for the government. Furthermore, on July 30 the administration announced that funds for dealing with the savings and loan crisis were nearly exhausted and that the cost of the bailout was projected to go as high as $100 billion for fiscal year 1991. As bad as this news was for the budget, the deficit situation was about to take a turn for the worse at the end of July.

In the tradition of the principle that "it is always something," on August 2 Iraq invaded Kuwait. While GRH permits its own suspension during an emergency, this did not provide a basis for suspension of the budget talks since American troops were not yet involved in an actual military conflict. Rather, the invasion in several ways exacerbated the nation's debt. First, the direct cost of the American troop commitment to Saudi Arabia was projected to be about $12 billion to $15 billion (in the absence of a shooting war). Even though American allies were eventually persuaded by secretaries James Baker and Nicholas Brady to pick up part of the cost, and even though the Defense Department could manage to cover part of the expense of the deployment through the transfer of funds within its own budget, the invasion had the effect of partially canceling out the peace dividend.[12] In a more subtle way, the Iraqi invasion and the American response put more strain on the budget. In the context of the American deployment in the Middle East, a number of defense programs for which there was no justification at the end of the cold war became vital components of the American defense establishment in the new, post-cold-war, national security environment. Furthermore, the budget deficit was likely to increase as higher oil prices resulting from the Middle East crisis contributed to a slowing economy.

By mid-August the fiscal year 1991 deficit was projected to be as high as $169 billion, with the consequent potential for a disastrous $100 billion sequester. The largest sequester in history to that point had been in fiscal year 1986 when $11.7 billion was withheld (only about 5 percent of outlays). If the government were required to cut $100 billion, discretionary domestic spending would be cut by about 25 percent and the military budget by as much as 41 percent. Because GRH provides for partially exempting the military budget from sequester in times of national emergency, the Iraqi invasion did provide political cover for avoiding part of the GRH deficit reduction target.[13] Nevertheless, with the invasion and the resulting increase in oil prices, it became almost a foregone conclusion that GRH would be repealed, reformed, or quietly put off until another year.

The most likely suggestion for amending GRH, it seemed, would be for Congress to adopt a five-year, $500 billion deficit reduction, with roughly $50 billion in savings slated for the first year. This plan had all the trappings of a grand compromise. It postponed even larger deficit reduction (almost ensuring further budgetary crises) and, at the same time, would permit members of Congress to go back to their districts in an election year, claiming they had voted "to cut the deficit by $500 billion." The fact that the government had failed to meet its deficit targets in fiscal year 1990 would not be mentioned, nor would incumbents hint at the likelihood that planned reductions after the first year could always be changed or put off again until a later time. In this way, members would be able to wriggle out of their commitments to meet mandated deficit targets.

In the absence of a budget agreement, the appropriations process was stalled on Capitol Hill. By September 7 the House had passed ten of its regular thirteen appropriations bills, while the Senate had acted on only two. Both houses of Congress were waiting for a budget agreement that would almost certainly call for deep cuts in appropriations and the passage of an entirely new package of taxes. Consequently the appropriations measures adopted up to this point were in some sense already obsolete. Members of the Appropriations, Ways and Means, and Finance committees despaired at the prospect that their work could be undone at the budget summit. This concern for the jurisdictional sensibilities of congressional committees was ultimately a constraint on the budget summit. Committee recommendations (and jurisdictional boundaries) had to be taken into account in order to win widespread congressional support for the budget plan.

With the October 1 deadline approaching, the budget summit was still stalled over the issue of new taxes. In general terms, it was clear that the compromise agreement was eventually going to mandate a roughly equal portion of taxes and budget cuts. The spending cuts would probably include, along with reductions in defense spending and discretionary domestic programs, reductions in entitlement programs (so-called uncontrollable spending), including Medicare. While there was agreement in principle on the budget-cutting side of the equation (although the numbers were still far apart), on the tax side, schisms existed not only along party lines but within the parties themselves. The Republicans, backed by the White House, again introduced the capital gains tax reduction proposal. The Democrats united behind a proposal to increase the tax rate on the very wealthy.

The basis for a relatively equitable compromise seemed to exist. Democrats would exchange the lowering of the capital gains tax rate for a higher income tax rate for the wealthy. However, when word of the impending deal was leaked, a number of House Democrats warned that they would not support any reduction in the capital gains tax rate, while Newt Gingrich, representing conservative Republicans, rejected any tax increase altogether. In early September he delivered a speech reiterating his call for a widespread reduction in taxes in order to stimulate the economy. While other participants in the budget summit opposed Gingrich's proposal out of hand (even other Republicans), there was reason to believe that quite a few House Republicans were inclined to agree with their minority whip.

The news leaks to the press and other members of Congress had a devastating effect. Given advance notice, different sides on the tax question had time to marshal their forces in opposition to any plan. Budget negotiators were hemmed in at every turn by vocal activists who sought to scuttle various components of the very delicate deal that was in the works. Consequently, when the budget summit reconvened on September 7, the location of the meetings was transferred to an officers' club on Andrews Air Force Base just outside the capital. In their desperation, summiteers had hoped that a change of scenery, the relative isolation, and the restricted access of an air force base would be conducive to agreement. But the talks remained stalled. The preliminary summit schedule called for an agreement by September 10 (leaving Congress twenty days to approve the agreement and adopt its appropriations bills), but on September 18 the summit broke up without reaching an agreement. It was announced that, as in the past, the main stumbling block was still taxes. On other issues the gaps had narrowed. For example, Republicans and Democrats were only about $30 billion apart (about 3 percent of the total defense budget over the next five years) on the issue of military spending reductions.

In the meantime, federal workers were informed during the third week of September that they were likely to be laid off as of October 1. On September 25, in anticipation of the summit's failure to reach a budget agreement, the House appropriations committees reported to the full House a continuing resolution that would temporarily waive GRH sequesters and provide stopgap funding for the government until October 20. The president, however, made it clear that he would veto any waiver of GRH sequestration that was approved before Congress adopted some sort of deficit reduction plan. Should Congress fail to adopt a plan by September 28, President Bush stated that "Americans will have to face a tough mandated sequester."

In late September three possible scenarios began to develop. The most optimistic scenario posited a breakthrough in the budget talks. Even if such an agreement were concluded soon enough, with Congress approving the compromise plan, it was still unlikely that Congress would be able to finish its work by the end of the fiscal year. Congress would not only have to approve the budget agreement and pass all thirteen of its regular appropriations bills by September 30 but also, at the same time, construct and pass a reconciliation bill that would require the reconsideration of appropriations measures already approved.

A second, more probable scenario was one in which some sequestration would occur, whether or not the budget summit reached some kind of agreement before the end of the fiscal year. If Congress passed a continuing resolution before reaching a budget accord, pursuant to the GRH law, sequestration would automatically take effect. If a budget agreement were to be approved, appropriations bills were to be reconciled and passed, and the president were to get a budget that either waived or met the GRH guidelines, sequestration would be lifted as soon the new budget was signed into law.[14]

Under the worst-case scenario, the outcome would be far less benign. If the budget negotiations were to fail and the president were to veto a continuing resolution, the federal government would simply cease to function. There would be no funds available. All nonessential federal employees would be laid off and their agencies closed down. Everything from the military to veterans hospitals and the nation's airports would be subject to closure. The speculation was that in the event of such a complete breakdown in the budget process, the president would call on certain statutory and prerogative powers to order essential government personnel back to work.[15] Even though the president would surely protect the military from a shutdown, the effects of a general work stoppage would be incalculable. Social Security checks would be withheld from the elderly,[16] passenger rail and air traffic would be delayed or grind to a halt, welfare recipients would go without payments, and so on.

On September 17, still without an agreement, the budget summit left Andrews Air Force Base and continued its negotiations at the Capitol. These talks had an ultimately fateful, distinguishing characteristic. In order to facilitate compromise, the number of participants was reduced from seventeen to eight. Excluded from this new "super summit" were all members of Congress except the majority and minority party leaders of both Houses. Of particular importance was the exclusion of the chairmen of both tax-writing committees (Dan Rostenkowski and Lloyd Bentsen), as well as the maverick minority whip, Newt Gingrich. While this move may have facilitated agreement within the summit, it generated resentment in Congress. There was certainly some question as to whether congressional leaders could impose a summit agreement on Congress under such conditions.

THE FIRST OCTOBER DEAL

Throughout late September the super summit met without agreement. The appropriations process remained suspended. By the last week of September it became almost certain that the nation would face at least a sequester. Then, at eleven o'clock in the morning on Sunday, September 30, at almost the last possible moment (thirteen hours before the end of the fiscal year), Richard Darman announced in the White House press room that the summit had reached an agreement. Congress, which had been forced by the delay and threat of government shutdown to stay in session, awaited the Speaker's call to convene, not to consider the budget agreement but to adopt a continuing resolution that would fund the government temporarily.

Only the barest outline of the agreement (whose finer points were still being negotiated) was made available to the press and Congress. The logjam had been broken, making an agreement possible, when the president dropped his demand for a reduction in the capital gains tax rate in exchange for concessions from the Democrats, who set aside their demands for an increase in income tax rates for the wealthy. The result was a four-part agreement intended to provide $500 billion in deficit reduction over five years, compromising the positions of both the right and the left.

For conservatives, the most controversial aspects of the plan were its tax provisions. While President Bush managed to maintain a degree of fidelity to his no-new-taxes pledge by protecting income tax rates from revision, the agreement did mandate the collection of $134 billion in "new revenues" over the term of the compromise. Congressional conservatives, who had vowed to oppose any new tax increase, were largely unwilling to accept the president's ruse. In order to collect the new revenues, the agreement called for the adoption of a ten cent per gallon tax on gasoline, a two cent per gallon tax on home heating oil,[17] new liquor and cigarette taxes, sales taxes on the purchase of luxury items, and a reduction in the amount of income-tax deductions for the wealthy. In exchange for dropping his insistence on a capital gains tax reduction—which the president hoped would stimulate the economy—the budget agreement also authorized the creation of new investment tax credits for small and medium sized businesses. These tax incentives, which represented a net loss to the Treasury, were offset by the increase in gasoline taxes and the reduction in deductible taxable income for the rich.

Liberals, too, were upset over the tax provisions of the plan. According to estimates released by Congress's Joint Committee on Taxation, the burden of the new taxes would largely fall on the lower middle class. For wage earners with annual incomes from $20,000 to $50,000, the new tax would represent a net increase of about 3 percent. For individuals with incomes in excess of $200,000, taxes would increase by only a third of a percent. Worst of all were projections that persons earning less than $10,000 would experience a whopping 7.6 percent increase in their taxes.[18] Liberals were outraged that in the aftermath of the Reagan revolution, with its increasingly regressive tax rates, the new summit plan was making taxes even more regressive.

Another aspect of the plan that was highly objectionable to liberals was the provision to reduce Medicare benefits over five years by a total of $60 billion. Other entitlements, such as Social Security, would be protected from any cuts. The response from liberals to this proposal was immediate and profoundly negative. Senior-citizen groups began to rally their forces in opposition to the plan.

On the expenditure side, the agreement called for more than $200 billion in savings from discretionary programs. Most of these cuts (about $170 billion) were to come from defense. Political conservatives were concerned about these cuts, particularly in view of American involvement in Operation Desert Shield. The agreement also called for a $12 billion reduction in agricultural price supports—a large cut in percentage terms—which alarmed members of Congress from predominantly agricultural districts. Even though most other discretionary programs were generally excluded from the cuts, the disparate combination of objections to the plan formed an unusual and wide-ranging coalition in opposition to the agreement.

Finally, the budget agreement was based on a set of economic assumptions set forth by the OMB that were considered completely unrealistic by many economists and members of Congress.[19] In order to reach its goal of deficit reduction, the agreement assumed that, even though the country was heading into a recession, the growth rate would nearly double in 1991, interest rates would drop, and the price of oil would fall in the next twelve months from $40 to $24.15 a barrel. If these economic projections were to prove incorrect, the deficit in the "out years" of the plan would be significantly larger than projected.

Nevertheless, the summiteers had reached a budget agreement just before the deadline. By four o'clock on Sunday afternoon, Congress was back in session to pass a continuing resolution designed to fund the government in the short term. There was some controversy on the floor concerning the duration of this resolution (since Congress needed time to pass thirteen appropriations bills and a reconciliation bill once the budget resolution was passed), but the president made it clear that he would not sign a continuing resolution that extended government funding beyond October 5, especially in the absence of congressional approval of the budget summit agreement. The president and his advisers hoped that this threat would assure quick consideration of the agreement and lead Congress to approve the entire package virtually intact. The less time Congress had to consider the budget package, they reasoned, the less time its opponents would have to marshal their forces. By threatening to veto any continuing resolution longer than five days, the president virtually assured that Congress would face another budgetary crisis within five days if the agreement were rejected.

On the afternoon of September 30 Congress quickly passed and sent to the president House Joint Resolution 655, a bill to provide for continuing appropriations until October 5. The bill put off the imposition of GRH sequesters until expiration of the continuing resolution. The president signed the legislation before midnight that evening, averting disaster, at least temporarily. The burden still remained on the president and the congressional leadership to convince an increasingly hostile membership of Congress from both sides of the aisle to support a painful, sure to be unpopular package of budget cuts and tax increases.

SUMMARY

From what started out as a relatively placid budget cycle, consideration of the fiscal year 1991 budget gradually degenerated into crisis. The fact that neither the president nor Congress was able to come to an agreement satisfying the requirements of the Gramm-Rudman-Hollings law was a demonstration of the principle that balanced budgets cannot be mandated by law. For many years Congress and the president had put off tough decisions that would have made it possible to meet deficit reduction targets in future years. In 1990 the president presented his budget to Congress as if it were business as usual. It contained all kinds of assumptions about economic performance that were highly unrealistic. Nevertheless, it looked as if the president and Congress might be able to meet their deficit reduction obligations for at least another year, if for no other reason than the peace dividend, which provided for significant and unexpected savings in the budget. Events conspired, however, to derail both Democratic and Republican plans for deficit reduction. First, the increased costs of the savings and loan bailout significantly raised the projected deficit. Then, by midyear, the economy began to slow down, rendering functionally useless the president's initial economic projections. The coup de grace to deficit reduction was delivered by the crisis in the Persian Gulf. Crude oil prices almost doubled, sending the economy further into decline. The president then committed American troops to a mission that was sure to eat up many of the budgetary savings presented by the collapse of the Warsaw Pact.

The budget summit that was finally convened encountered serious difficulties in arriving at an agreement. These difficulties were exacerbated by the worsening economic situation but were based on ideological and philosophical differences that separate the political parties in the United States. The philosophy of the Republican party was reflected in the president's insistence on reducing the capital gains tax. Higher taxes, to the wealthy in particular, are anathema to most Republicans on the grounds that they punish successful individuals and discourage investment in industries that generate jobs and prosperity. Many Republicans at the summit believed that imposing higher income tax rates without lowering the capital gains tax rate would send the country into recession, with American capital flowing abroad in search of a more hospitable economic environment.

The philosophy of the Democratic party, on the other hand, was reflected in its insistence on imposing a more progressive system of taxation. Throughout the 1980s the tax system had become increasingly regressive, helping to produce a widening gap between the richest Americans and the poorest. Some Democrats believed that reducing the capital gains tax rate would result in a further separation between rich and poor, and that a heavier tax load on the poor and the middle class would help create a permanent underclass unable to finance an education, obtain proper medical care, invest in business, or otherwise advance. Democratic opposition to the capital gains tax rate reduction is based on more than abstract principles. Many Democrats believe that creating investment incentives for the wealthy would simply make the deficit grow larger. It was precisely this Republican commitment to supply-side economics (countering deficits with tax cuts), according to Democrats, that created the huge budget deficits of the 1980s.

These ideological differences came to a head at just this time due to a confluence of events. Heretofore, budget negotiators had been able to finesse the GRH deficit targets by simply cutting fat out of the budget, selling governmental assets, harming politically powerless constituencies, or creating phony economic scenarios. But in 1990 the GRH targets were so far below the size of the deficit, the economy was so weak, and too many of the politically easy cuts had already been made that, in combination with the inevitable budgetary crises that occur in the course of any fiscal year, the annual budget cycle set off one of the most meaningful political debates in American history. Negotiators were confronted with imposing budget cuts and tax increases on some of the most important and powerful political constituencies in the country. The budget summit stalled not over minor disagreements and the unwillingness of its participants to compromise but over the issue of taxation, reflecting fundamental philosophical differences. Whether the leadership of both parties would be able to defend the compromise it ultimately reached would reflect not only the quality of political leadership in the federal government but, more importantly, the true ideological divisions within American society.

NOTES

1. See Aaron Wildavsky, *The Politics of the Budgetary Process* (Boston: Little, Brown, 1964); and Allen Schick, "Incremental Budgeting in a Decremental Age," in Albert C. Hyde, ed., *Government Budgeting,* 2d ed. (Pacific Grove, Calif.: Brooks/Cole, 1992), 410-425.
2. The "administrative savings" in the president's budget were to be realized from procedural reforms in various federal bureaucracies.
3. The argument goes something like this: the government should reward an investor for incurring risks, especially if those investments create jobs and profits and thus higher government revenues. Furthermore, treating capital gains as wages discriminates against investors. If an investor buys $60,000 worth of securities and sells them ten years later for twice the price, he has to pay a capital gains tax on his $60,000 profit. Under the 1986 reform, the investor would have to pay taxes on this amount as if it were part of his salary. The problem is that because the investor earned that money over a ten-year period, inflation, not to mention the cost of having the original investment tied up in the form of securities, has cost the investor a certain amount of profit. Treating his $60,000 as straight income could be considered unfair discrimination against investors as compared to wage earners.
4. Supply-side economists argue that in the long run a capital gains reduction will generate more revenues than it loses because it stimulates more overall business activity.
5. Congress eventually raised the bulk of the needed revenues by raising Social Security taxes and seeing to it that those new funds would be counted as part of general revenues. See HR 3299, the Omnibus Reconciliation Act of 1989.
6. Richard G. Darman, "Director's Introduction to the New Budget," in *Budget of the United States Government, Fiscal Year 1991* (Washington, D.C.: U.S. Government Printing Office, 1990), 7.
7. Ibid., 15.
8. Ibid., 19-20.
9. Ibid., 20. Surpluses accrued in the Social Security Trust Fund were being used to offset the budget deficits in regular government spending accounts. Senator Moynihan proposed to cut Social Security taxes and, at the same

time, take the Social Security Trust Fund (and its surplus) off budget.

10. Ibid., 20-21.
11. This would be less true in the Senate. Since Democrats controlled only fifty-five seats, they would never have been able to muster the sixty votes necessary to squelch debate if the Republicans had decided to filibuster a Democratic-sponsored budget agreement.
12. Prior to the Iraqi invasion, cuts in the defense budget pursuant to the collapse of the Warsaw Pact were probably going to be no more than $20 billion to $30 billion per year.
13. President Bush did announce that expenditures for military personnel were to be exempted from sequestration.
14. In order to understand how this scenario would work, it is important to recognize that sequestration is not applied all at once but is instead imposed over the course of the fiscal year. In fact, there was a precedent for such a sequester. In 1989 funds had been sequestered for almost six weeks after October 1 until Congress and the president finally approved a budget. As it turned out, the 1989 sequester had the effect of cutting more than $16 billion from the budget for the 1989 fiscal year. Program cuts caused by a sequester kick in at the beginning of the fiscal year and result in a certain reduction in services representing the size of the percentage cuts. For example, with a projected $100 billion sequester in 1990 and a resulting 25 percent reduction in nonexempted domestic programs, offices of the Social Security Administration would have closed at least one day a week, reducing but not discontinuing services. Thus a sequester would be painful but not disastrous, and the negative effects of such a cut could be reversed.
15. This act would have the potential of provoking a constitutional crisis. The Constitution mandates that "no money shall be drawn from the Treasury, but in Consequence of Appropriations made by Law." The law providing for most appropriations would have expired as of September 30. What then would the president be empowered to do?
16. Social Security payments were exempt from sequestration, and the Social Security Trust Fund is solvent independent of general revenue receipts. Nevertheless, the administration of the Social Security Trust Fund *was* subject to sequestration and dependent on annual appropriations. Thus the money was there to cover Social Security checks, but no one would be in the office to process the payments.
17. The original agreement did not include new taxes on heating oil—an issue that was important to congressional members from the Northeast—but Sen. Lloyd Bentsen of Texas, chairman of the Senate Finance Committee, insisted that energy taxes be extended to include heating oil and be more equitably distributed across the nation. Bentsen's involvement in this issue was but an opening salvo in what was to become a scramble to alter the agreement. See Martin Tolchin, "Why Heating Oil Is Taxed After All," *New York Times*, October 2, 1990, A22.
18. Joint Committee on Taxation, reprinted in Jason De Parle, "Crux of the Tax Debate: Who Pays More?" *New York Times*, October 15, 1990, B9.
19. See Peter Passell, "Aches Aside, An Eclectic Accord that Economists Say Seems to Fit," *New York Times*, October 2, 1990, A23.

CHAPTER 4

October 1990: The Failure of Leadership and the Success of Governing

In the waning days of the 101st Congress the legislative process did little to instill public confidence in American government. Important legislation, affecting the lives of millions, was hurriedly adopted in the wee hours of the morning with little more than a cursory debate. Nevertheless, the final result was a compromise on the budget that was in many ways an elegant solution sensitive to the demands of macroeconomics, the realities of the legislative process, and the requirements of fairness. The real story behind the passage of the fiscal year 1991 budget was how American government managed to muddle through. What was remarkable and not a little reassuring about this result was the fact that the process was driven by institutions that could operate, as they were designed to do, without enormously competent or coherent leadership.

WHERE HAVE ALL OUR LEADERS GONE?

Predictably enough, surveys of public opinion conducted in October 1990 indicated that the American people sensed a lack of leadership in government at the federal level. Although surveys commonly show a lack of public confidence in Congress as a whole—citizens tend to love their senators and representatives but hate Congress—there was also a substantial drop, in a very short period of time, in public confidence in the government, particularly in the president's performance. Indeed, if the making of the budget in the fall of 1990 demonstrated nothing else, it validated the public perception of an occasional lack of leadership in the White House and an almost endemic lack of leadership on Capitol Hill. Whether or not the American public really wants to be led is another question.

There are some very logical structural and historical reasons why no one in government seems able to take the lead on matters of national importance such as the deficit. Nevertheless, the government manages to muddle through. The events of October 1990 and the surprisingly positive outcome demonstrate both the strengths and weaknesses of our American political system. Several fundamental reasons explain why our political system fails to lead but succeeds in governing.

The Framers of the Constitution set out to design a government that did not work very well and, by and large, they were enormously successful.[1] The evidence of their success is displayed in the chronic disorganization of the governmental process. So concerned were they about the problems inherent in a "mobocracy" that they built into the Constitution a number of safeguards designed to prevent the unimpeded rule of the masses. Among other things, the Framers made sure that the voting franchise was limited, that the House of Representatives was the only institution at the federal level to be elected directly by the citizenry, and that the powers of the House were to be restricted mainly to domestic policy (the Senate and the president were almost exclusively to share the foreign policy function). In addition, the Framers made sure that, through a system based on the separation of powers and checks and balances, the different branches of government would curb one another, so that if a faction (even a majority faction) seized one branch of government (or one house of Congress), it could be thwarted by the opposition of other branches.

Over the years, many of the constitutional provisions designed to defeat democracy or the rule of the masses have fallen by the wayside. The franchise is now virtually unrestricted for all citizens above eighteen years of age. Since 1913, the Senate has been popularly elected. The lines delineating the constitutional powers of the Senate and the House of Representatives have begun to blur. This more democratic tendency is probably all to the good, as modern sensibilities viewed the original Constitution as a design that too heavily favored rich white males. Nevertheless, there is a danger that in making the system too representative, as James Madison feared, a democracy could degenerate into mob rule (resulting in the violation of minority rights) or the rule of faction (violation of the rights of the majority).

Democratization is a very powerful concept. It has led to the admirable expansion of the voting franchise and, at the same time, to a less beneficial derogation of leadership in Congress. Congressional leaders depend on their ability to persuade and their capacity to sanction. The sanctions available to them are a function of party rules and those of the House and Senate. Because Congress makes its own rules, and because what is good for the individual is not necessarily good for the institution, the tendency of late has been to lift the sanctions available to party leaders in a decentralized Congress. Consequently, party leaders in both houses are left with little more than persuasion as a tool to enforce party principles. Some party leaders are more effective than others at the art of persuasion. House Speaker Sam Rayburn and Senate Majority Leader Lyndon Johnson were famous in their day for the ability to "twist arms" and "educate" the rank and file. The presence of such great persuaders, however, cannot be depended on for consistent leadership. Indeed, in the 101st Congress Speaker Tom Foley for the Democrats and Minority Leader Bob Michel for the Republicans were well liked and respected by their colleagues, but they failed dismally at the art of persuasion in the fall of 1990.

Party leaders used to have virtual control over the legislative process through their manipulation of committee referrals[2] and control of the legislative schedule on the floor. The rank and file may now petition to have a bill discharged from committee and brought directly before the House.[3] All these changes and more have had a democratizing effect in the sense that members now compete on a more equal footing for a piece of the legislative agenda, thereby gaining a more influential legislative voice earlier in their careers than ever before. This may well serve the interests of the individual, but it does not serve the interests of the institution. Policies are promoted that advance narrow interests, and party leaders are more often than not powerless to impose any overall intelligence on policy making.[4]

The price we pay for this democratizing process is a loss of policy coherence and representation of the broader public interests. Thus the public hates Congress but loves its representatives.[5] Members of Congress do an excellent job of mirroring the interests of their constituencies but a poor job of representing national interests. This fact is reflected in the paradox that public opinion polls register a high degree of dissatisfaction with the institution, while, at the same time, the reelection rate since 1980 has generally been in excess of 80 percent in the Senate and 90 percent in the House.

In mirroring the public's concerns, Congress reflects both the unity and disunity of public opinion. The same surveys that continue to show the public's dissatisfaction with its political leaders also reveal that the public is somewhat ambivalent on the issue of balancing the budget. The type of policy required to balance the budget would almost certainly impose sacrifices that the public is not yet willing to make. On the one hand, the public clearly is concerned about the budget deficit. On the other hand, public opinion surveys indicate no clear direction as to where it would be appropriate to cut the budget or impose higher taxes (or a combination thereof). Congress, being a relatively representative institution, merely reflects this ambivalence.

It is ironic that the expansion of the franchise has become something of a liability. When the franchise was limited, there was much greater unity not only in terms of policy but also perspective. Now, even though in absolute numbers the membership of the House and certainly the Senate is not a total reflection of American society, the voices of their constituents are much more diverse. It is hard for members to discern from this cacophony exactly what the "public" wants. Thus, in becoming more democratized, our legislative waters have become murkier.

In particular, there is no clear consensus in the American political arena as to the meaning of leadership. Most people, if asked to select a list of the most respected leaders, would probably choose historical figures such as George Washington, Abraham Lincoln, Winston Churchill, or Franklin Roosevelt, who were in many ways ahead of their times. In many cases, those leaders now held in high regard were reviled by their contemporaries. We now recognize in those individuals qualities of leadership, such as innovation and a firm commitment to ideals in the face of fierce opposition, that we do not applaud in the behavior of our own representatives. In some ways, the style of leadership of the past was both nonrepresentative and nondemocratic. Do we really want our representatives to hold fast to their ideals in the face of spirited public opposition? Are we willing to support innovative leadership that may just as likely lead to disaster as to success?

At the national level, about the only institution generally capable of exercising "heroic" leadership is the presidency. But when the president fails to lead, as he did in October 1990, chaos can be the result. Effective leadership is not only a function of creativity and persistence; it is also a function of sanction and persuasion. Presidential scholars have noted the decisive importance of the power of persuasion associated with the presidency.[6] In foreign affairs, the presidency relies mainly on broad authorities provided under the Constitution. But because the constitutional presidency (as compared with Congress) is relatively weak in domestic affairs, a president with even the best-conceived domestic program will be unable to implement his plans if he fails to use his office to frame the public agenda and convince the citizenry and leaders in Washington to support his proposals. George Bush failed to enunciate a clear position on the budget agreement in the fall of 1990. In the vacuum that remained, Congress managed to fill the void.

As rudderless as is the American ship of state, there is enough unanimity in our politics to produce compromise in times of need. Repeatedly we will see in the following chapters certain moments of truth in the legislative process when the divided Congress has come together to produce occasionally elegant solutions. Just such an extraordinary set of circumstances occurred in October 1990. What makes this story of the budget agreement remarkable is not so much the striking absence of effective leadership in Congress and at the White House, but the ease with which, in time of need, Congress arrived at a solution.

The Budget Odyssey: October 1

The first budget summit agreement was in trouble almost from the beginning. On September 30 when the president announced the agreement to the press in the White House Rose Garden, Newt Gingrich, who had earlier in the day told the president he wasn't going to support the package, was noticeably absent. Gingrich (the second-ranking Republican in the House) was not alone in opposing the plan. Congressional Democrats on the left also made it clear that they were not pleased with either the regressive tax increases or the size of the cuts in Medicare. Given the fact that both the left and the right were unabashedly opposed to the plan, the president and the Democratic leadership were charged with the task of finding enough votes from the political center to gain passage for the agreement. The leadership of both parties (Newt Gingrich excepted) thus began an all-out campaign for the support of their membership. The failure of their efforts graphically demonstrates the weaknesses of party leadership in the modern era.

On October 1 the president began to telephone Republican members of the House requesting their support. In addition, White House Chief of Staff John Sununu traveled to Capitol Hill to drum up support in the Republican party caucus. Sununu, a former governor of New Hampshire, was so used to browbeating members of his state legislature that at the conclusion of his remarks it was natural for him to suggest that the president was prepared to retaliate if support from the membership was not forthcoming. Members of Congress, who were unaccustomed to being bullied and knew that the president was in no position to carry out these threats, were outraged. Sununu lost more support than he had gained.[7] By the end of the day, early head counts showed that 57 of 176 House Republicans were already firmly opposed to the plan. The size of this opposition was crucial, as prospects for passage of the measure depended on the support of a Republican majority. Democratic leaders had already indicated their unwillingness to support the plan unless a majority of Republicans also favored it. In other words, the Democrats were only willing to support a bipartisan tax increase.

On October 2 the president began to lobby groups of Republican congressmen in the White House. Democratic leaders, in the meantime, informed their congressional membership that the vote on passage of the summit agreement was a test of party loyalty that would be duly noted for future reference. This was to be the case despite the fact that liberal members of the party's congressional leadership, including Deputy Whip Marty Russo of Illinois, had already publicly opposed the plan.

Sensing that the budget package was in trouble, the president took the dramatic step on October 2 of quickly scheduling a nationwide broadcast in an effort to stir up popular support for the summit agreement. It is the ultimate weapon in the president's arsenal to go over the heads of Congress to call for public support. Many times during the previous administration, President Reagan had utilized his impressive ability to deliver a message from a prepared text to win popular support for his programs. President Bush, however, was not nearly so forceful nor was his message very appealing. Moreover, he labored under the burden of having to support a position he had rejected only months before. His speech was a direct repudiation of his "no new taxes" pledge.

Predictably, the speech did not have its intended effect. The president was cast in the strange political position of having not only to go back on a campaign promise but also to ask the public to support incumbents, including many Democrats, who supported the budget plan. The president said:

> I ask you to understand how important, and for some, how difficult this vote is for your congressmen and senators. Many worry about your reaction to one part or another. But I know you know the importance of the whole.... I ask you to take this initiative, tell your congressmen and senators you support this deficit-reduction agreement.[8]

The next day congressional offices were flooded with messages from constituents who opposed rather than supported the plan. The president's speech had merely drawn the nation's attention to the fact that its taxes were about to be increased. As a result, public opinion polls began to register a precipitous drop in Bush's popularity.[9]

By October 4 it became increasingly apparent that the leadership of both parties lacked the votes to gain passage of the budget summit plan. With the October 5 deadline for expiration of the continuing resolution and the concomitant cutoff of federal funds fast approaching, Speaker Tom Foley announced that the guidelines in the budget plan were for "illustrative purposes" only and were subject to change according to the inclinations of the individual committees. This promise, Foley hoped, would bring on board committee and subcommittee chairs who felt slighted by the summit's deal.

Foley's initiative was an attempt to smooth ruffled jurisdictional feathers. Never before had there been such a detailed budget resolution. As previously noted, a certain tension had always existed between the budget committees, which are oriented toward fiscal responsibility, and the appropriations, taxation, and authorization committees, which have policy responsibility. By making the budget agreement so detailed, the summit had intruded on the jurisdictions of virtually all the committees of Congress. Policy committee and subcommittee chairs not only resented the raids on their areas of responsibility but particularly objected to the fact that this jurisdictional incursion had been orchestrated, in part, by players outside both the institution and the party—specifically, the White House. Speaker Foley hoped that this last-minute bid to reclaim the support of the committee chairs would swing most Democrats toward favoring the bill. Indeed, Dan Rostenkowski, who chaired the House Ways and Means Committee and had jurisdiction over Medicare and the repeal of special-interest tax breaks that were part of the summit package, announced that he planned to alter the agreement as a precondition for his support. Rostenkowski, bolstered by the Speaker's promise, eventually supported the package, as did other prominent Democrats.

Foley's statement, however, did nothing to assuage the concerns of House Republicans. Because the Democrats controlled all the committee and subcommittee chairs, the Speaker's assurance that the agreement could be altered in committee did nothing to satisfy the demands of congressional Republicans. In fact, because a number of congressional committees display a high degree of partisanship, Republicans feared that the budget agreement would be changed for the worse if the committees were given an opportunity to alter the plan. The House leadership was in a bind with seemingly no way out.

As midnight approached on October 4, the leadership had run out of ideas and was quickly running out of time. Even if the budget agreement were to be passed that evening, Congress would still have only twenty-four hours to finish its budget work before the continuing resolution expired. In an act of desperation, the leadership decided at approximately 1:00 a.m. on October 5 to bring the budget deal to a vote. Votes on the floor can be unpredictable, the leadership reasoned, particularly close ones. Members might experience a last-minute change of heart, or party whips could have made a mistake in counting. Furthermore, if the final margin of defeat was fairly close, it was always possible for the leadership to engage in some last-minute deal making that might alter the balance. The dynamics of voting in the modern Congress, however, conspired against the leadership's strategy.

Ever since the electronic voting system was installed in the House chamber, it has been fairly easy for members to follow the course of voting even as it is taking place. Each voting member is given a coded identification card that can be inserted into any one of a number of slots located around the chamber. Members can push a button that will register their vote (Yes, No, or Present) on an electronic scoreboard located above the Speaker's podium. This technological advance has had some interesting effects, many of which are, again, to the detriment of the leadership.

Members are called on to record their vote by electronic device hundreds of times a year.[10] With so many different issues, members cannot possibly be completely informed about them before casting their votes. They therefore often rely on cues or helpful hints from friends, the party leadership, or other members of their state delegation.[11] Before electronic voting devices were installed, during a vote running tallies were kept almost exclusively by party leaders represented by the bill's floor manager. Members who arrived on the floor during a vote had to rely on the advice of the leadership as to how to vote (unless they were lucky enough to run into a trusted colleague). Now members take their cues and make their decisions with much more sophistication. They can look up at the electronic board to see how their friends and enemies, recognized experts, or members from similar districts have voted. They can also get a sense of how the running vote tally is going. The member who withholds his or her vote on an important issue until the last moment is in a prime position to strike a deal with the leadership should the vote be very close. Similarly, if a motion is heading toward an overwhelming defeat or victory, the member can vote his or her conscience (or more likely his or her constituency's conscience) without affecting public policy.

On October 5 it was the Democrats who held back, refusing to be sucked into a vote for a massive tax increase unless a majority of Republicans also went along. As the Republican vote began to register and it became apparent that the summit package was headed toward a stunning defeat within the president's own party, Democrats began to weigh in. Republicans and Democrats voted in almost equal proportions against the plan. The budget resolution was rejected three to two (179-254). The congressional leadership of both parties had succeeded in marshaling only 40 percent of the House, including their own votes.

The failure of the summit agreement was a dismal loss for the leadership at both ends of Pennsylvania Avenue. Rank-and-file Democrats thought they could get a better deal, and conservative Republicans, with Newt Gingrich in the lead, refused to abandon the no-tax cornerstone of their party's platform. It is a testament to the powerlessness and decentralization of leadership at the national level that on an issue so dear to the White House and congressional leadership barely 40 percent of the House of Representatives was willing to comply. In a parliamentary system, the government would have fallen and the party leadership might well have been replaced. But in the U.S. Congress, there were few recriminations. The leadership is accustomed to losing from time to time.

NECESSITY AS THE MOTHER OF INVENTION: OCTOBER 6-19

In the tradition of muddling through, Congress in the early morning of October 5 proceeded to the next order of business, passing another continuing resolution that would fund the government until an agreement could be reached. The Senate quickly approved the new resolution.[12]

The president, however, was in no mood to wait. True to his word, Bush vetoed the new continuing resolution the next day. The House failed to override the veto and the government shut down.[13] Fortunately for federal employees who were likely to be furloughed by the funding disruption, the country had just entered the long Columbus Day holiday weekend. Congress would have until Monday to work out a deal with the president before the federal shutdown had profound effects on government services nationwide. The president authorized essential federal personnel, such as air traffic controllers and federal law enforcement officers, to continue to work, at least temporarily. The military was also not affected.[14] The Park Service, however, was shut down, leaving tourists in the nation's capital no access to museums or monuments. Paradoxically, the only federal tourist attraction still open to visitors was the Capitol itself. Consequently, the visitors' galleries of both Houses were packed for most of the weekend's budget debate.

The first order of business to get government back on track was the negotiation of a new budget agreement. If the summit agreement was unacceptable and the Republicans could not produce a majority for any type of tax increase, the Democrats would have to write their own budget agreement. On the morning of Saturday, October 6, Democratic (the Republicans refused to participate) conferees from the House and Senate met to work out a new plan. The president had indicated that he would sign another continuing resolution only if Congress passed a budget plan or a continuing resolution permitting GRH sequesters to kick in. Rather than allow for sequestration, the Democrats were determined to produce a budget agreement on their own.

As the Democratic conferees worked through the day, they were guided by the fact that the most important tactical failure of the summit agreement was its violation of committee jurisdictions. Budget resolutions were never intended to make policy, as the 1974 budget reform had made clear, and yet the summit agreement had done just that. Thus the conferees simply set overall levels of spending and reduction, leaving it up to the committees to determine how those levels were to be achieved. The conferees were very careful to adhere to the deficit reduction targets already specified by the summit plan, as the president and a number of congressional Republicans had already agreed in principle to those numbers. In addition, the new Democratic budget resolution would permit a lowering of the capital gains tax rate, if Congress were so inclined. The conferees hoped that enough Democrats would be won over to the new budget proposal by the degree of freedom it provided for committee action and that some Republicans would accept the plan for no other reason than that it specified levels of cuts and revenues they had already agreed to and held out a possibility of lowering the capital gains tax. The conferees, as it turned out, were right.

At 2:30 in the morning on Sunday, October 7, the House passed the new budget resolution (H. Con. Res. 310). A bare majority of the House, 218 Democrats, voted in favor of the plan. They were joined by thirty-two Republicans, who added a substantial cushion (and something of a bipartisan flavor) to the winning margin. Senate approval for the package soon followed, and almost ten months after the process began, Congress produced a budget resolution. As a final note in the weekend drama, Congress approved another continuing resolution (H.J. Res. 666) that would keep the government running until October 19. President Bush, satisfied that Congress had met his requirements for a new budget resolution, signed the new continuing resolution into law.[15]

With the budget disaster averted for the moment, the legislative process returned to its more or less normal course. The focus of budgetary politics again shifted to the congressional committees that had received their allocations for spending, cuts, and taxes under the newly adopted budget resolution. The task now facing Congress was to write a reconciliation bill that would put into statute the agreement achieved under the budget resolution.

THE PRESIDENT STUMBLES

In the normal course of events, the president exercises influence over the legislative process in three ways. First, he is responsible for enunciating a clear, relatively unambiguous position on the legislation under consideration. Members of Congress then have some kind of guideline as to what type of legislation the president will or will not sign. The implicit threat in all of this is that the president may veto any legislation that deviates too far from his stated position. The presidential veto, therefore, is at least as important as a threat as it is in actual use. Once the president makes his position clear, Congress must have the votes to override the president's veto, design legislation sensitive to the president's demands, or execute the purely symbolic maneuver of passing legislation that is clearly unacceptable to the president. In the last instance, the president will be directly blamed for legislative failure. It takes very little congressional support for the president to exercise influence over the legislative process in this way. All the president needs is one-third plus one vote in either House to block passage. Because the Republicans hold more than one-third of the seats in both houses of Congress, a threatened presidential veto has considerable credibility despite the fact that the Republicans are in the minority.

Second, the president must explain his position to the American people. Popular support is a powerful weapon that can be used to influence congressional proceedings. Because the president speaks with one voice and has a national constituency, he is naturally the focus of media attention. A skillful president can easily outmaneuver his opponents in Congress and monopolize the national policy agenda. If the president's position is popular, that is all the more to his advantage. If the position is ambiguous, complex, or unpopular, it is a greater test of the president's ability to sway public opinion.

Finally, to sway congressional votes, the president must use the political and constitutional tools at his disposal, which include much more than the power to veto legislation. As chief executive, the president exercises a high degree of influence over the interpretation and execution of the law. Members of Congress know that the president can delay or block the implementation of programs vital to their districts. Furthermore, as head of the party, the president has considerable influence over the electoral process. A popular president can be a substantial political asset or a threat for congressional incumbents seeking reelection. This weapon in the president's arsenal is particularly potent during an election year.

In early October, President Bush displayed a surprising ineptitude in his attempt to influence the legislative process. First, his message wasn't clear. Several times in the week of October 9-12 he seemed to shift his position on taxes. At a press conference on October 9 Bush indicated that he would support a deal on taxes that would provide for a lowering of the capital gains tax rate in exchange for a rise in the top rate for taxes on the wealthy: "If it can be worked out in the proper balance between the capital gains rate and the income tax changes, fine." [16]

That same afternoon Sen. Pete Domenici, ranking minority member of the Senate Budget Committee, emerged from a meeting with the president at the White House, saying that Bush had indicated that the tax rate-capital gains deal was off. While jogging on a campaign visit in North Carolina the next day, Bush responded to questions about his position on taxes by saying, "Read my hips" as he ran past reporters. This cryptic remark was widely reported in the press, adding to uncertainty about the president's position. On October 11, House Republicans emerged from a meeting with the president and suggested that he would, indeed, support a deal that included a higher income tax rate in exchange for lower capital gains taxes. Later that same afternoon, however, White House Press Secretary Marlin Fitzwater told reporters that he did "not believe that such a compromise was possible" and that it would be "a waste of time" to pursue such a deal.[17] Democrats were elated at the seeming disarray at the White House, while Republicans had no guidance as to the president's position. The field of tax reform was thus abandoned to the Democrats.

Without a clear message as to his preference, the president's failure to employ his other tools of persuasion seemed almost superfluous. As Bush's popularity slipped in the polls, Republican candidates throughout the country no longer welcomed his campaign support, and a number of them publicly denounced the president's shift on taxes. As Rep. Mickey Edwards, chairman of the Republican Policy Committee, explained to reporters when asked why House Republicans were unwilling to support the president, "We work with the president but not for the president." A number of Republican candidates openly began to adopt the Democrats' message of tax fairness. The president had failed to set the agenda. Specifically, he had never made a clear case for capital gains tax reductions nor had he explained his position on tax fairness. Thus he had failed to lead.

CONGRESS FILLS THE VOID

With the president largely absent from the political arena, Congress began to work on a budget reconciliation agreement that was to be almost entirely of its own invention. Without the effective involvement of the president, which often adds a complex dimension to the legislative process, the structural distinctions between the two houses of Congress became much more evident.

The Senate, being a much smaller body than the House, tends to be much more informal. For example, it is a time-honored tradition that senators are permitted to speak for as long as they want on the floor, which gives them the opportunity to filibuster, or talk a bill to death should they so desire.[18] In an important departure from tradition in 1975, the Senate amended Rule XXII, or the cloture rule, to permit debate to be terminated by a vote of at least three-fifths of the members (sixty votes). Cloture had previously required a two-thirds vote. In the 101st Congress the Republicans controlled forty-five seats in the Senate, so they were fully capable of resisting any attempts to silence them on the floor. Thus the threat of a filibuster was a very real possibility. Moreover, without a rule governing debate, Senate legislation is to a greater degree subject to amendment on the floor.[19] Consequently, Republicans in the Senate, even without the president's support, had much more influence over the adoption of a reconciliation bill in October 1990 than did their colleagues in the House.

The Senate reconciliation bill was subject to a number of amendments, most of which were defeated. One of the most important amendments adopted by the Senate was a package of procedural reforms sponsored by Majority Leader George Mitchell. He proposed that the spending and taxing targets of the five-year plan adopted pursuant to the budget resolution be made mandatory. Furthermore, any bill passed by Congress in the next five years that reduced taxes or increased the cost of entitlement programs or discretionary spending would require a corresponding increase in revenues to make up the difference or would necessitate cuts in other programs across the board to make up the shortfall.[20] The most controversial aspect of the mechanism was that the OMB, the president's budgetary arm, would have the final say as to how much these new congressional initiatives were likely to cost. A number of senators, particularly liberals, objected that giving this authority to the OMB would transfer tremendous budgetary power to the executive branch. The OMB was known to be quite partisan in its submission of estimates, so that if it overestimated the cost of a particular bill it did not favor, it would create a powerful disincentive to adopt the legislation. At the very least, a number of members argued, the CBO should be given some say. The opposing arguments notwithstanding, Mitchell's amendment was easily adopted.

The Senate then approved the final version of its own reconciliation bill. In addition to the Mitchell amendment enforcement provisions, there were substantial differences between the House and Senate versions of the plan. Because House districts are drawn up according to the principle of proportional representation, the workings of the House are heavily influenced by members from urban centers in the Northeast and on the West Coast. In the Senate, however, New York and California have the same amount of representation as do North Dakota and Alaska. The resultant rural and Western bias of the Senate, plus the greater influence of the Republican minority, produced a Senate reconciliation proposal that tended to be much less progressive (in terms of income distribution) and much more reflective than the House measure of the concerns of an agricultural and mining economy. For example, the Senate bill allowed for tax breaks that would specifically benefit the uranium processing industry, energy producers (including ethanol and petroleum producers), as well as Western-based airline corporations.[21] Thus the final hurdle that stood between passage of appropriations bills and final adjournment was the formation of a conference committee to resolve the differences between House and Senate reconciliation bills.

The House, with its larger membership, tends to be much more formally structured than the Senate. After all, were all 435 members given their say on every issue, the House would never complete its work. Thus the rules of the legislative process in the House are much more extensive and strictly enforced.[22] House proceedings are driven by majority rule because a majority of the members can at almost any moment terminate, limit, or in a number of other ways control debate. For example, all bills considered on the floor are governed by a rule, which has been adopted in a vote separate from the legislation itself and determines the length of debate over a bill, as well as the types of amendments and the degree to which they will be permitted. The House can adopt an open rule, which permits any and all types of amendments to be considered that are in order.[23] It can also adopt a closed rule, which mandates an up or down vote on a bill with no changes permitted on the floor. It is also possible to adopt a modified closed rule, which permits the consideration of only certain predetermined amendments. The House Rules Committee reports the rule under which each major piece of legislation is to be considered. This committee, whose membership is closely guarded by the House leadership, is very much a tool of the Democratic party leadership. The majority party in the House thus has some control over the legislative process and, indirectly, over public policy. Given the right set of conditions (in this case, the absence of a clear presidential position and disarray in the minority party), the majority party in the House is more likely to dominate the legislative process than in the Senate.

In the case of the House reconciliation bill, the rule adopted permitted consideration of only two versions of a deficit reduction plan.[24] To the consternation of House Republicans, the Rules Committee would not allow the submission of a Republican alternative.[25] Under a liberal plan reported by the Ways and Means Committee, new taxes adopted would be much more progressive than provided for by the budget summit (increasingly shifting the tax burden to the rich); cuts in Medicare would be much fewer, and most pro-business tax incentives would be dropped. Under an alternative fall-back plan proposed by the Democratic leadership, new taxes would still be progressive, but the package would be designed to be more acceptable to moderate Republicans. The Democratic leaders were still not sure they could keep their own troops in line. Furthermore, the rule adopted permitted the two plans to be voted as complete packages with no amendments allowed. This kind of rule, sometimes known as a "king-of-the-mountain" rule, permits the leadership to submit to the floor a number of packages, each to be voted on in turn. Under this type of rule, the last package adopted supersedes all other votes.[26] The leadership generally introduces its plan last, so that if it holds its members in line, it can be sure to dominate the legislative proceedings.[27] Thus the House Democrats set their own agenda, one that reflected their success in capturing the national debate on the fairness issue. The House passed both packages of amendments (the leadership package prevailed under the rule) and sent their bill on to the Senate.[28]

OBRA 1990: THE END GAME

Conference committees operate under the general principle that they negotiate within the boundaries of the provisions established by the bills passed by both houses. For example, if a House appropriations bill sets a spending limit above a companion Senate appropriations bill, the conference committee is responsible for somehow splitting the difference. On rare occasions a conference committee will write into legislation a statute with an entirely unique construction.[29] In the case of the 1990 reconciliation bill (OBRA—Omnibus Budget Reconciliation Act), the conference committee was as concerned with settling differences between the House and Senate versions as it was with mollifying the factions that were capable of derailing the bill. In this case, the demands of the House Democrats had to be reconciled with the natural tendencies of the Senate as well as the interests of Senate Republicans.

The conference report, or the final bill on which the vote is taken, was in most cases a compromise between House and Senate differences. Income tax rates for the wealthy were raised from 28 to 31 percent. The Senate bill had not changed the rates, but the House had raised them to 33 percent. The top tax rate for capital gains stayed at 28 percent to protect the capital gains rate from the increase in the top income-tax rate for the wealthy. Gasoline taxes were raised 5 cents a gallon. The House bill had provided for no increase in gasoline taxes, whereas the Senate had stipulated a 9.5 cent per gallon increase. Reductions in Medicare benefits, an item vital to House conferees, remained at the House bill level. Differences on most other provisions were either divided roughly down the middle or, at the insistence of one side or the other, provisions vital to powerful factions were preserved. In addition, the conference approved a modified version of the procedural changes that had been introduced by Senator Mitchell. The end result was a reconciliation bill that was projected to reduce the deficit by $496.2 billion over the succeeding five years and $42 billion for fiscal year 1991. Both houses approved the conference report on October 27 and sent the final legislation on to the president, who had already indicated that he would sign the bill.

With a budget agreement firmly in hand, between October 22 and October 28, Congress passed all of its regular appropriations legislation. On October 26 and 27 Congress passed a total of eight major bills. In most cases, without the text of final legislation in hand, members were forced to vote on measures about which they had only the barest information—sometimes little more than one-page outlines summarizing multibillion dollar packages. In addition, Congress also passed another continuing resolution, the fourth, that would continue funding the government until the clerks of the Congress had time to draw up all the legislation just passed and send the final measures on to the president.

It is not unusual for Congress to adopt a spate of legislation at the very end of a session. As adjournment approaches, members are faced with the stark choice of either passing imperfect legislation or doing without, which often leads to compromise. While the end of the 101st Congress was somewhat more frenetic than usual, the quantity of legislation and the rapidity with which it was passed at the very last moment were not entirely atypical. Besides the regular appropriations measures, the members passed in the last three days of the session a major clean-air act, a crime bill, a child-care measure, a substantial revision of the immigration law, and authorization bills for defense, housing, farm programs, and education.[30] This final flurry of legislation established the second session of the 101st Congress as one of the most active in modern times.

THE FAILURE OF LEADERSHIP

Where, then, was the failure of leadership? The most substantial failure here was in the absence of presidential leadership. The final reconciliation bill was almost entirely reflective of congressional concerns. Only in the barest outlines of the agreement—the five-year reduction plan targeted to save close to $500 billion—did a semblance of the original summit plan remain. There was also a more subtle failure of leadership in the final agreement. Blame for this failure could be placed on both Congress and the president. With the midterm elections only a week away, little was made of the fact that the reconciliation bill constituted a functional repeal of GRH, with a deficit reduction for fiscal year 1991 of little more than $42 billion—well below the levels mandated by GRH at the beginning of the year.

Otherwise, congressional Democrats dictated the outlines of the plan within the limits agreed on at the summit. Table 4-1 demonstrates the degree to which the principle of fairness, as defined by the Democrats, was built into the final plan.

POSTMORTEM

October 1990 was a remarkable month in the history of the U.S. Congress for several reasons. In a very unusual move, Congress had voted to raise taxes in an election year—less than two weeks, in fact, before the election. Furthermore, this was a direct tax increase. There

TABLE 4-1 Change in Individual Tax Rates under Budget Reconciliation

	Change in Federal Taxes			
Taxable income	Summit	Senate bill	House bill	Final
Less than $10,000	+7.6%	0.0%	−1.3%	−2.0%
$10,000 to 20,000	+1.9%	−2.3%	−1.6%	−3.2%
$20,000 to 30,000	+3.3%	+2.7%	+1.0%	+1.8%
$30,000 to 40,000	+2.9%	+2.8%	+1.0%	+2.0%
$40,000 to 50,000	+2.9%	+2.8%	+0.8%	+2.0%
$50,000 to 75,000	+1.8%	+1.9%	+1.4%	+1.5%
$75,000 to 100,000	+2.1%	+2.5%	+1.5%	+2.1%
$100,000 to 200,000	+1.9%	+3.5%	+0.7%	+2.3%
$200,000 and over	+1.7%	+3.7%	+7.4%	+6.3%
Average	+2.4%			+2.1%
Total additional revenues	$20.4[a]			$18.3[a]

Source: Joint Committee on Taxation.

[a] Billions of dollars.

was no subterfuge behind which members could hide, arguing that this was anything but an increase in the public's tax burden. More often than not, in an election year Congress shies away from controversial, politically damaging legislation.

Second, what happened in October 1990 was fairly unusual in that Congress seized the legislative initiative. In the modern era, with the advent of the powerful executive and the electronic media, it is very rare for Congress to seize the national agenda from the presidency. What made this event all the more remarkable was that the issue over which Congress asserted itself was, for the first time, the fundamental controversy in the public forum. It is not unusual for Congress to assert itself in areas peripheral or relatively unimportant to national policy. However, on an issue as central as the budget and as divisive and controversial as distributional fairness, the 101st Congress stands out as one of the most assertive since the end of the Vietnam War.[31] As we have seen, this congressional assertion was more a function of presidential failure than of legislative success. Nevertheless, the initiative shown, particularly by leaders of the House when confronted by a revolt of their rank and file, was a singular example of the *potential* for leadership invested in congressional parties.

Also unusual was the fact that the legislation set forth in a fairly detailed fashion budgetary politics for the next five years. American politics, driven by the biennial electoral cycle, is not renowned for its capacity for advanced planning. Most public policy formulated by American government is reactive. The budget plan adopted in 1990 was designed to have far-reaching effects, not only in deficit reduction but also in setting spending priorities for the long term. Whether Congress would adhere to this five-year plan was another question. One suspects that in an institution that makes its own rules, the strictures of the past are easily forgotten, as were the GRH deficit reduction targets.

Finally, in a move that was little trumpeted by the press, Congress revised its budget process in the most significant way since passage of the 1974 Budget and Impoundment Control Act. As we shall see, the fiscal year 1991 Reconciliation Act deleted more than the previous GRH deficit reduction targets. In a major change of emphasis, the bill passed in the waning days of the 101st Congress changed the emphasis in federal budgeting from *deficit* control to *spending* control. This was no minor alteration, especially in view of the fact that, after all the political maneuvering and even with the new budget reduction package factored in, the fiscal year 1991 budget deficit was projected to be as high as $300 billion—more than the budget deficit (when not controlled for inflation) for any year in history.[32]

NOTES

1. Special thanks to Dr. David Prindle at the University of Texas, who has made this point so cogently.
2. Bills once introduced are referred to committee by an officer of the House who is a subordinate of the Speaker. The Speaker has the choice of making either a hostile or favorable referral by sending a bill to a committee that is either sympathetic or hostile to its contents.
3. A discharge petition requiring the signatures of 218 members (or a majority) requires that a bill be discharged from committee and brought directly to the floor. Successful discharge petitions are rare, but the mere threat of such a petition may spur a committee into action.
4. For more on this, see Lawrence C. Dodd, "Congress and the Quest for Power," in Glenn R. Parker, ed., *Studies of Congress* (Washington D.C.: CQ Press, 1985), 489-520.
5. See Glenn R. Parker and Roger H. Davidson, "Why Do Americans Love Their Congressmen So Much More Than Their Congress?" *Legislative Studies Quarterly* 4 (February 1979): 53-62; and Timothy E. Cook, "Legislature vs. Legislator: A Note on the Paradox of Congressional Support," 43-52 in the same volume.
6. See, for example, Richard E. Neustadt, *Presidential Power*, 2d ed. (New York: John Wiley, 1980); and more recently, Jeffrey K. Tulis, *The Rhetorical Presidency* (Princeton, N.J.: Princeton University Press, 1987).
7. The White House, it turns out, was prepared to play hardball. Ralph Regula, a Republican from Ohio, told the administration that he was not supporting the summit agreement. He was later informed by the White House that his

plans to take his wife and four constituents to see a play from the president's box at the Kennedy Center had been canceled. Regula voted against the plan.

8. Text of President Bush's October 2 speech to the nation reprinted in "Bush Touts Bipartisan Spirit, Appeals for Public Support," *Congressional Quarterly Weekly Report*, October 6, 1990, 3249.
9. In an October 8-10 *New York Times*-CBS News survey of public attitudes toward the Bush presidency, the president's approval ratings dropped 16 percent and his disapproval ratings rose 15 percent from his standing in the first week of August. While the situation in the Middle East apparently contributed heavily to his drop in approval, the economy and the budget largely accounted for his higher negative ratings. Michael Oreskes, "Economy and Mideast Standoff Bring Drop in Bush's Standing," *New York Times*, October 14, 1990, 1.
10. Between 1981 and 1988, the House averaged about 450 recorded votes a year (the Senate about 100 less), or almost 1,000 votes for every Congress. Because recorded votes take fifteen to thirty minutes for each vote cast, this means that every Congress spends 300 to 500 hours just *voting*. See Norman Ornstein, Thomas E. Mann, and Michael J. Malbin, *Vital Statistics on Congress: 1989-1990* (Washington, D.C.: AEI/Congressional Quarterly Inc., 1990), 158.
11. See John W. Kingdon, "Models of Legislative Voting," *Journal of Politics* 39 (August 1977): 563-595.
12. House Joint Resolution 660. The Senate concurred by voice vote.
13. The override attempt failed by only six votes in the House. Of those present and voting, only 260 members voted to override the veto. Nine Democrats, or more than the margin needed for an override, voted to sustain the president's veto. Conversely, twenty-five Republicans defected from the president's (and their party's position) and voted to override the veto.
14. There is a constitutional question associated with the president's powers in this regard. Although it seems clear that as commander-in-chief the president can mobilize the nation's resources in case of emergency, it is not clear that the president can, as Bush did, choose the programs he wishes to keep operating in the event of a funding cutoff. In the absence of a national security imperative, the president's decision to keep air traffic controllers at their jobs, for example, might have been a violation of Congress's authority to make appropriations.
15. P.L. 101-412.
16. Transcript of President Bush's October 9 press conference reprinted in *Congressional Quarterly Weekly Report*, October 13, 1990, 3447-3449.
17. Marlin Fitzwater, quoted in George Hager, "Parties Angle for Advantage as White House Falters," *Congressional Quarterly Weekly Report*, October 13, 1990, 3398.
18. Time limits on debate in the Senate can be imposed only by unanimous consent or the agreement of all members present, including members of the minority party.
19. Including the inclusion of nongermane riders.
20. Mitchell's amendment divided the federal budget into three parts: entitlements, discretionary spending, and revenues. Legislation that reduced revenues in one area of the budget would subject that area to corresponding cuts. Thus, for example, any increase in discretionary spending would either have to be accompanied by a revenue increase or would automatically result in a corresponding cut of the amount of the shortfall from all other

discretionary programs.

21. Sen. Lloyd Bentsen of Texas, a state heavily dependent on oil drilling, was the chairman of the Finance Committee, which was largely responsible for writing the tax provisions of the plan. Eleven of the twenty members of the committee came from states west of the Mississippi (excluding California). Senator Dole, the minority leader and a member of the committee, managed to exempt all airplanes costing less than $250,000 from a luxury tax that was part of the tax provisions. Kansas, Senator Dole's state, is the home of Cessna Corporation, a manufacturer of small private airplanes that generally retail for less than $250,000.
22. The rules of the House comprise more than a thousand pages, while the rules of the Senate are less than one hundred pages in length.
23. Under the rules of the House, amendments that are not germane to the legislation being considered may be ruled out of order by the presiding officer. House Rule XVI, clause 7.
24. H. Res. 509.
25. The Republican alternative, which contained no new tax increases, was excluded because it was about $100 billion short of the $500 billion five-year deficit reduction target.
26. See Roger H. Davidson and Walter J. Oleszek, *Congress and Its Members,* 3d ed. (Washington D.C.: CQ Press, 1990), 320.
27. Such a rule contributes a political bonus because it permits members to go on record supporting a number of different plans, even packages that have no prospect of final adoption.
28. H.R. 5835.
29. For instance, the 1974 budget reform procedures were, for the most part, written in conference.
30. S. 1630, S. 1970, S. 5, S. 358, H.R. 4739, S. 566, S. 2830, and H.R. 7 respectively.
31. At the time, there was an attempt in Congress to muzzle the presidency, particularly in the area of foreign policy.
32. It should be noted that, for accounting purposes, Social Security surpluses were removed by the reconciliation bill from the positive side of the ledger. Thus, the fiscal year 1991 deficit, projected to be close to $300 billion, would in actuality have been more like $240 billion if the old accounting procedures had been followed (the Social Security Trust Fund was slated to have a $60 billion surplus in 1991). Parenthetically, this was another area in which congressional Democrats prevailed. No longer could the president claim for accounting purposes Social Security surpluses, which could not, by law, be used as general revenues.

CHAPTER 5

November and December 1990: Politics, Policy, and the New Budget Process

The December recess provided a chance to review the details of the budget agreement just concluded. Known as the fiscal year 1991 Omnibus Budget Reconciliation Act (OBRA), it put into statute a number of important changes in budget policy and process. This chapter will discuss the outlines of those changes, including the suspension of Gramm-Rudman-Hollings, the change in emphasis from deficit reduction to spending reduction (they are *not* the same), spending caps for both discretionary and entitlement spending, pay-as-you-go budgeting, provisions for economic forecasting, and new accounting principles for applying loan and credit guarantees.

CALM ON THE HILL

When Congress adjourns, Capitol Hill, and of course the rest of Washington, take on a different, less frenetic character.[1] Congressional staffers stroll the halls of the Capitol Hill office buildings dressed in jeans and sneakers (with more businesslike attire tucked away in their cubicles just in case the member or an important constituent walks through the door). Vacations, weddings, elective surgery, and all other personal matters are scheduled during the intersessional break or after final adjournment. These plans were disrupted by the budget imbroglio that had enveloped the 101st Congress in its final days. Nevertheless, with lightning speed, calm returned to the Capitol complex in the aftermath of congressional adjournment.

For members of Congress, however, the storm had just begun. The end of the session meant returning to their districts to explain and justify what they had just done. Stepping back and viewing the final result would reveal a budget package that was in many ways a genuine improvement, but in the context of midnight sessions, backroom deals, and the inevitable last-minute compromises, the members had a lot of explaining to do. They had "won dirty," and the benefits of their success would not become apparent until well after the 1990 elections. Consequently, while congressional staffers were casually beginning to evaluate the effects of the new budget reform, incumbents were scrambling at home to create a favorable spin for an election year tax increase.

THE ELECTIONS

As it turned out, the congressional elections of 1990 were, on the surface, a reaffirmation of business as usual. Incumbents were reelected at a rate close to or exceeding normal expectations. Members of the modern House are generally reelected at a rate somewhat in excess of 90 percent. The election of 1990 was no exception; close to 97 percent of House incumbents who ran for reelection were returned to office. In the Senate, all but one of the thirty-two incumbents seeking reelection were successful. The president's party suffered more or less normal losses for a midterm election, with the Republicans losing nine seats in the House and one in the Senate.

Midterm congressional elections have a completely different character from those same races in presidential election years. The most important single factor in determining the outcome of congressional races, particularly in off-year elections, seems to be the quality (in terms of experience, skill, reputation, and resources) of the candidates who choose to run against an incumbent. Challengers will evaluate their prospects very early in the political season to determine whether they have a chance of victory. Should conditions be unfavorable, strong challengers will choose not to run and those challengers who do emerge will find a dearth of campaign contributors. The conditions surrounding the 1990 elections were particularly unfavorable for challengers. In general, the redistricting that was about to occur in the aftermath of the 1990 census would mean that, even if they were victorious, House challengers would quite likely have to run for reelection in 1992 from an altered (sometimes substantially) congressional district. Moreover, quality Republican challengers are generally reluctant to run against Democratic incumbents when historical patterns so clearly show that members of the president's party are at a substantial disadvantage in midterm elections. Finally, in general, quality challengers from both parties have been discouraged from running against an entrenched incumbent given the fact that, for the last few decades, all incumbents in all elections for Congress have been getting tougher to beat.[2]

Senate elections are markedly different from House races and, in general, are quite a bit more competitive. For one thing, Senate challengers don't face redistricting. In addition, because Senate districts (which are, after all, states) can't be tailored by a political process for the benefit of an incumbent, the demographics of a state may change in the course of a six-year term. This demographic shift can be damaging to an incumbent. Furthermore, a six-year election cycle means that a senator elected in a presidential election year will have to run for reelection in an off-year, or vice versa, thus facing a dramatically different electoral environment from one race to the next. Finally, Senate incumbents tend to be much more visible in their legislative activities, which makes it much more difficult for them to finesse an unpopular political stance, as House members would do by concentrating on constituency service.

Consequently, challengers to Senate incumbents tend to be much better positioned and financed than candidates for the House. As a result, the turnover caused by electoral defeat is historically much higher in the Senate, and Senate elections seem to be much more sensitive to such factors as a weak economy. For example, on average in an off-year election, the president's party experiences losses of roughly one Senate seat for every two seats it holds. There are, however, some anomalies that make each Senate election unique. Since only a third of the Senate is up for reelection in any given electoral cycle, the "class" facing the voters at the polls may be subject to special circumstances. For example, in 1980 a number of Republican senators were elected from normally Democratic constituencies on the coattails of Ronald Reagan's landslide victory over Jimmy Carter. Many of the same freshmen Republicans elected that year were defeated in 1986 when President Reagan was no longer able to influence the outcome. Thus the Senate elections of 1980 and 1986 displayed higher than normal turnover rates.

In 1990, however, fewer Republicans than Democrats were running for reelection, and those members who had been initially elected in 1984 were far less dependent on Reagan's coattails than their predecessors had been in 1980.[3] Thus Republican losses were much smaller than would have been expected on the basis of historical trends, although party leaders were disappointed at losing even one seat in a year when they expected a popular president and a strong economy, along with a number of impressive challengers to Democratic incumbents, to produce a modest gain and perhaps even a majority.

Overall, despite the fact that the reelection rate in the House was 96.9 percent, only about 2 percent lower than in the previous election, margins of victory for incumbents were much lower than in 1988. Eighty-five incumbents won their elections with less than 60 percent of the vote.[4] This was close to double the number of close elections that had occurred in the previous electoral cycle.[5] The average vote percentage for Democrats in 1990 was 65.8 percent (down from 68.8 percent) and for Republicans was 59.8 percent (down from 67.5 percent). This was particularly ominous in a mid-term, preredistricting election year in which incumbents should have been in a much more powerful position than usual. In addition, voters in California, Colorado, and Oklahoma voted to limit the terms of incumbent legislators.[6]

As bad as these trends were for all incumbents, they were particularly bad for the Republicans. With one less seat in the Senate, Republicans were even less likely to capture the Senate in the 1992 election. Furthermore, for President Bush the outcome was even more ominous. When he was elected in 1988, he had a smaller percentage of his own party in Congress than any other president in history. The 1990 elections only exacerbated his problems.

THE NEW BUDGET PROCESS

It was not altogether a bad deal. The Omnibus Budget Reconciliation Act (OBRA) produced a budget plan that was sensitive to the demands of economic trends and the requirements of public policy, and, being a political compromise, it produced a reform of the budget process that was relatively enforceable. In going against the conventional wisdom, Congress had passed in an election year a substantial tax increase. The following is a brief summary of the major reforms mandated under the October budget agreement.

Going into the winter of 1990-1991, the American economy was in recession. The Commerce Department's measure of economic activity, the Index of Leading Economic Indicators, dropped 1.2 percent in August—the sharpest decline in that yardstick since the October 1987 stock market crash.[7] The August figures were followed by another 0.8 percent drop in September and a 1.2 percent decline in October.[8] Had the Gramm-Rudman deficit targets for fiscal year 1991 been met, the corresponding deficit reduction for a year in which the budget shortfall was projected to be close to $300 billion would have had to be well in excess of $200 billion. The consequences of such a reduction in government spending, not to mention the impact of such cutbacks on government programs, would have been disastrous for the economy. After all, the *entire* budget for discretionary spending for 1991 (the primary target of deficit reduction) was projected to be only about $490 billion. Close to one out of every two dollars for defense, government operations, and foreign aid would have been eliminated, or tax revenues would have been raised 15 percent or some combination thereof (with the requirement being that this reduction take place all in one year).

Recognizing that the magnitude of reductions and tax increases necessary to comply with GRH would produce an economic calamity worse than the deficit itself, Congress deemphasized the deficit reduction approach to budgeting. Heretofore, Congress and the president had produced a veneer of compliance with *deficit reduction* targets. Hereafter, Congress and the president would attempt to comply with *spending* targets. The importance of this shift in the philosophy of federal budgeting should not be understated. Because the GRH deficit reduction approach to budgeting was simply unworkable, massive, across-the-board cuts in spending were not a credible threat; budgeting at the federal level had become a game in which the primary goal of fiscal policy making was not necessarily to reduce spending (which was impossible anyway given the unrealistic targets imposed under GRH). Rather, the goal of budgeting under GRH became blame avoidance (when the inevitable shortfalls occurred), shifting spending obligations off-budget, and producing phony economic predictions that would make budget deficits seem less substantial than they really were.

Under the new plan, the focus of budgeting would be on limiting spending (regardless of the deficit). In other words, as we shall see, Congress imposed limitations on the parts of the budget it could control and, with the rest of the budget, let the cards fall where they might.

The first task for budget process reform under the Budget Reconciliation Act was to produce a set of realistic deficit targets. By the middle of 1990, the best guess of economists in both the OMB and the CBO was that the economy in its weakened state could sustain no more than $50 billion (as opposed to $64 billion or more pursuant to the old GRH) of deficit reduction for the next fiscal year. Consequently, the policy makers' first decision in the budget summit was to aim for that $50 billion reduction. The final result under the Reconciliation Act was intended to produce $42.5 billion in savings, which was fairly close to the summit goal. The further lowering of deficit reduction targets was a response to the economy, which had suffered more shocks related to an increase in the price of oil caused by the crisis in the Middle East.[9]

A second task to be accomplished by budget reform if, in essence, GRH was to be revised, was the imposition of a new set of budgetary guidelines and enforcement provisions. Because the new emphasis was to be on spending reduction rather than deficit reduction, OBRA established a five-year plan of spending caps to replace the GRH structure of deficit reduction targets. These caps were to be the limits beyond which Congress could not go in appropriating funds.

In addition, spending caps were to be divided into five separate accounts: entitlement programs, three separate areas of discretionary spending, and interest on the debt. The discretionary spending account was to be divided into three ledgers: defense, domestic, and international assistance. A pay-as-you-go discipline was to be imposed on all new spending and revenues. No new entitlement could be approved or discretionary spending or tax expenditure passed without a commensurate reduction in other services delivered or taxes imposed in that same account. Furthermore, impenetrable fire walls were to be set up between spending accounts. Savings in one account could be applied only to deficit reduction and could not be transferred to another account.

If this seems like an enormously complex approach to budgeting, it is. However, the administration of a budget that was to be in excess of $1.3 *trillion* is simply not conducive to the meat-ax approach to budgeting that had existed under GRH. After all, GRH was not sensitive to economic trends or the demands of policy, nor was it geared to sanctioning only wasteful programs. The efficient and just program was just as likely to suffer in the same way and in the same amount as was the inefficient, wasteful program. This dynamic made GRH essentially unfair and, in many ways, undemocratic.

Gramm-Rudman-Hollings and Son of Gramm-Rudman-Hollings

It is not entirely accurate to say that the GRH law disappeared as a result of the 1991 Reconciliation Act, but rather that under the new law, sequestration for the purpose of deficit reduction had become much less likely. As was done in 1987, Congress revised upward the deficit reduction targets under the law in recognition of the fact that there was a certain value in maintaining targets that would serve as benchmarks for measuring new spending measures, entitlement enhancements, and tax increases or reductions. After all, in the five years since GRH had been in effect, budget deficits, when controlled for inflation and measured as a percentage of GNP, had been reduced. If for no other reason than the fact that deficit levels were an important standard by which to measure the success or failure of the budget process, the outlines of GRH were preserved. Table 5-1 shows how GRH deficit reduction targets were amended over time.

There were some important changes in how the GRH deficit reduction targets were to be imposed. The most significant was that for 1991-1995 targets were to reflect "current economic and technical assumptions."[10] This meant that deficit reduction targets would be adjusted according to changes in economic forecasts. For example, if the inflation rate were to increase unexpectedly (above initial projections) in any given year, deficit reduction targets would automatically be revised upward to reflect the relative decrease in the value of the dollar. The same logic would apply if the economy were to show an unexpected downturn (with the resulting decline in revenues and increased costs in entitlements). GRH sequesters could be applied only in cases in which

TABLE 5-1 Original and Revised Deficit Targets (in billions of dollars)

Fiscal year	*1985 Gramm-Rudman-Hollings*	*1987 Gramm-Rudman-Hollings*	*1991 Omnibus Budget Reconciliation Act*
1986	171.9		
1987	144		
1988	108	144	
1989	72	136	
1990	36	100	
1991	0	64	253
1992		28	277
1993		0	195
1994			109
1995			101

Source: Congressional Budget Office, December 1990 interim assessment.

there were so-called policy violations or changes in law that violated spending limits set by Congress in other parts of the Reconciliation Act.

These changes in procedure were somewhat controversial. For one thing, the amended GRH law (dubbed "son of GRH") mandated that the economic assumptions used in estimating the president's budget in January could not be changed in the course of that fiscal year. This would prevent the recurrence of the so-called midsummer surprise when the president altered his economic projections during the course of the fiscal year (usually in July). However, this would also raise the possibility that Congress might act on the basis of what had become, by the middle of the summer, wildly inaccurate economic assumptions. There was also concern that because the OMB had the primary responsibility for providing the economic estimates governing overall budget projections, the president could use those assumptions as a tool to control the budget process in Congress. To many members of Congress, one of the most egregious aspects of the original GRH law had been that the OMB (and thus the president) had an inordinate amount of influence on the decision making in Congress.

It did not escape the notice of fiscal conservatives that the amended GRH deficit reduction schedule revised upward the allowable deficit for fiscal year 1991 from $64 billion to $253 billion (including the Social Security surplus, although it was to be excluded under the new law). Thus, while members were back in their districts trumpeting their success in reducing the deficit by $500 billion, as a matter of fact, they had allowed the deficit to rise to its highest level in history.[11]

In addition, "son of GRH" directed that in the final two years of the new five-year plan (1994 and 1995), the rules under which sequesters were imposed were to revert to the original law. In other words, unless the president opted to adjust the deficit targets for 1994 and 1995 (an option that was written into the law), deficit amounts in excess of $109 billion in 1994 and $101 billion in 1995 would automatically have to be cut from all nonprotected programs in the budget regardless of policy or economic considerations.[12] This component of the law aroused some controversy, especially among the original opponents of the GRH approach. As suggested above, GRH sequesters are not sensitive to the requirements of policy making in a democracy. Nevertheless, three years in the life of a piece of legislation is an eternity, and in an institution that makes its own rules, mandates imposed in one year can be changed in another.[13]

To some extent, GRH survived the fiscal year 1991 budgetary crisis. Nonetheless, substantial changes were made that largely obviated the sequester threat, at least in the short run. This change in GRH was reflective of the new overall tenor of budgeting law. To reiterate, under the new enforcement provisions of the Reconciliation Act, new and primary emphasis in budgeting was to be transferred from a primary concern for deficit reduction to an emphasis on spending control.

DISCRETIONARY SPENDING

In recognition of the fact that the discretionary portion of the budget had little to do with the increase in the deficit—the previous year's increases were due in roughly equal proportions to the slowdown in the economy and cost overruns associated with the savings and loan crisis—summit negotiators had determined early on in the summer of 1990 to protect discretionary accounts from automatic and indiscriminate budget cutting. While the budget summit was still meeting at Andrews Air Force Base, staffers representing Sen. Robert Byrd (D-W.Va.), chair of the Senate Appropriations Committee, and Sen. Jim Sasser (D-Tenn.), chair of the Senate Budget Committee, negotiated with White House representatives on possible changes in the enforcement procedures associated with the new budget agreement. The president was asking for some form of line-item veto (or at least an enhanced impoundment authority), while congressional negotiators, particularly from the Appropriations Committee, were seeking some kind of separate protection from the sequestration of discretionary spending.[14] The president never got his enhanced veto power. Congressional negotiators, however, did get a change in the way discretionary spending would be handled.

As we have seen, enforcement provisions similar to those agreed on in the summit were reintroduced by Senator Mitchell in the form of an

TABLE 5-2 Discretionary Spending Limits (budget authority in billions of dollars)

Fiscal year	*Defense*	*International*	*Domestic*
1991	$288.9	$20.1	$182.7
1992	291.6	20.5	191.3
1993	291.7	21.4	198.3

Source: Omnibus Budget Reconciliation Act of 1990.

amendment to the reconciliation bill in the closing stages of the Senate debate. Those changes were largely included by the conference committee in the final legislation. Title XIII of OBRA, better known as the Budget Enforcement Act of 1990 (BEA), was the result.

Pursuant to the BEA, all discretionary spending was divided into three separate accounts: defense, international, and domestic spending. Over each account was imposed a series of *spending* caps. Across the first three years of the agreement, defense was cut $180 billion below the baseline (current spending plus inflation); international assistance was held constant; and approximately $20 billion was added above the baseline to domestic spending. The spending caps for each of the next three years are shown in Table 5-2 (in the final two years of the package only deficit targets were specified).

If total appropriations in any one of these three accounts were to exceed their caps, a mini-sequester would occur, that is, a sequester (or across-the-board cut) would be ordered for all programs within that account.[15] For example, spending for education that pushed the discretionary account over its cap would cause reductions in law enforcement, health, environmental enforcement, and other components of domestic discretionary spending. One advantage to this scheme was that domestic programs would not be made to suffer as the result of a violation of spending caps in defense or foreign aid. Foreign aid and defense, in turn, would be protected from excesses in the other two accounts. Furthermore, all discretionary spending would be protected from excesses in other parts of the uncontrollable budget, including entitlements and taxation. One major objection to this scheme was that just as domestic programs were protected from increases in defense, defense programs were protected from the pressures of other parts of the budget. By legislative fiat, the "guns versus butter" paradigm in budgeting no longer applied.

This provision was considered a major victory for the appropriations committees (and subcommittees), which were no longer subject to sequesters caused by the machinations of the uncontrollable entitlement budget. By the same token, this agreement was viewed as greatly diminishing the power of the budget committees. Because spending levels were mandated by law for the next three years, annual budget resolutions would have little meaning. After all, the appropriations committees already had their marching orders (spending limits they had imposed on themselves during budget negotiations). In addition, the fire walls that protected defense appropriations from being transferred to domestic accounts were considered a loss for congressional liberals, advocates of lower levels of defense.

Defense Spending and the Baseline Budget

There were a number of objections to this process as it was constructed. First and foremost were objections to the spending levels set by the law, especially in the area of defense. House Democrats, in particular, were concerned that spending levels for defense were too high and that the spending caps did not represent real cuts in defense spending beyond what would normally have occurred had there been no Reconciliation Act.[16] In other words, House liberals believed that defense advocates had managed to obtain a relatively inflated defense budget (relatively unaffected, that is, by the collapse of the Warsaw Pact).[17]

This controversy was related to the disputed notion of what constitutes a baseline budget. For the purpose of determining the amount of deficit reduction associated with spending caps, the spending limits mandated by the law were to be deducted from the baseline budget. This budget is "a set of projections showing the levels of spending and revenues that *would* occur for the upcoming fiscal year and beyond if existing programs and policies are continued unchanged, with all programs adjusted so that existing levels of activity are maintained."[18] The problem with estimating the baseline budget for defense, especially in the aftermath of the cold war, was that it was unclear what providing for defense "at existing levels" would mean in the absence of a viable Warsaw Pact. Obviously the cost of defense would be less under those conditions, but how much less was not clear. For the purpose of inflating or creating the appearance of deficit reduction (and for the purpose of providing much higher levels of defense spending than some members of Congress thought necessary), many on the Democratic side believed that the baseline for defense spending had been set much too high. Thus some of the deficit reduction through spending cuts claimed as a result of passage of the Reconciliation Act was probably not a real reduction.

Economic Forecasting

Another problem in the new plan was how changes in the economy were to be factored into the discretionary budget. For example, if the economy were to enter a period of unexpected inflation, spending limits set in previous years would have very little meaning. In that case, spending caps would be adjusted according to the OMB estimates of the rate of inflation for that year. There was some concern that in its economic assessments accompanying the president's budget, the OMB would be able to manipulate the discretionary accounts. In order to prevent this, Title XIII established an elaborate procedure through which the OMB was to consult with the CBO in arriving at its estimates. In addition, there was some concern among Democrats that fire walls in the Reconciliation Act separated defense from other forms of spending—amounts deducted from defense could not be applied to increases in domestic spending or entitlements. This was a victory for the administration and advocates of relatively high levels of defense spending.

Declared Emergencies

Another controversy in the new system for discretionary spending was the process through which supplemental appropriations would be figured into the overall budget in order to determine the size of the deficit and thus deficit reduction. For example, for the purpose of determining spending caps, the costs of Operation Desert Shield (soon to become Desert Storm) were not to be included (the same principle held true for the costs of the savings and loan bailout). In fact, under the law, if the president were to designate a particular supplemental appropriation as an emergency, and Congress agreed, none of those funds would be counted against spending caps. The cost of an emergency supplemental would simply push yearly deficit targets upward. If the costs of the savings and loan bailout were to increase unexpectedly, requiring an emergency supplemental, the deficit target mandated by "son of GRH" for that year would be adjusted accordingly. All other *nonemergency* supplementals would be counted against spending caps. Not only was there a potential for abuse in this procedure (the concept of "emergency" being left up to the discretion of the president), there was also the potential for a significant increase in the power the president wielded in the budget process, as well as for a substantial increase in budget deficits beyond the control of the new appropriations process.

Because the new procedure regulating discretionary spending emphasized *spending* control rather than *deficit* control, there was reason to believe that huge deficits would continue unabated. These deficits would simply become the product of emergency supplementals or off-budget appropriations and poor economic performance. While the president would retain the power to reimpose sequestration (particularly in fiscal years 1994 and 1995), there was every reason to expect that he would be pressured to waive sequestration if the withholding of those funds meant a substantial reduction in needed services or damage to the economy. The result could well be huge uncontrolled deficits for the foreseeable future.

GETTING TO THE SOURCE OF THE PROBLEM

A number of positive things could nonetheless be said about the reformed discretionary spending procedures. For one thing, discretionary spending would no longer be subject to sequester as the result of overruns in other truly uncontrollable areas of the budget that are the result of disasters or fluctuations in the economy. By and large, increases in discretionary domestic spending were not the cause of most of the large deficit increases of the 1980s. A powerful argument could be made for the proposition that discretionary accounts should not be held exclusively liable for deficits to which they do not contribute. In addition, built into the new appropriations process was a dynamic as old as the Constitution itself. By ensuring that an increase in one area of a spending account results in a decrease in another area (pay-as-you-go budgeting), interest is pitted against interest for the purpose of spending reduction. This resembles, in principle, the design concept behind the separation of powers. The great advantage of this principle of decision making is that the interest of one group is held in check by another, creating a dynamic tension that is both sensitive to policy (the process cannot be dominated by any one interest) and to the demands of deficit reduction (the total spending in any account cannot go beyond its cap). Finally, the new budget process was designed to meet the demands of policy making in the relative long term. Accounts were allotted modest increases that are adjustable according to the performance of the economy. The overall package was more policy sensitive and less sensitive to trends outside the control of Congress, and thus more democratic than the appropriations process that had existed under GRH.

ENTITLEMENTS

The flip side of making discretionary spending immune was the treatment of increases in other areas of the budget. This meant that entitlements were also slated to stand on their own—to be made to work on a pay-as-you-go basis. This meant that any policy change resulting in an increase in entitlement spending for one program would cause a corresponding decrease in entitlement spending for other nonexempt programs in the entitlement account. For example, if benefits were to be increased under Medicare, all other nonexempt entitlement programs (such as farm price supports) would suffer a corresponding decrease. Alternately, Congress could order any combination of reductions as long as they were taken from entitlement spending. It should be noted that the Social Security Trust Fund was to be excluded from the entitlement account, and Social Security recipients would not be made to suffer decreases in benefits regardless of the activities taking place in other parts of the entitlement budget.

The pay-as-you-go discipline imposed on entitlements was based on the same principles that were to govern discretionary spending. Increases in entitlements would pit interest against interest. There was, however, one major difference. Because there is no way to plan in advance exact levels of entitlement spending (citizens qualify for entitlements according to demographic shifts and changes in the performance of the economy), there were to be no spending caps on the entitlement account except for the overall deficit reduction targets imposed by "son of GRH." However, since the deficit targets under the amended GRH law were subject to change according to the performance of the economy, there was very little in the way of an effective limit to entitlement spending. This was clearly a controversial outcome, especially to those officials who saw deficit reduction as the primary goal of budget process reform. If the economy were to slip into recession, as it was bracing to do in late 1990, entitlement spending would increase tremendously, even without changes in the law. Nevertheless, entitlement benefits were so important (or politically untouchable) that they were to be the last source of government spending to be cut.

Another controversial aspect of the new approach to entitlement spending was the way in which the costs of providing a new service were to be determined. Should Congress decide to expand an entitlement benefit, the costs of that expansion, in terms of determining the size of cuts in other entitlement accounts, were to be a function of economic forecasts. After all, applications for entitlement benefits are a function of the state of the economy (and also of demographics). Because, under the law, the OMB was to make projections concerning the costs of new entitlement programs, the White House was given a particularly potent weapon to influence the expansion of new entitlement programs. After the adjournment of Congress, contingency plans were already being made on Capitol Hill to counter this threat to Congress's policy-making jurisdiction.[19]

TAXATION

Taxation was also to be made accountable to a pay-as-you-go approach to budgeting. Any tax benefit (expenditure) would have to be made up through increases in other areas of the federal tax code. This constituted a revolution in taxation politics. Heretofore, tax expenditures were a politically popular way to deliver benefits to individual constituencies. Since these expenditures did not show up as a drain on the budget until the loss in revenues was experienced sometime in the future, tax breaks could be delivered more easily because they required only a change in policy, not in appropriations. Thus very costly tax expenditures had a way of entering the tax code through the Ways and Means Committee even as the budget and appropriations committees were trying to reduce the deficit. The new pay-as-you-go principle would naturally produce constituencies opposed to new tax expenditures. As new tax breaks were granted, they would create an immediate increase in the rates of taxation of other groups. Here again the Madisonian principle of pitting "faction against faction" was incorporated as part of the law.[20]

FEDERAL CREDIT AND LOAN GUARANTEES

The federal government insures most of the savings deposits (up to $100,000 per depositor) held in the nation's banks and savings and loan institutions. If such an institution were to become insolvent, the federal government would cover the losses of its depositors. This system worked well as long as federal regulators kept a close watch on the investment activities of federally insured savings and loan institutions.

In the wake of the deregulation of savings and loan institutions in the 1980s, many thrifts began to drift into insolvency. This occurred because the newly deregulated entities began to compete with one another to attract depositors by offering generous interest rates. In order to pay for this, many thrifts made increasingly risky investments. (Prior to deregulation, savings and loan institutions were limited to making a small range of investments and to paying a relatively low interest rate.) For the federal government, the failure of thrifts incurred a financial obligation to depositors, which signified potential drains on the Treasury without any corresponding offsets in appropriations. In other words, federal loan guarantees (such as for government-insured student loans) or deposit insurance represented a potential for net expenditure that had not been accurately included as a debit on the government's books. Although under the new budget agreement the initial costs of the savings and loan bailout were to remain off the books for the purpose of estimating the deficit, a number of similar programs were to be subject to new and more accurate procedures.

At the same time that the scope of the savings and loan debacle became apparent, a number of troubling trends (and losses) began to emerge in other government programs providing loans and guaranteeing payment of loans made by private institutions. Some process had to be designed to put the true costs of these programs into the budget. Under the Reconciliation Act, Title V (the Federal Credit Reform Act of 1990) was added to the Congressional Budget Act. In order to avoid the misstatement of the costs of federal loan and deposit guarantees, the new law mandated that for the purpose of determining the true value (or cost) of a loan guarantee, new accounting procedures would be used. Specifically, the cost of direct loans would no longer be counted as a function of cash flows.

Heretofore, when a loan was made by the government to an individual, the amount of that loan was counted as a debit against the federal Treasury in the dollar amount of the loan. As the loan was repaid, those payments were counted in the budget as assets. This accounting procedure had the effect of overstating the cost of direct loans, at least in the short run. As a consequence, direct loan programs were politically very difficult to authorize. Under the new plan, the economic cost (or subsidy cost) of direct loan programs was to be immediately charged to the budget in the form of the percentage of the loans that were expected to be defaulted. Since the default rate of direct loans is a very small percentage of the total, the cost of these loans would be measured more accurately. By virtue of this reform the approval of direct loan programs became less politically costly and would provide Congress with another option should it decide to lend the government's money to deserving individuals.

By contrast, the cost of loan *guarantees* was understated. Losses associated with these guarantees did not show up until a loan was defaulted and the government was left with the responsibility of covering the loss. As a consequence, loan guarantee programs were artificially less costly in the short term and thus more politically appealing. Yet these programs had cost the government billions of dollars. Private institutions that distributed federally guaranteed loans had little incentive to engage in fiscally sound practices with this money because their losses were guaranteed to be repaid by the government. Under the new law, the projected default rate was to be immediately charged to the budget, and a loan guarantee program could proceed only if an appropriation was passed by Congress to cover the expected loss. It was hoped that the requirement that an appropriation be approved as a precondition for implementing a new loan guarantee program would lead to more responsible administering of these programs.

GOVERNMENT SPONSORED ENTERPRISES

Finally, pursuant to the credit reform package, the Treasury Department was ordered to report to Congress on ways to reduce liabilities with respect to government-sponsored enterprises (GSE). GSEs are private enterprises sponsored by the federal government that provide credit to be used for a number of socially desirable objectives (such as home ownership and small business investment). GSEs are operated according to standard business principles except for the fact that the federal government is expected to step in and insure their losses. This, of course, can lead to massive federal financial obligations and may also contribute to irresponsible behavior of GSEs that are insulated from the discipline of the market. The Treasury Department was charged with the responsibility of presenting to Congress a plan for preserving the fiscal soundness of GSEs.

FISCAL OUTLOOK

While no one on the Hill or in the White House was completely happy with all the provisions of the Reconciliation Act, there was some reason to be optimistic in the aftermath of the 1990 budget battle. In fact, it seemed likely that the corner had been turned in the budget crisis. Very simply, the 1990 Omnibus Budget Reconciliation Act dictated a set of more or less realistic spending limits and enforceable procedural reforms. While budget deficits were projected to remain high in the short term, there was some reason to believe that in the near future deficits would return to a manageable level—all of this made possible without undue economic dislocation or political restructuring (constitutional amendments or massive delegations of power to the executive).

DEFICITS

For fiscal year 1991 the deficit was projected to be in the range of $300 billion. This was to be, in dollar amounts (uncontrolled for inflation and with the Social Security surplus excluded), the largest deficit in history. In early December the CBO issued a set of projections for the deficit in the years beyond 1991, which showed that as a result of the 1990 reforms, the deficit was going to decline both in real terms and as a percentage of GNP. Because CBO projections are generally given more credence than any other economic projections produced by the government, the outlook, for the first time in quite a while, was optimistic. Based on the best currently available economic forecasts in

TABLE 5-3 Preliminary Deficit Projections (in billions of dollars)

Year	*Projected deficit* [a]	*Deposit insurance* [b]	*Percentage of GNP*
1990	$277	$ 56	4.1
1991	320	91	4.5
1992	337	107	4.3
1993	252	28	2.6
1994	156	−44	0.8
1995	143	−29	0.4

Source: Congressional Budget Office, December 1990.

[a] Excluding Social Security surplus (pursuant to the new law).
[b] Savings and loan bailout (included in overall projections).

December 1990, the CBO projected that, after a slight rise in fiscal year 1992, the deficit would begin a precipitous decline. This projection was dependent on the accuracy of the economic forecasts used by the CBO, a fairly stable political environment, and the willingness of Congress to abide by the provisions of the newly passed reform package. See Table 5-3 for deficit projections according to the CBO in December 1990.

There were, of course, some clouds on the horizon. First and foremost, it was still not clear in December whether the United States would be involved in a war in the Middle East within the next few months. Even in the absence of war, the projected costs of the deployment in the Persian Gulf were continuing to rise. For example, on December 10, 1990, the administration announced that the costs of the deployment in the Middle East could go as high as $30 billion, almost twice the previous estimate.[21] While these costs would not be counted against any of the budget's spending caps (they were to be approved as separate emergency supplemental appropriations), they represented real costs to the taxpayers. Second, there was no certainty that Congress would not continue to adjust the law. If deficit projections were to ease, as they were slated to do, there would be enormous pressure on Congress to approve new programs or change spending limits in order to meet needs left in abeyance during the previous high deficit years.[22] Finally, there was no guarantee of the accuracy of the economic assumptions under which the CBO was operating. The economy could go into decline (as it eventually did), throwing out previous CBO projections not only in the current year but in future years through increases in the interest on the debt. If deficits were to show a massive increase beyond projections, tremendous pressure would be exerted on the agreement as a whole.

Nevertheless, optimism prevailed in December. Congress had passed a number of reasonable reforms that were enforceable. Projected tax revenue increases resulting from the changes made in the reconciliation bill were, for the most part, realistic. In addition, spending caps imposed were much more likely to be adhered to than the previous GRH deficit reduction targets, which, if imposed, would have resulted in fiscally unthinkable and politically impossible spending cuts. GRH was simply not a credible threat, whereas the mini-sequesters to be imposed if spending caps were exceeded were entirely plausible.

DECEMBER POSTSCRIPT

As the 1990 calendar year was ending, the new fiscal year had already begun. In the Executive Office Building the OMB was already hard at work preparing the president's fiscal year 1992 budget submission due to be presented to Congress some time in early February. On Capitol Hill the 102nd Congress was being organized even as the 101st was performing its final act. In response to the president's decision to more than double troop strength in the Middle East, the Armed Services Committee in the Senate and the Foreign Affairs Committee in the House held hearings to investigate and participate in the formation of the administration's diplomatic and military strategy.

In the meantime, freshman members of Congress began to arrive in Washington to set up their offices and hire their staffs. In the basement of the Rayburn Building, in an area of temporary cubicles set aside for freshman members, hopeful job applicants distributed their résumés and waited for interviews. Incumbent members vied for better office space or vacated their offices while workmen added new carpet and another coat of paint. The halls were littered with the debris of renovation.

The Democratic and Republican caucuses met in late November and early December to elect new leadership. Members jockeyed for better committee appointments and freshmen waited to see what their initial committee assignments would be. Although there were no upsets in the almost universal reelection of party leadership in both caucuses, there was a surprise change in committee chairmanships. In a reaffirmation of the 1970s subcommittee reforms that made ineffective or autocratic full committee chairmen vulnerable to a challenge, Frank Annunzio (D-Ill.) of the House Administration Committee and Glenn Anderson (D-Calif.) of the Public Works Committee were deposed by the Democratic caucus. With most of the new committee assignments made, the 102nd Congress returned home, awaiting the beginning of the new session on January 3.

NOTES

1. For 1990, when Congress adjourned *sine die* (having "adjourned finally," as opposed to having gone into recess), the members adopted a provision that empowered the leadership of the House and Senate to call Congress back into session should the president decided to attack Iraq without first consulting congressional leaders.
2. See Gary C. Jacobson, *The Politics of Congressional Elections,* 2d ed. (Boston: Little, Brown, 1987), particularly chapters 3 and 6.
3. Ibid., 179-180.
4. A marginal race in one election year generally produces a stronger and better-financed opponent in the next. Although it is a hard concept to measure, the closer to 50 percent the percentage point lost is, the more costly the race is.
5. See Chuck Alston, "Warning Shots Fired by Voters: More Mood than Mandate," *Congressional Quarterly Weekly Report,* November 10, 1990, 3796-3797.
6. The Colorado measure limited the terms of all its state and national legislators. This led to a court challenge as to whether the state had the constitutional right to limit the terms of members of Congress, which are set by the Constitution. The Oklahoma and California measures limited only the terms of state officials.
7. Commerce Department, Bureau of Economic Analysis. The Index of Leading Economic Indicators is derived from the average of eleven seasonally adjusted economic statistics.
8. "Leading Indicators Down 1.2% in October," *Washington Post,* December 1, 1990, D12.
9. The reduction from the summit's target also reflected the difficulty associated with gaining even modest reductions in the budget through the political process. Practically every spending account and every target of new taxation has a constituency ready to fight for its interests.
10. Subtitle A, Public Law 101-508, The Omnibus Budget Reconciliation Act of 1990.
11. Even the CBO projections for the deficit may have been understated, particularly for future years. This is because of the reverberation effect of previous years' deficits. If the CBO's projections were too low for 1991 and 1992 (as they would be if Congress were forced to pass a larger than expected supplemental appropriation to support Operation Desert Shield), the effect of higher than expected deficits would reverberate through the deficit in future years by increasing the expected costs of interest on the debt. As it turned out, Operations Desert Shield and Desert Storm were not a drain on the budget because of the offsetting contributions of our allies.
12. The major programs exempted from sequestration are: Social Security (including disability benefits); veterans' compensation and pensions; federal military and civilian retirement benefits; interest on the national debt; outlays from prior year appropriations; earned income tax credit; family support payments; child nutrition; Medicaid; food stamps; Supplemental Social Security Income; Women, Infants, and Children (WIC); Aid to Families with Dependent Children; and state unemployment benefits.
13. In fact, this element of the reform, the reimposition of GRH three years down the line, made it almost certain that the 1990 budget package would be a three-year deal. There was no prospect that it would be any easier to

impose GRH in 1994 than it had been in 1990.

14. Discretionary spending not exempt from GRH sequesters had been inordinately affected by sequestration. Representatives of the appropriations committees, which were largely responsible for discretionary spending, reasoned that inasmuch as this wasn't part of the problem, it shouldn't be part of the solution to deficit spending. The undeserving were being punished by GRH sequesters applied in the current form.
15. The resulting sequester would be in the amount of the overage, with the costs being imposed equally (in percentage terms) across all other programs in the account.
16. It should be noted that for the purposes of outlining defense appropriations under the Reconciliation Act, the Desert Shield operation was to be treated as an entirely different entity. Appropriations for Desert Shield would not be counted against the spending caps, nor would costs of the operation above the allied contributions be applied against the deficit for the purpose of sequestration.
17. Under the budget law, because defense spending levels were basically held constant, defense would suffer, in reality, only about a 4 percent annual reduction over the next three years (reflecting the erosion of inflation). A number of Democrats had called for as much as a 25 percent cut at the earlier stages of the defense authorization, reflecting the prevailing appetite for a peace dividend.
18. United States Senate, Committee on the Budget, *The Congressional Budget Process: An Explanation*, 100th Congress, 2nd Session, S. Prt. 100-89, 15.
19. For example, projections of costs could be written into the statute, authorizing the creation of a new entitlement benefit.
20. It should be noted that the great proponent of the separation and balance of powers, to whom the Framers referred, was the Baron de Montesquieu in his book *The Spirit of Laws*.
21. Molly Moore, "U.S. Troop Deployment May Cost $30 Billion in 1991, Aides Say," *Washington Post*, December 11, 1990, A18.
22. There were also still supply-siders in Congress who favored tax cuts as a way to stimulate the economy. If the economy were to go into decline, there would be significant political pressure to reduce taxes and thus potentially add to the deficit.

CHAPTER 6

January and February 1991: The Gathering Storm

January is a time of beginnings in Congress. The session opens, new members are sworn in, the committees organize, and the president presents his budget. The winter of 1990 was a little bit different and a little bit the same. Overshadowing increasingly somber economic news and budget projections was the outbreak of a shooting war in the Middle East. But behind the scenes, beneath the excitement generated by the war, legislative business continued as usual. The rhythm of congressional life perseveres regardless of external disruptions because of the imperatives imposed by the schedule of the fiscal year.

THE SWEARING IN

On January 3, House Minority Leader Bob Michel (R-Ill.) stood at the Speaker's podium and held the gavel. This biennial ritual is the only time the minority leader ever presides over the House of Representatives. The irony of the moment was not lost on the membership as they gave Michel a warm reception and an even warmer send-off. It was Michel's duty to introduce the incumbent Speaker of the House, Tom Foley, who was continuing the thirty-six-year tradition of a Democratic majority in the House. Michel had never served as a member of the majority. Indeed, by January 1991, no congressional Republican then in office had ever served as a member of the majority. At the conclusion of a pro forma vote in which Foley was elected Speaker, Michel was given the gavel and an opportunity to deliver a graceful concession speech that belied the sense of frustration existing just below the surface. As House Republicans not in control, in an institution where the rules and procedures are dictated by the majority party, they had little prospect of grabbing the brass ring of power—then or in the foreseeable future.

At no time was this Republican frustration more evident than in the debate that followed the swearing in of the Speaker and the rest of the House, for it is on the first day of the new Congress that the institution adopts its rules. This procedure rarely generates much debate. The swearing in is a festive occasion. Members celebrate the end of an arduous campaign and the beginning of a two-year term before the next election. Friends and families of the newly elected members crowd the House chamber; young children play in the aisles. Parties celebrating the new Congress are planned for the afternoon. On this day, however, when the House leadership introduced its package of rules changes to be adopted by the 102nd Congress, the floor erupted into acrimonious debate. Of particular concern to Republicans was a seemingly innocuous provision that would require the Congressional Budget Office to render a cost estimate of any legislation likely to generate an expense. Without such an estimate, the bill would be subject to a point of order—to be ruled ineligible for consideration by the chair.

Why would the Republicans get so upset about a seemingly inconsequential provision? In an institution that makes its own rules, rules determine outcomes, and in requiring that CBO estimates be used to anticipate the costs of spending and tax measures, the Democrats had issued a challenge to the Republican-controlled White House.

The story behind this controversy is complex. Pursuant to the hard-fought 1990 budget agreement, the president's Office of Management and Budget was given the authority to estimate the cost to the federal government of any legislation to be considered in Congress. As we have seen, this was a source of controversy in 1990 because Democrats feared that the OMB would overestimate the price of programs the president did not favor. The OMB's projections were particularly important in estimating the cost of adjustments in entitlements and taxation.[1] The House Democrats simply wanted to prevent OMB dominance of budget estimates by ensuring that CBO estimates would also be included as part of any spending or revenue package before the measure left the House.

Republican members were apoplectic. It was not that CBO estimates are highly partisan to the benefit of the Democrats but rather that the proposed rules change was a direct challenge to the authority of the White House and a threat to the delicate compromise represented by OBRA.[2] From the Republicans' perspective, the budget deal was being amended on the very first day of the new Congress. Democrats countered that they had never agreed to give the OMB complete control over making estimates. This was one of the areas of controversy, they argued, that had been left unsettled in October 1990 as negotiators struggled to arrive at a budget agreement before the government ran out of money. Predictably the Republicans lost. In a vote that followed party lines, the Democrats overwhelmed their opposition, serving notice that in the 102nd Congress the minority status of the Republican party would have largely the same effect it always had. The Republicans could not help but be disappointed at this reminder of their relative powerlessness.

THE ECONOMY SLUMPS

On January 6 the Bank of New England was seized by the federal government. One in every seven depositors in New England held accounts in the bank. Its failure was, in part, the result of the collapsing economy in New England and the concomitant collapse of prices in the region's real estate market. The insolvency of the Bank of New England generated concerns that the entire banking system was in trouble.[3]

On January 8 the *Washington Post* reported that the recession, which even the Bush administration admitted had begun, would add an additional $50 billion to the deficit. As recently as October 1990, the deficit projection was on the order of $320 billion, but the new deficit estimate for fiscal year 1992 could approach $400 billion. Even worse, the recession would begin to put pressure on elected officials to counter the effects of the downturn, thus raising the amount of government spending. Moreover, recessions and their attendant higher levels of unemployment also increase pressure on the entitlement portion of government spending. There was some fear that these political and structural pressures would prematurely kill the budget deal so dearly fought for a few months earlier.

Under the budget agreement, the Congressional Budget Office was required to issue a low growth report if the economy showed a negative growth rate for at least two quarters in a row. Under the law, if such a report were issued, the majority leader in the Senate would be required to introduce a joint resolution (presidential signature required) to temporarily suspend the budget agreement and its caps on spending.[4] By early January it was clear that the economy was in recession and that the technical criteria for the issuance of a low growth report had been met.

When in late January the CBO issued its low growth report, there was some fear that members of the Senate, particularly on the left, would take the opportunity to bury the budget deal. To put it simply, the October agreement did away with the trade-off of "guns versus butter." Savings realized in the defense account could not be transferred under the OBRA agreement to any other areas of spending. The left, in particular, chafed at this restriction. In their view, the defense buildup in the 1980s had left unmet the crying need for federal assistance to social programs. Indeed, to some extent, President Reagan had managed to shift budget priorities from domestic discretionary spending to defense (entitlement payments continued to grow unabated). The 1990 budget agreement, in effect, locked in that transformation through the construction of fire walls. The left was willing to sink the budget agreement in order to do away with these fire walls.

A collective fatigue, however, ruled the day. No one in the leadership was willing to reopen the debate. From both sides of the aisle in the Senate the leaders let it be known that even though they were required by law to introduce a bill to suspend the 1990 OBRA, they were completely unwilling to support the measure. This commitment was given despite the fact that the deepening recession made the 1990 budget deal seem less relevant (by late winter some estimates of the budget deficit were in the $400-$500 billion range).

CONGRESS ORGANIZES ITSELF

The congressional schedule for January 1991 originally called for a long intersessional break. Members would attend the ceremonial swearing-in ceremony and then recess until early February. The president's new budget was not to be submitted until then, as he had asked for and received an extension. Without the budget submission, there would be little to do—or at least it seemed that way. Events outside the capital, however, conspired to keep Congress in town. With more than 400,000 American troops dispatched by the president to the Persian Gulf, members of Congress demanded that they be given a forum to participate in the decision to go to war. Thus, immediately after the swearing in, members of the Senate began an unscheduled debate on the deployment of troops to the Middle East.

THE COMMITTEES ORGANIZE

While events in the Middle East may have removed economic news from the headlines, there are behind-the-scenes proceedings that must take place in a new Congress whether or not the nation is in crisis. Committees must be organized and subcommittees appointed by the time the president's budget—the starting gun of most of the legislative process—is presented to Congress.

The process of making committee assignments had begun as early as December, when some of the most sought-after appointments were made to the Appropriations and the House Ways and Means committees.

Each committee is organized in a different way. Committee organization, rules, and even norms of behavior are a function of tradition and the structure of the committee itself. One of the most important determinants of a committee's character is the degree to which its membership tends to turn over. It is a principle of congressional as well as human behavior that people tend to relate differently to one another depending on how long they plan to interact. Political scientists refer to this behavior as the politics of the "supergame."[5] In a long-term relationship, the concession or compromise the individual makes today will presumably be returned tomorrow. In other words, the expectation of a long-term relationship will have a moderating effect and also establish more regularized patterns of behavior.

Turnover rates vary widely among congressional committees. In addition, since some committees are exclusive, while others are nonexclusive (members can serve on only one exclusive committee), there is a tremendous variation in the degree of commitment to and the average length of service on a committee.[6] For example, the House Administration Committee is a nonexclusive and relatively undesirable committee, which tends to have a high turnover rate. Although there is a certain overriding pressure in Congress to maintain comity within committees, nonexclusive and semi-exclusive committees tend to have a high degree of partisanship and heavy-handed leadership. Republicans, even more than Democrats, tend to shuttle off the House Administration Committee because of its partisanship. However, on an exclusive, highly sought-after committee, very few members leave except when they retire or are not reelected. Members of these committees tend to treat one another with a certain amount of respect, circumspection, and much less partisanship.

Becoming a member of the Appropriations Committee involves a heavy commitment of time and resources and also a long-term commitment to interact successfully with other members who are likely to serve on the committee for the rest of their congressional careers. The committee, therefore, has become a kind of institution within an institution, whose membership, regardless of party, often has more in common than it does disagreement.

The rules of the Appropriations Committee are structured and arcane. For example, unlike other committees where subcommittee jurisdictions are very fluid, these subcommittees have set responsibilities that are rarely subject to change. Subcommittee chairmanships rarely become open, except on the death, defeat, or retirement of the chair. Holders of these posts are therefore enormously powerful, knowledgeable, and influential within their area of responsibility. For example, Rep. Jamie Whitten (D-Miss.), who is also the full committee chair, has been the chair of the subcommittee on Agriculture for many years and, deservedly has become known as the "permanent secretary of agriculture." Indeed, Whitten's control over agriculture appropriations makes him much more powerful than any presidential appointee in the conduct of national farm policy.

By contrast, on other committees such as Foreign Affairs, subcommittee chairmanships are much more fluid not only in terms of personnel but also jurisdiction. This dynamic detracts from the institutional memory and consistency and, as a result, the influence of Foreign Affairs subcommittees.[7]

The distinguishing feature of the selection of Appropriations subcommittee chairs is that members are allowed to "grandfather" from one Congress to the next at least two of their subcommittee slots. This means that members of the Appropriations Committee accrue seniority on their subcommittees in the same way that they achieve positions of seniority on the full committee. The practical effect of this rule is a significant amount of stability within the Appropriations Committee itself.

By contrast, subcommittee selection on the House Foreign Affairs Committee is made by straight seniority. A very senior member of the majority party on this committee can choose to jump from one subcommittee to another. Consequently, on Foreign Affairs, by virtue of being the first to choose that subcommittee, the senior member becomes the chair. Therefore, subcommittee chairmanships on Foreign Affairs and most other semi- or nonexclusive committees are subject to frequent change. By comparison, since members of the Appropriations Committee can grandfather their subcommittee appointments, even the most senior member cannot replace a more junior subcommittee chair who chooses to remain.

Because of the rules and the long-term nature of subcommittee service on the Appropriations Committee, the initial choice of subcommittee assignments is a crucial and strategic decision for members of the committee. For example, when at the end of the 101st Congress, Bernard Dwyer (D-N.J.) decided to drop two of his subcommittee assignments and instead become the lowest-ranking member of the subcommittees on Energy and Water and Defense, he was making a career decision. It just so happens that the Defense subcommittee has jurisdiction over the largest portion of the discretionary budget, and the Energy and Water subcommittee has jurisdiction over the kind of water projects that his district in New Jersey so desperately needs.[8] Clearly, Rep. Dwyer has an interest in using his subcommittee positions to serve his district. More than that, however, members have to weigh their chances of moving up the subcommittee ladder.

Appropriations subcommittee chairs hold virtual fiefdoms in their thirteen separate areas of jurisdiction (each being responsible for one of the regular appropriations bills). Because of the selection process and the rules of subcommittee assignment, the Appropriations Committee has among its leaders some of the most senior members in Congress. In 1991 the three most senior members of the committee had a combined total seniority of 117 years. As a result, for a junior member of the majority, choosing a subcommittee is largely determined by what prospects it offers to become a "cardinal" (as the Appropriations subcommittee chairs are known) early in one's career. This is a daunting choice. According to one of the newest members of the committee in the 102nd Congress, David Skaggs (D-Colo.), the prospect of moving up the seniority ladder on Appropriations is "like climbing Mt. Everest."[9]

THE PRESIDENT'S BUDGET

The legislative process begins in earnest with the presentation of the president's State of the Union address. While most presidents use this opportunity to lay out some kind of agenda for the coming year, Bush's annual speech was overshadowed by what had become a shooting war in the Middle East. Sandwiched between statements concerning the progress of the fighting and the president's plan for a "New World Order" were several relatively vague references to his plan for domestic spending. The two specific points emphasized were a reintroduction of the plan to reduce the capital gains tax and a proposal to return some federal programs to the administrative control of the states. Beyond those proposals, any mention of education, health care, or repair of the nation's infrastructure was made in passing without any major initiative or proposal attached. It was as if the president was completely distracted by the war. And yet the necessity of the budget submission would not wait.

On Monday morning, February 4, the president released his 1,700-page fiscal year 1992 budget plan. Although the contents of the plan had been leaked in advance, there was a scramble on Capitol Hill that morning to respond to the president's proposals. It would take weeks to analyze his plan in detail, but in its barest outlines the budget projected something in excess of $1.45 trillion in spending, about $36 billion above the previous year's levels, or an increase of 2.5 percent. The deficit was projected to be $281 billion.[10] According to the president, his budget represented an actual cut in spending when controlled for inflation. This cut below the baseline was not controversial in and of itself. What was controversial was not *what* the president proposed to do with the budget but *how* he proposed to do it.

Washington is a city of "spin." In the battle for the headlines, each party attempts to place its own interpretation in the press. By 2:30 p.m. on that afternoon the House Democratic leadership had already issued its response to the president's budget proposals. Titled "The President's Budget: Meeting Commitments Abroad, Ignoring Problems at Home," House Majority Leader Richard Gephardt's communiqué outlined "talking points" to be used by the Democratic membership of the House in responding to questions from the local press.

On the recession, the "bullet"—the position the Democrats hoped would be picked up in the press—was "a million Americans have lost their jobs." On education, the focus was "on education spending that does not keep pace with inflation," and so on. For members from districts with a large population of senior citizens, the emphasis would be on the proposed cuts in Medicare.[11] For rural districts, the member would highlight the president's proposed cuts in farm programs, veterans' programs, or mass transit funding for cities with populations of less than 100,000.

The administration responded with a series of statements defending the budget. The president's mind was clearly elsewhere, but so was the public's attention. The result was a general lack of focus on the new budget. Nevertheless, the administration countered the Democratic critique by stressing the deficit reduction component of the budget and, to offset anticipated Democratic criticism that the budget favored the rich, announced that many of the entitlement reductions were to be taken out of the pockets of individuals who earned in excess of $125,000.

Secretary of the Treasury Nicholas Brady opened the administration's Capitol Hill defense on February 7 before the House Budget Committee. He argued that the president was in no position to propose massive new changes in the budget's configuration because the deficit, the new budget law with its spending caps, and the need to keep federal programs operating without massive disruptions had constrained the administration's planning.[12] In some sense, Brady was right. The fact is that much of the budget was locked in, permitting very little room for maneuver. There was nothing the president could do about the federal government's obligation to service the debt. For 1992, the total interest on the debt was projected to be close to $206 billion, or 14 percent of total spending. Fully another 41 percent of the budget was tied up in payments to individuals under existing law or entitlements. Even though the administration had proposed a fairly large decrease in payments for farm price supports and Medicare (two large components of the entitlement account), those reductions were to be much less than 2 percent of the total budget, and, even at that, such reductions would be highly controversial and were dependent on legislative action.

Even more subtle restrictions on the president's latitude to act existed in the discretionary budget. Democrats had argued for two years that, particularly in areas of foreign policy and defense, the president proposed a "sleepwalker's" budget that did nothing to respond to changing conditions, particularly the end of the cold war. The demise of the Warsaw Pact had obviated some of the need for historically high levels of defense and foreign aid expenditure, the war in the Persian Gulf notwithstanding. Nonetheless, even in areas of so-called discretionary spending the president's hands were tied. In the area of defense, for example, the president was proposing a real reduction (when controlled for inflation) of 3 percent. Even this relatively small reduction would impose on the military, among other things, an obligation to reduce its active-duty forces by about 88,000 people. These reductions in force would impose a hardship on the economy if for no other reason than that they represented a huge layoff of service personnel in a relatively short time who would have to be absorbed by the private sector. Even a temporary layoff of this size costs the government a tremendous amount of money as claims rise for unemployment compensation and job-training assistance. In other words, changes in the federal budget can only be made incrementally regardless of the state of the international environment.

Some areas of the discretionary budget, of course, are more flexible than others. In the foreign assistance account, for example, the president has a certain amount of flexibility, at least to the extent that reductions in foreign aid do not have substantial direct effects on the domestic economy. But the foreign aid budget is small (about $20 billion, or a little more than 1 percent of total expenditures), and in this area, too, there are powerful constituencies opposing change. In 1990 the president and Congress had experienced significant disagreements about the makeup of foreign aid, particularly in view of the changes taking place in Eastern Europe. It was particularly in this area of foreign assistance that the president was accused of submitting a nonresponsive budget.

The foreign aid budget has essentially two components: economic support funds and military assistance. Other programs contribute to the economic and military sides of the equation, but the essential distinction in the foreign assistance account is "guns versus butter." In view of the changes taking place in Eastern Europe, the administration was finding it increasingly difficult to argue that military assistance should be emphasized over economic aid in order to counter a quickly declining global Soviet threat. It was also becoming more difficult for the administration to argue that the countries receiving foreign aid were the most deserving. Israel and Egypt, clearly not the poorest of countries, are the two largest U.S. aid recipients, partly as a result of the Camp David accords. Other large recipients such as Turkey and Pakistan are deserving but are clearly not the most needy countries either.

The Congressional Black Caucus argued that sub-Saharan Africa had long been ignored, even with the area in danger of becoming one of the most economically devastated places on earth. At the same time many other members of Congress reflected the view, largely shared by the American public, that needs at home were much too pressing to allow for a significant foreign aid commitment.

All these pressures, however, were put on hold upon the outbreak of the war in the Persian Gulf. Almost immediately after the beginning of the crisis, Turkey and Egypt were compensated for their active participation in the coalition against Iraq. Egyptian debts ($7 billion) were forgiven, while the powerful American-Israel Political Action Committee and Hill and Knowlton, one of the most influential lobbying firms, stalked the halls of Congress on behalf of the Israeli and Turkish governments respectively. The result was very little change in the configuration of the foreign aid budget. Even in the area of foreign assistance, change would have to come incrementally.

Of course, much of the lack of maneuverability in the budget was due to the size of the deficit. The fact that the 1990 budget agreement put aside the deficit question by shifting the emphasis in the budget process away from deficit reduction to spending control changed the dynamics of the budget debate in Congress to a remarkable degree.

No longer were budget negotiators obsessed with the size of the deficit. In fact, one of the major changes in the character of the 1990 as opposed to the 1991 budget debate was the almost complete absence of any mention of the size of the deficit. The Republicans had no desire to discuss the mounting deficit totals that would rightly or wrongly draw attention to what could be construed as presidential fiscal mismanagement. The Democrats avoided the issue as well, recognizing that the only solution to the problem would be reducing spending or raising taxes—unpalatable choices that would draw attention to perceived Democratic weaknesses in financial management. Thus the debate proceeded in Washington with a certain sense of unreality. It was almost as if, by legislative fiat, the deficit, which had seemed so important in previous years, no longer mattered. A number of items, such as the savings and loan bailout, the costs of Operation Desert Shield, and a reduction in Social Security taxes, were discussed as if they made no contribution to the deficit simply because through an accounting gimmick they were to be considered off budget for the purposes of scoring.

What mattered to decision makers was not so much the size of the deficit but how the administration chose to allocate expenditures within the spending caps. The Democrats argued that many of the Bush proposals emphasized priorities that were misguided or simply wrong. For example, while the Bush budget proposed a $200 million increase in funding for WIC (Women, Infants, and Children), the budget also reduced by $600 million income assistance to help the poor pay for home heating. The president proposed a reduction in federal operating assistance for mass transit while at the same time recommending an increase for highways, to be drawn from the Highway Trust Fund. Conflicts were inevitable and heightened as a result of the budget agreement that pitted one program against another through the pay-as-you-go principle. If government were really to contract spending, tough decisions would have to be made.

CONGRESS'S TURN

The full Appropriations Committee very rarely meets. In fact, the activities of the Appropriations Committee are so concentrated at the subcommittee level that it does not even have its own hearing room. On the rare occasion when the full committee meets, the other committees of the House are more than willing to clear the way for Chairman Whitten's committee. For congressional insiders, the meeting of the full Appropriations Committee is one of the most impressive events in the legislative year. Lined up along the chairman's right is the College of Cardinals—members who more than any others in a body of 435 equals hold the reins of power. Far below, behind tables temporarily set up for the committee overflow (its fifty-nine members make it the largest committee in Congress), sit the most junior members of the committee.

When Whitten begins to speak, he does not use the microphone, and even though almost nobody can hear him, no one is willing to interrupt. Every once in a while the chairman raises his pitch and in his deep Mississippi drawl discernibly reviews the history of federal investment policy since the 1940s. Whitten's accent and seniority belie his progressivism. He has not risen to his position of power without political acuity. In Whitten's politics the old and new South meet. The strain of progressivism that catapulted Franklin Roosevelt to his second and third terms can still be distinguished in Whitten's politics. He is an unabashed New Dealer who has no problems using his position to deal goods to his constituents and still call it investment. In his opening remarks Whitten harangues the administration's witnesses, accusing Budget Director Darman of cutting government assistance just when the economy is in recession. At one point, ranking minority member Joseph McDade (R-Pa.) attempts to cut in. "Just a minute," says Whitten, and McDade falls silent. Such is the power of the last of the "mossback turtles."[13]

After the chairman's and the ranking minority member's statement, the committee's witnesses get their chance. Michael Boskin, chairman of the Council of Economic Advisers; Nicholas Brady, secretary of the treasury; and the president's budget director, Richard Darman, each make their case for the president's budget. Boskin, a professional economist, argues that the proposed budget is the best fiscal alternative available given the current recession. Brady stresses the deficit reduction element of the proposal, but the star of the show (and this committee hearing is little more than theater) is Richard Darman. Backed by a series of mounted, poster-sized charts, Darman highlights massive increases in entitlement spending, mainly for the middle class. His purpose in pointing this out is to defend the president's proposal to trim some $47 billion (over five years) from entitlement programs, mainly Medicare. Even so, the budget director projects that in 1992 alone more than $600 billion will be spent on entitlements.

As the committee begins its questioning, it is soon obvious why the full Appropriations Committee rarely meets. The U.S. budget is so massive and the full committee so large that there is little coherence to its work. Each member in order of seniority, alternating from one party to the other, is given about five minutes to question the witnesses. The questioning jumps from one subject to another as each member explores the area of his or her subcommittee's jurisdiction. Rep. Sidney Yates (D-Ill.) explores funding for the fine arts; Rep. David Obey (D-Wis.) at first examines the education budget and then jumps to foreign operations, the jurisdiction of the subcommittee over which he presides. The most junior members must wait their turn until last and may be skipped if they leave the room. Nancy Pelosi (D-Calif.), the most junior Democrat on the committee, waits almost five hours to get her five minutes of questioning. She then challenges Darman on the president's allocation for AIDS treatment and research.

These full committee hearings are highly scripted as they are the "theater" of Congress. Occasionally something may happen in a public committee hearing that is dramatic enough to affect the legislative process. In the main, however, committee hearings are for public consumption, as a member battles with 534 others in Congress for a piece of the limelight. While the committee hearings are going on, however, behind the scenes the dissection of the president's budget begins in earnest.

THE APPROPRIATIONS SUBCOMMITTEES

The real work of the Appropriations Committee takes place in subcommittee. It is at this level that the chairman's mark is prepared—the benchmark that represents the chairman's funding proposals—which will be used as a reference throughout the entire process. This early stage, sometimes occurring as early as February, is crucial to decisions made as late as the end of the fiscal year. Yet the hearing rooms in which many of these multibillion dollar deliberations take place are no larger than an office suite, often located in some out-of-the-way corridor in the Capitol. In theory, these meetings are open to all, but rarely is the general public well represented.

The first subcommittee to meet, even before submission of the president's budget, is the Subcommittee on the Legislative. An informal agreement between Congress and the Executive Office of the President permits each branch to run its own affairs so long as it leaves the other branch alone.[14] If the president were to veto the legislative-branch appropriation, it is likely that the White House budget would attract extra scrutiny in Congress.

On the House side, Vic Fazio (D-Calif.) is the chair of the subcommittee responsible for overseeing legislative-branch appropriations. As such, he is known as the "mayor" of Capitol Hill. Fazio is the model of what an Appropriations subcommittee chairman should be. Reappropriating money for the Government Printing Office or the Architect of the Capitol is not the stuff of grand strategy, but Fazio can be a detail man if called on to play that role. He has been through this process before, and as each agency comes before the subcommittee to ask for its incremental increase, Fazio gently questions the agency representative. Such occasions demonstrate the value of the much reviled seniority system, which ensures that the committee chairs will preserve the institutional memory of Congress. Fazio and the next chair of the Subcommittee on the Legislative will always have a relatively sophisticated background in areas pertaining to its jurisdiction.

The procedure in this subcommittee is characteristic of the hearings that will occur in other subcommittees as soon as the president presents his budget. The main difference between the responsibilities of the Legislative and the other subcommittees is one of scale. In contrast to the "mere" $1.7 billion in funding authority available to the Subcommittee on the Legislative, the Defense and Military Construction subcommittees oversee the allotment of more than $300 billion.

It is difficult to conceive of such an overwhelming task. Some idea of how complex the annual job of appropriating for defense is can be obtained by dividing a $300 billion budget into a thousand separate line items that would result in an average expenditure of $300 million per line item. Even at that level of complexity, the Defense Subcommittee does not have the time to micromanage the expenditure of such large sums of money. Consequently, the oversight process in committee is basically hit or miss, particularly in the appropriation of funds for the largest, most expensive programs. If irregularities are taking place, the committee will either get lucky and discover the waste on its own or a whistle-blower in the bureaucracy or private sector will call attention to the mismanagement of funds by an agency. Micromanagement, in any practical sense, is impossible for any congressional committee charged with overseeing a $1.45 trillion budget.

THE COST OF DESERT SHIELD

On occasion, everything else in Congress is swept aside by an overarching issue. In this case, the crisis in the Middle East eclipsed the budget crisis at home. On January 10 when Congress began its debate on the president's request for authorization to use force in the Persian Gulf, the House of Representatives launched what turned out to be the longest and one of the most free-form debates in American history. Under the rule adopted by the House, members would consider three different resolutions: two advisory concurrent resolutions relating to the continuance of sanctions and a joint resolution formally authorizing the use of force. In theory, there was supposed to be a limit on debate, but the leadership recognized that the issue of war and peace was so pivotal that virtually every member deserved the opportunity to "go to the well" (speak before the full House assembled) and explain his or her position on the war. When the votes were finally counted, almost two and a half days after the talking began, the Senate narrowly and the House by a wider margin approved the use of force.

In September 1990 the Defense Department predicted that the cost of Operation Desert Shield, in the absence of a shooting war, would be $15 billion for the fiscal year 1991. By early January unofficial estimates of the cost of the operation in the Middle East had nearly doubled. These were merely unofficial estimates, however, inasmuch as the administration refused to release to Congress its revised projections of the cost. The White House argued that the president was no more obligated to give Congress a running account of the costs of Desert Shield than it was to consult with Congress about the strategy of deploying troops in the field. In other words, maintaining secrecy about the cost of the military operation was permissible under the powers of the president as commander-in-chief.

House Budget Committee chairman Leon Panetta (D-Calif.) was in no mood to wait. On January 4, the day after Congress went back into session, Panetta held a hearing in his committee to review the cost of Desert Shield. Conspicuously absent were representatives from the Departments of State and Defense, who had been invited by Panetta but declined to attend. From those who did testify, however, the figures were sobering enough.

Charles Bowsher, comptroller general and director of the General Accounting Office (Congress's investigatory arm), predicted that the cost of Desert Shield for fiscal year 1991 alone could be as high as $130 billion. He predicted that $100 billion of the cost would be directly incurred by the intervention and another $30 billion would represent the loss of savings that would have occurred had the Operation never taken place.[15] (In the wake of the demise of the Warsaw Pact, the military had planned to scale back its operations drastically.) In addition, the United States had forgiven $7 billion owed by Egypt, not to mention other foreign assistance that would be directed to allies such as Turkey who had aided in imposing sanctions against Iraq.[16] As high as these estimates were, they would be costs incurred only in the absence of a shooting war. Lawrence Korb, a former assistant secretary of defense in the Reagan administration, estimated that if a shooting war developed, the cost in dollars (not to mention human lives) would be somewhere in the range of $1 billion to $3 billion a day![17]

Under the 1990 budget agreement, Desert Shield costs were to be designated emergency supplemental appropriations, to be considered outside the regular appropriations process. Under OBRA, when the president and Congress agree that a supplemental appropriation is required to meet an emergency, those funds will not be "scored" against spending caps or deficit reduction targets. ("Scoring" is the term used to describe the process by which programs are counted against spending caps.) In other words, if Operation Desert Shield were to cost $100 billion for fiscal year 1991, that year's deficit reduction target would automatically be adjusted upward by $100 billion. Accordingly, the regular defense spending cap would not be affected by a Desert Shield supplemental appropriation. There was some concern that the Defense Department would be tempted to charge against the costs of Desert Shield other expenses it would have incurred had there been no crisis. This would create room under the defense spending cap for programs that the department had previously been forced to reduce or discontinue. Furthermore, the crisis in the Persian Gulf imposed indirect costs by generating additional interest on the debt, offsetting some of the peace dividend, increasing the price of oil as well as the cost of pay for reserve forces called to active duty, and generating additional costs for our non-oil-producing allies such as Egypt, Turkey, and Israel, which would probably have to be made up in foreign aid.

OBRA specified that as much of the cost of Operation Desert Shield as possible was to be recovered by reprogramming funds in the Defense Department account and obtaining contributions from our allies. Accordingly, the Defense Department was planning to recover about $5 billion (or a very small percentage) through reprogramming, and by mid-January our allies had pledged approximately $10 billion (of which only about $3 billion had been paid).

THE DESERT STORM SUPPLEMENTAL APPROPRIATION

Proceeding along an entirely different track from regular appropriations legislation were two administration requests for supplemental funds to offset the initial costs of the war. The first supplemental appropriations to be considered under OBRA, they were, consequently, the first and most serious test of the new budgeting regime. Because the 1991 budget contained no funding per se for Desert Shield (the operation had been using contingency funds or existing accounts drawn down at the expense of other items), it was necessary for the president to return to the new Congress and ask for additional funding.

Under the terms of the 1990 budget agreement, the direct costs of Operation Desert Shield were automatically to come to Congress as an emergency supplemental. The "emergency" designation was crucial in this case because, under the new budget arrangement, appropriations specified as emergencies by Congress and the president would not be scored against the spending caps and thus would not count against appropriations of a similar type.[18] Legitimate, direct costs of the operation would not automatically result in sequestration. There was no way to avoid the possibility that the costs of the military operation in the Middle East would contribute to the debt. However, as long as Desert Shield expenses were designated as part of the emergency, they would not count against other items in the Defense Department's account.[19]

The Appropriations, Budget, and Armed Services committees launched investigations of the administration's Desert Shield request. Of particular concern were three items in the president's wartime budget. First, there was a request for extra compensation for the military to offset their additional expenses resulting from the increase in the price of oil resulting from the crisis. This additional request for $2.8 billion, no small increment, was perceived to be grossly unfair since every other government agency had to absorb this increase. Moreover, inasmuch as oil prices by the end of February were already at their prewar level, it was not clear that the administration's request was accurate or necessary.

The administration also requested weapons purchases that exceeded their replacement rate. For example, in the supplemental request, the military asked for an additional 500 Patriot missiles to replace the ones that had so successfully defended Saudi Arabia and Israel against Iraqi SCUD missile attacks. In fact, the military had fired fewer than 200 missiles in the course of the entire war. Finally, members of Congress were concerned about the way the administration proposed to handle foreign contributions to the Desert Shield/Storm operation. The administration proposed to place these contributions in an account that would be at the direct disposal of the secretary of defense (subject to review by the Office of Management and Budget).[20] In essence, this meant that Congress would have no say in the way these funds were spent. Even congressional Republicans objected. Members of the Senate Appropriations Committee, notably the ranking minority member, Mark Hatfield (R-Ore.), were opposed. Without consulting Congress, Hatfield argued, the administration would be subverting Congress's constitutional authority to make appropriations.[21] Ultimately, in order to protect its prerogatives, Congress opted to make specific line-by-line provisions for the expenditure of the donated funds.

CONCLUSION

By the end of February, the budget process had more or less returned to normal as it became clear that a successful war would not unduly overextend the budget. The burden of the war would be especially light if the allies made good on their pledges of support and if the war was quickly and successfully ended, as seemed likely at the time.[22]

The year had begun with high drama, as befits a capital city on the brink of war. There is nothing quite so awesome in American government as the power of the presidency in time of war. The first month and a half of 1991 were dominated by President Bush. As chief diplomat he organized and led an international coalition in support of the war effort; as chief of state he dominated the media and public pronouncements; and as commander-in-chief he decided when and how to take the nation into battle. By contrast, there is no institution in government quite so underwhelming as Congress in time of war. Not only is there a lack of information available on the status of the troops in the field, but very few members of Congress are willing to go on record and thereby seem to second-guess and perhaps undercut a wartime president, particularly a popular one.

But the bill for the war must eventually come due, and then there is no way for the president to avoid the prying eyes of congressional committees. January and February, therefore, provided the preamble for the coming budget debate. This was the case not only because of the war but also because the president's budget was presented to Congress in February. As we shall see, the success of Operation Desert Storm did nothing to settle the debate over budget priorities at home. In fact, the success of the American war effort added fuel to the debate over the allotment of the budget for future years. Was President Bush's "New World Order" to require new defense expenditures at home and abroad? Would the conclusion of the war and the demobilization of troops intensify the recession, putting new pressures on government spending?

NOTES

1. The money that Congress appropriates for a program determines its cost. However, for entitlements and taxation, changes in the laws result in costs that are very much a function of economic and actuarial projections.
2. In fact it is an informal tradition in Congress that the directorship of the CBO alternate between Republicans and Democrats.
3. Albert E. Crenshaw, "Questions Remain for Other Banks: Some in 'Second Tier' Said to Be Insolvent," *Washington Post,* January 8, 1991, C1, C3.
4. Section 258, Title XIII, 1990 Omnibus Budget Reconciliation Act, U.S.C. The purpose of this provision was to ensure that in the event of a recession the spending caps would not impede government action to compensate for the effects of the economic downturn.
5. See Nelson Polsby, "The Institutionalization of the U.S. House of Representatives," *American Political Science Review* 62 (March 1968): 144-168; it is applied to individual committees by Richard F. Fenno, "The House Appropriations Committee as a Political System: The Problem of Integration," *American Political Science Review* 56 (June 1962): 310-324; John F. Manley, *The Politics of Finance: The House Committee on Ways and Means* (Boston: Little, Brown, 1970); and James T. Murphy, "Political Parties and the Porkbarrel: Party Conflict and Cooperation in House Public Works Committee Decision Making," *American Political Science Review* 68 (March 1974): 169-185.
6. The exclusive, semi-exclusive, and nonexclusive designations apply only to House committees. In the Senate, some committees are designated "major" committees. Senators are guaranteed at least one major committee assignment. Most of them sit on three and can sit on as many as five committees.
7. In addition, Foreign Affairs subcommittees have no direct control over the appropriation of monies, which detracts from their influence.
8. See Dan Morgan, "How to Make the Sun Shine on the Passaic: Switch Seats on Appropriations," *Washington Post,* March 1, 1991, A13.
9. Quoted in Morgan.
10. Pursuant to the 1990 budget agreement, this deficit projection did not include the Social Security Trust Fund, which had a surplus, and a $15 billion "placeholder" that represented preliminary estimates of the cost of the war in the Persian Gulf; most of these costs were hopefully to be accrued during the 1991 fiscal year rather than extended into fiscal year 1992.
11. The president proposed approximately $25 billion in "savings" (a euphemism for cuts) in Medicare over a five-year period.
12. See the prepared testimony of Nicholas Brady before the House Budget Committee, February 7, 1991.
13. "Mossback turtle" is the term used to refer to the committee chairmen who dominated the House from about 1920 to 1970. Most of them were from the South and rather advanced in years. The subcommittee reforms of the 1970s did away with the power and even some of the committee chairs, who were deposed. It is a testament to Whitten's political acuity that he not only survived the era of subcommittee reform but also adjusted to changes in the South that had significantly altered his constituency.
14. Formally, the Treasury, Postal Service and General Government Subcommittee has jurisdiction over White House operations. However, consideration of the president's salary and other staffing requests is almost always pro forma.
15. Written testimony of Charles Bowsher, comptroller general of the United States, submitted to the House Budget Committee, U.S. House of Represen-

tatives, January 4, 1991.

16. Turkey was granted certain waivers by the administration for its textile exports to the United States.
17. Written testimony of Lawrence Korb submitted to the House Budget Committee, U.S. House of Representatives, January 4, 1991.
18. Omnibus Budget Reconciliation Act, Section 251 (b)(2)(D).
19. It should be noted that just because an item is designated an emergency and is not scored against its own account, it is not the same as being held off budget. Off-budget items such as the Social Security surplus are not scored at all and do not affect the spending caps, trigger sequestration, or lead to an adjustment of the deficit reduction targets.
20. See the testimony of Richard Darman before the Senate Appropriations Committee, February 26, 1991, 4.
21. Ibid.
22. Projected direct costs of the war had been dramatically scaled down. With estimated costs at $50 billion and allied pledges at about $53 billion, the intervention would be paid for in full if the coalition partners met their financial commitments. See the testimony of Robert D. Reischauer, director of the Congressional Budget Office, before the House Budget Committee, February 27, 1991.

CHAPTER 7

March and April 1991: The Pace Quickens

Once the president submits his budget, the appropriations process can begin in earnest. As soon as the OMB clears their annual requests for funding, agencies can make a case for their allocation before their designated appropriations subcommittee. By and large this presentation is pro forma, as most ongoing agency funding is incremental or a clear reflection of previous levels of funding. Congress has an ongoing commitment to most agencies, and, more importantly, most agencies develop powerful constituencies inside and outside the legislative process. With respect to administrative expenses, the budget process at this stage is relatively noncontroversial. What programs the agencies will ultimately administer is another matter. Which roads will be built? Which harbors dredged? Whose post office will be built? These decisions are the mother's milk of congressional politics.

It is at this early stage, the preparation of the chairman's mark, that much of the real competition for funding occurs behind the scenes. Not every request can be funded. Members, both on the Appropriations Committee and off, vie for a piece of the appropriations pie. The chairman is inevitably caught in a bind. Because there are limits to funding, there must be winners as well as losers. If a program or individual request for funding is left out of the chairman's mark, it is likely that the program will die then and there, at least until the next fiscal cycle.

More in the public eye is the activity on the floor. Spring is the season for authorizations, which are supposed to precede the appropriations process. The first major legislation to come to the floor at the beginning of a congressional session is therefore likely to be an authorization package. However, there are characteristics of the authorization process that make this stage of the legislative process less important than meets the eye.

It is likely that about the middle of March a supplemental appropriations bill (or several) will emerge. Fiscal year 1991 was no exception. While the process and subject matter of those 1991 supplementals were somewhat unique, this does not mean that the consideration of separate, freestanding appropriations measures in the middle of a fiscal year is at all uncommon. In fact, the passage of such bills in the spring is more the norm than the exception. As March is roughly the midpoint of the fiscal year, unplanned gaps in funding then begin to appear in the budget. What makes the consideration of the Desert Shield/Storm supplementals so special as a case study is that this was the first appropriations measure to go through the entire legislative process under the provisions of the October budget agreement.

Finally, April 15 is supposed to be the deadline for the adoption of the congressional budget resolution. However, Congress almost never meets this deadline, and 1991 was no exception. As we have seen, in the previous year Congress failed to adopt the budget resolution before the very end of the fiscal year in September. More commonly, floor consideration of the budget resolution gets postponed to late April and May.

AUTHORIZATION

The structure of the authorization and appropriations process reflects the fundamental choice members have to make every day between budgetary considerations and policy. In general, authorization bills are the product of the collective judgments of expert legislative committees as to how and whether the federal government should pursue a particular activity. In addition, authorization bills set general ceilings for funding.

The appropriations committees, on the other hand, look at the problem differently, assessing authorized legislative activities in light of budgetary demands. In other words, an activity that may seem worthwhile in theory may be impractical in terms of funding. It is possible and, in fact, common for programs to be authorized but not funded. For all intents and purposes, an authorized program that is not funded never exists. The authorization stage is merely the first and not always an absolutely critical part of the appropriations process.

In theory, spring is the time for Congress to pass its authorization bills in anticipation of passage of the appropriations bills later in the summer. As often as not, however, the authorization process is much less predictable. For one thing, many authorizations are reapproved on a multiyear or more or less permanent basis rather than annually, reflecting the fact that not all policies operate on a yearly cycle.

Before 1960, most authorizations were permanent. When a department or agency was created, there was usually an open-ended fiscal authorization attached to the law to the effect that "there are hereby authorized to be appropriated such sums as may be necessary" to conduct an agency's function. The appropriations committees then established yearly funding levels for the agency. The problem with this style of authorization was that agencies never went out of existence. Moreover, the authorization committees, once they established an agency with a permanent authorization, ceded much of their control to the appropriations committees. Consequently, there was an incentive to reestablish authorization committee control by making agency review periodic. Now major authorization bills come due for reexamination with a certain regularity.

Also contributing to the unpredictability of the authorization process is the fact that authorizations can be supplanted by policy statements made through appropriations bills. The requirement that appropriations be preceded by authorizations is an institutional, *not* a constitutional requirement. Therefore, because Congress is an institution that makes its own rules, the authorization requirement is sometimes short circuited, especially when authorization bills become too controversial and fail to survive the legislative process.

For example, in most years (including 1991), Congress is unable to pass a foreign aid authorization bill (an annual authorization). Foreign aid is immensely unpopular in Congress and is a policy fraught with partisanship. Yet most members would admit in private that there is a real need for most American foreign assistance. What members need, therefore, in voting for foreign assistance legislation is political cover, which is provided in the annual ritual that ends with the rejection of the foreign aid authorization measure. On that bill, members are allowed a generally free hand to attach the kinds of amendments that make the final legislation palatable enough for constituents and at the same time unpassable. But because money can be appropriated without authorizations, foreign aid authorization is sacrificed on the altar of electoral politics.

To be more specific, foreign aid authorization generally collapses in the Senate. This is principally because the Foreign Relations Committee is heavily influenced by ranking minority member Sen. Jesse Helms (R-N.C.), one of the most conservative members of Congress. Any bill likely to emerge from the Senate committee would be much too conservative for the full Senate, much less the House. Alternately, if the bill were to be amended on the Senate floor to delete Helms's influence, it is likely that the North Carolina Republican and his allies would jam up the Senate's schedule in protest. Consequently, Senate foreign aid authorizations are rarely brought to the floor. The appropriations committees write the authorization language through their distribution of funds in the foreign operations appropriations bill.[1]

This points up the major difference between the authorization and appropriations processes. *Appropriations bills are much too important to fail.* Without an appropriations bill, agencies would be forced to close, federal employees would be laid off, programs would be interrupted, and citizens would not receive their government benefits.

Authorization bills, on the other hand, are fragile creations. Because of this, some of the most controversial legislation is attached to appropriations rather than authorization measures. For example, restrictions on government funding for abortion, most significantly the Hyde amendment forbidding federal funding of abortions, are generally attached to appropriations bills. If such controversial provisions were attached to authorization bills, those bills would fail either because they could not withstand a presidential veto, or because members could feel safe in voting against them since programs can be funded without an authorization. Thus, because many authorization bills are not must-pass bills, they are much more likely to be vetoed or voted down and are much less likely to be subject to compromise.

Because the appropriations process is not dependent on the size or even passage of authorizations, *authorization bills can contain high, sometimes unrealistic, levels of spending.* First, because authorization levels do not have to be fully funded, members can vote for exorbitant levels of spending safe in the knowledge that those appropriations will never be made. Second, because authorization bills are not absolutely crucial, they often fall into the realm of theater rather than public policy making. As constituents rarely understand the distinction between authorizations and appropriations, members find that votes in favor of exorbitant authorization levels are free votes. Members can claim credit for voting full funding for the parochial demands of constituents without necessarily busting the budget. Furthermore, when the appropriations committees fail to meet authorization levels of spending, the member can blame someone else (the appropriations committees or the president in case of a veto) for the failure to fund policy decisions made through the authorization process.

Finally, authorization bills are often not passed in sequence. Appropriations bills sometimes precede the authorization process if only because these bills are must-pass legislation. The authorization process proceeds at a desultory pace, to be put aside in moments of crisis or at the end of the fiscal year. Nevertheless, to pass an appropriations bill before an authorization bill requires some delicate negotiation. In order to avert the opposition of authorization committee members (who are, after all, a majority in the House and Senate), appropriations bills passed before authorization bills require some prior clearance. For example, authorization committee members resent earmarks and limitations in appropriations bills that infringe on their jurisdiction.

A classic case in the use and difference between authorization and appropriations bills occurred in the spring of 1991. Rep. Les AuCoin (D-Ore.) introduced an amendment to the Defense Authorization Act that permitted military hospitals abroad to perform abortions. Predictably, the president threatened to veto the entire bill for this and other reasons. The threat was entirely plausible, but not entirely awe-inspiring. The president wasn't going to allow the military to go out of existence, and the military could get along without a defense authorization for a year. It was not much of a sacrifice, therefore, for AuCoin to drop his amendment on the authorization for the greater good of getting the legislation past the presidential veto. But when the AuCoin amendment was attached to the defense appropriation, that was an entirely different matter. The president could threaten to veto the appropriation, but the threat was not entirely credible. Would the president really veto an appropriations bill and allow the military to go out of business in order to keep military hospitals from performing a few abortions? This was unlikely. The logic of the appropriations process would protect the AuCoin amendment if it survived.

It would be perfectly reasonable to inquire at this point why AuCoin would bother with the authorization process at all. The answer lies in the fact that most earmarks and limitations language attached to appropriations bills expire at the end of the fiscal year. Authorization language is more or less permanent. While the funding allowed in authorization bills is for a specified period, the policy changes are permanent. Although appropriations bills may include some language that has the effect of legislation, opponents can take solace in the fact that much of this policy will expire at the end of the fiscal year. This is one reason why the president may be willing to accept appropriations bills including language with which he disagrees.

Even though all governmental activity is in some way connected to spending money, the connection is often quite tenuous. Policy decisions must be made. For example, in the spring of 1991 Congress considered a reauthorization of the Federal Surface Transportation Act, better known as the highway bill. One of the more controversial issues was allowing LCVs (Long Container Vehicles) or trucks pulling up to three trailers on interstate highways. This is just one of many regulations considered governing the use of the nation's highways that are almost certainly the province of authorization or policy-making committees rather than the spending authorities in Congress.

PREPARING THE CHAIRMAN'S MARK

About the beginning of April, if Congress is to get its appropriations work done by the end of September (and take a long recess in August), the House must begin to clear all thirteen regular appropriations bills. (There is a constitutional requirement that the House initiate all tax and spending legislation.) Each of the more controversial measures, not to mention their accompanying authorizations, can take up to a week or more of legislative time. Consequently, the subcommittee chairs must prepare their "mark" early if there is to be any hope of timely passage of legislation. It is in the preparation of the mark that the power of the appropriations cardinals reaches its zenith. The mark is the subcommittee chair's plan for budget allocations for its area of jurisdiction and is functionally the last time a subcommittee member can have a significant impact on appropriations legislation. At the full committee level the cardinal's mark is rarely significantly changed. On the floor of the House, appropriations bills are generally considered under a closed or modified closed rule that forbids the inclusion of extraneous or minority sponsored amendments.

On the Senate side, although appropriations bills are more likely to be subject to amendment, there are political problems in trying to alter something in the bill that the chair has already rejected. In other words, if the subcommittee chair refuses to include an item in his mark, an attempt to reverse his decision on the floor is a politically dangerous maneuver. If it does happen, it may well be a one-shot deal. A senator amends an appropriations bill at the cost of a significant amount of political capital. Such an amendment is not only likely to lose but may also alienate some of the powerful appropriations subcommittee chairs, making it not a smart tactic in the long run.

Finally, while appropriations bills can be changed in conference, appointed conferees include subcommittee chairs who generally preside over the conference committee. As we shall see, in order to arrive at a compromise, the chairman of the conference has enormous latitude in including or deleting funding proposals. Thus the preferences of the chairman's mark are likely to survive the legislative process largely intact.

The much preferred strategy for getting an item into an appropriations bill is to include it in the chairman's mark from the beginning. Obviously every spring the chair and the subcommittee staff are deluged with requests for funding. The selection process is a study in the hierarchy in both houses of Congress. As the chair has a limited pool of money under the budget resolution, requests for funding must be ranked according to some kind of formula. One factor to be considered is the power and stature of the member making the request. Jamie

Whitten, as chair of the full committee and the subcommittee on Agriculture, is much more likely to get his request included in some other chairman's mark than is a junior member of the Republican minority who is not a member of the Appropriations Committee. Other considerations include (not necessarily in this order) personal relationships, the existence of relevant authorizing legislation, and, of course, public policy concerns. According to that formula, after the chairman's requests are met, the chairman's mark reflects a complex mixture of institutional and public policy concerns.

BLOOD IN THE WATER—THE DESERT STORM SUPPLEMENTAL

One of the most feared events at sea is a feeding frenzy. Stimulated by blood in the water, sharks became so frenzied that they may even attack one another or anything that moves in an attempt to get at their prey. In some ways, Congress is prone to such frenzies. On occasions when the largesse of the budget is available to all, members will engage in an undisciplined scramble to get as much as they can for their own constituents. Such a frenzy occurred in 1981 with the passage of President Reagan's tax reform proposals.

Buoyed by his landslide victory in 1980, the new president aimed to stimulate the economy by providing taxpayers, particularly the wealthy, with tax relief. Democrats in Congress, rather than fight the proposal of a newly elected, popular president and reeling from the loss of the presidency and the Senate, decided to go along. The Democratic leadership adopted the general thrust of the proposal but, in an attempt to one-up the administration, proposed even greater tax breaks than those of the president.

With both Republican and Democratic members favoring tax cuts, the Democratic strategy set off a frenzy of revenue reduction. Politically vulnerable incumbents saw the 1981 tax act as an opportunity to reward their constituents with the rare blessing of both the president and the Democratic leadership. Congressional analysts predicted that over the decade the 1981 Tax Reform Act would cost the federal government as much as $2 trillion in lost revenues. Indeed, ten years after the frenzy subsided and the 1981 Tax Reform Act was passed, the country had almost tripled its yearly deficit and quadrupled the debt (to almost $4 trillion).[2] The lion's share of the shortfall could be traced directly to the feeding frenzy set off by President Reagan's 1981 tax reform proposals.

Most of the reforms in the budget process adopted since then were designed in one way or another to prevent another such feeding frenzy.

This is a particularly difficult trick to perform in an institution that makes its own rules, especially when the political incentive exists to defect from deficit control. It is generally to the benefit of individual members of Congress to subvert overall budget control. Therefore, it was quite likely, even in the early spring of 1991, that the reforms of the 1990 budget agreement would be unable to restrain the natural inclinations of members of Congress who have the power to circumvent the spirit of the law.

The first great test of the 1990 reforms came even before the beginning of much of the regular budget process for fiscal year 1992. When supplemental appropriations for financing Operation Desert Storm/Shield were being considered, the budget agreement of 1990 almost immediately came under pressure.

FUNDING DESERT SHIELD/STORM

Supplemental appropriations bills occur with regularity because Congress can never completely plan in advance for all contingencies. Most incremental costs beyond existing levels of appropriations must be covered by a transfer of funds or a separate supplemental appropriation passed in the course of the fiscal year. Supplementals have been increasingly common of late because of the deficit reduction requirements imposed on Congress by the 1974 Budget Reform Act and Gramm-Rudman-Hollings. One of the fictions perpetrated by the forced deficit reduction law is that the demand for services of programs subject to forced deficit reduction would disappear. Nothing could be further from the truth. Funding is understated for many programs at the beginning of the fiscal year for the purpose of deficit reduction, only later to be restored by supplemental appropriations. After all, the demand for government services does not simply disappear because of a lack of funding.

In 1987 President Reagan and budget negotiators from both parties in Congress agreed that supplemental appropriations bills would not be allowed unless they were adopted in the wake of a "dire emergency." (They would be adjudged out of order and/or the president would exercise his veto.) It was not entirely clear what constituted a dire emergency. However, if the president and Congress agreed that there was a need for emergency funding, supplemental appropriations would be allowed to stand. Although this agreement had a certain dampening effect on the size and frequency of supplemental appropriations, it did not succeed in ending the practice.

There is never going to be absolute agreement about what circumstance constitutes an emergency. Regardless of external conditions, Congress will often attempt to restore, through supplemental spending, funding for a program the administration does not favor. In such an instance, if the administration and Congress do not both agree to designate a supplemental appropriation a dire emergency, the regular rules of the budget process apply. Supplementals will be scored against deficit reduction targets and, as of 1990, spending caps. Prior to the October 1990 budget agreement, because the president does not have a line-item veto, items he opposed could be attached to his requests for supplemental spending. The president would then have to veto the entire appropriation or sign the bill.

Since the passage of OBRA, both the president and Congress formally have to designate an item as an emergency in order to exempt it from spending limitations.[3] This provision of the October accord became a controversial issue almost immediately. On February 14, 1991, Budget Director Richard Darman indicated in a letter to the ranking minority member of the House Budget Committee, Willis Gradison (R-Ohio), that if an appropriations bill was passed that the OMB did not deem an emergency or a direct cost of Operation Desert Shield, a sequester in the amount of the appropriation would be ordered. Darman was anticipating an attempt by members of Congress to use the Desert Shield/Storm supplemental as a vehicle for pork-barrel spending. The OMB, therefore, was serving notice that it intended to be the final arbiter of what constituted an emergency. The president and his budget director would then be able to select those nonemergency, nonexempt items out of any appropriations measure to calculate sequesters.[4] This interpretation would eventually serve as the equivalent of a functional line-item veto and, as a result, would become a matter of some controversy.

The politics of the dire-emergency designation took on a life all its own. Under the new budget agreement, Congress not only had to satisfy the Bush administration that the items it requested in a supplemental appropriations measure were in response to an emergency but also had to justify each supplemental expenditure item within the supplemental as an emergency in order to avoid an OMB-ordered sequester. As we have seen, the 1990 budget agreement specifically excluded the incremental costs of Operation Desert Shield/Storm from being counted against the spending caps. In effect, the president and Congress agreed in advance that the costs of the military operation in the Persian Gulf were indeed an emergency and thus exempt from scoring. There were, however, disagreements as to the definition of these costs.

Budgeting for Desert Shield at Home and Abroad

In order to ensure the expeditious passage of funds for troops deployed in the Middle East, the White House and congressional leaders agreed to consider the dire-emergency supplemental appropriations for Desert Shield in two separate bills. Those items that were clearly appropriate for the support of troops in the field would be passed in a single package. This, the larger of the two bills in terms of dollar amounts, was intended to fund the military operation in the Gulf. By agreement, it would be a relatively clean bill, exempt from riders that might delay its passage and restrict resupplying the military.

The other bill was to consist of a grab bag of items, most of which were described as the indirect domestic and international costs of operations in the Persian Gulf. Items were to be considered either emergencies or costs of Operation Desert Shield, while other items were to be scored as regular appropriations to be applied against the spending caps. Because of the controversy over what was to be considered an emergency or direct expense of Desert Shield, this second supplemental appropriations measure became a much more controversial piece of legislation. There were plans afoot in many congressional offices to use the dire-emergency designation as a way to exempt from spending limits a number of special appropriations items. As a result, the second measure was in danger of becoming what is known in Congress as a "Christmas tree"—a bill that members use as a vehicle to carry their own individual "ornaments" or pork-barrel projects.[5] It would be almost unpatriotic to hang an ornament off the military Desert Shield supplemental (and thus delay its passage). However, no such constraint existed with regard to the domestic dire-emergency supplemental. Consequently, the second, much smaller supplemental would become the first major test of the new budgetary procedures adopted pursuant to the October 1990 budget agreement.

The Domestic Desert Storm

Of particular concern with regard to the dire-emergency domestic supplemental were two items that could burst the spending caps: veterans' benefits and aid to Israel. In the postwar euphoria (when the final votes for the Gulf War supplementals were cast), a number of members of Congress sponsored legislation to expand veterans' benefits, perceiving the dire-emergency supplemental as an opportunity to expand these benefits without triggering sequesters that would normally occur in the regular appropriations process. Others may have seen the sponsorship of increased veterans' benefits as an opportunity to seek political cover from the fallout of their prewar votes against the president's use of force in the Persian Gulf.

The groundswell of support for these benefits put the administration in a difficult position. If Congress were to pass the most prominent of these proposals, only about 20 percent of the expenditures would be collected by veterans of Operation Desert Storm. In reality, there would be little reason to argue that these new veterans' benefits were a direct expense associated with Operation Desert Storm. In addition, while these expenditures would be used to fund important veterans' needs, they in no way constituted an emergency according to the meaning of the term in the 1990 budget agreement or the previous agreement with President Reagan. If these benefits were approved, President Bush would either be forced to veto the legislation, and thus appear to be denying veterans' benefits to troops in the field, or to sign the legislation and allow the emergency designation in OBRA to be violated in its first test.

There was a third alternative. The president could sign the legislation and the OMB could designate the measure as "nonemergency." The OMB would then sequester funds in the amount of the additional veterans' benefits. However, because most veterans' benefits are located in the nondiscretionary entitlement account, sequesters triggered by the passage of this new spending would have to be taken out of the accounts of other veterans' programs, Medicare, and farm crop subsidies, among other entitlement programs. Ultimately the president and his budget director chose to threaten to use this course.

Despite the president's warnings, and despite the fact that the measure was opposed on the floor of the House by Budget Committee Chair Leon Panetta (D-Calif.) and his ranking minority member, Willis Gradison, the House Appropriations Committee included the new veterans' benefits in the emergency portion of the dire-emergency supplemental. Eventually the House-Senate conference included some $58 million in additional veterans' spending in the emergency portion of the bill. After some negotiations with the OMB, in which the new benefits were reduced to $37 million, the administration permitted it to pass despite its objections. After all, the appropriation was a minuscule portion of the overall multibillion-dollar package.[6]

Another, much larger controversy involved aid to Israel, which had suffered the effects of forty SCUD missile attacks from Iraq. Although Israel never retaliated against Iraq, Israeli defense forces had been forced to maintain the highest state of alert preceding and during the war. Supporters of Israel in Congress asked for an additional foreign aid appropriation of close to $1 billion, arguing that other front-line states such as Jordan had been compensated for their expenses out of a fund set up by the Persian Gulf Cooperation Council and other partners in the coalition against Iraq (including Western Europe and Japan). In addition, Egypt had been given $7 billion in debt relief in partial repayment for cooperating with the anti-Saddam Hussein coalition. Because the Gulf States would not countenance having their funds used to compensate Israel, only the United States and, to a lesser extent, Western European countries could be relied on to help Israel.

Besides the fact that there is always a certain amount of resistance in Congress to foreign aid, particularly to Israel (the single largest foreign aid recipient), an incremental $1 billion in emergency appropriations could threaten the integrity of the entire OBRA process. The alternative to declaring such a level of aid to Israel an emergency would be a sequester applied against all other recipients in the foreign aid discretionary account, whose total funds are about $20 billion. All other recipients of U.S. foreign aid could expect a 5 percent cut as a consequence of the sequester. Again, the administration was caught in a bind.

To approve additional aid to Israel could quite possibly touch off just the kind of feeding frenzy the OMB and congressional budget leaders hoped to avoid. Supporters of other interests, particularly those within the United States, could argue that if the United States was willing to deliver assistance to Israel at this time, shouldn't the government also meet the needs of American citizens at home? On the other hand, if the administration failed to support additional aid to Israel or actively opposed such aid, it would not only face a serious domestic political backlash but also lose influence over the appropriations process (supporters of Israel probably had the votes to pass the aid). Moreover, it would also lose leverage over Israeli policy, particularly settlement policies on the West Bank and in Gaza. Supporters of Israel in Congress were already preparing legislation to aid Israel should the Bush administration fail to act.

Within the House Appropriations Committee, efforts to aid Israel were being stymied by a powerful subcommittee chair. Jurisdiction over foreign aid normally falls within the purview of the Foreign Operations subcommittee. The chair of that subcommittee, David Obey (D-Wis.), has rarely been supportive of high levels of American aid to Israel. He was clearly unenthusiastic about attaching additional aid to Israel to the Desert Shield appropriation, especially if the administration was opposed and the integrity of the 1990 budget agreement was threatened. Obey would have found it particularly difficult to have to "front" for Israel if the administration was unwilling to join in and deflect some of the inevitable criticism that aid to Israel always attracts.

Owing to the difficulty of attaching to Obey's bill any items that he opposed, there was some talk among supporters of Israel on the Appropriations Committee of adopting the very risky strategy of bypassing the chair. It might be possible to solicit the support of Defense Subcommittee chair John Murtha (D-Pa.), who would introduce aid to Israel in his Desert Storm defense proposal as military assistance rather than foreign aid.

Obey is one of the youngest cardinals and highest-ranking members of the Appropriations Committee. As it is quite likely that he will be chair of the full committee in the next few years, it is very dangerous for a member of the committee to get on Obey's wrong side. Reciprocity works both ways in Congress. Favors are returned and so are insults. To do an end run around the jealously guarded jurisdiction of the Foreign Operations subcommittee would not only be an insult, it would be a challenge to the effectiveness and authority of the subcommittee chair. In the end, it did not seem worth the risk for Israel or its congressional supporters to bypass Obey, even in the unlikely event that Murtha would agree.[7]

The best course, therefore, was to have aid for Israel included as part of the chairman's proposal or, failing that, to have the president include a proposal for aid in his Desert Storm request to Congress. The administration often has to be lobbied just like Congress. Grass-roots contacts must be informed of the issue and asked to contact the president's office and his cabinet secretaries. High-level contacts have to be utilized as well. The Israeli government both in the United States and abroad, as well as pro-Israeli groups at home, contacted administration officials at all levels.

In the meantime, Obey's subcommittee approved a request for domestic dire-emergency supplemental funding that contained no money for Israel. The chairman's budget included only $6 million, earmarked for the evacuation of Agency for International Development (AID) employees from the Middle East. With the chairman's request already submitted, the only way Israeli aid could be attached to the domestic Desert Storm supplemental would be to add the funds to the bill in full committee. (Remember, most appropriations bills come to the floor under a closed rule that does not permit amendment.) Of course, amendments in the full committee are rare. Subcommittee chairs generally protect their turfs. Consequently, cardinals will generally be unfavorably disposed toward amendments in the full committee, if only to preserve the integrity of the subcommittee structure. That being the case, an amendment to add foreign aid to Israel that was not supported by Chairman Obey would likely attract the opposition of almost all the other subcommittee chairs, not to mention other members unwilling to vote against the institutional interests of the cardinals. Nonetheless, proponents of aid to Israel prepared to take their request to the full committee.

At the same time, negotiations proceeded at the White House and in the State Department. The administration stated its willingness to request the aid if the Israelis would agree to certain conditions. With little more than an hour before the full committee was scheduled to meet, the administration and the Israelis finally came to an agreement.

The White House would request a one-time-only emergency aid package of $650 million ($350 million less than the Israelis wanted), provided that the Israelis not submit another request for aid before the end of the fiscal year.[8] The emergency designation was particularly important in that it would protect the rest of the foreign aid account from sequestration.

The logjam was broken. With the administration willing to make the request, Obey would recommend to the full committee that his own subcommittee's request be altered to include $650 million in emergency assistance.

The Full Committee Markup

The Appropriations Committee can decide to hold its markup sessions in any room. Markup sessions, however, are some of the most free-form, uncontrolled events in congressional life. Members of Congress would prefer not to be in public view without some kind of script or spin control. Therefore, while access to this event is generally not absolutely restricted, the committee did manage to find itself a room in the Rayburn House Office Building that was so small as to limit the size of the audience. The seating could barely accommodate the fifty-nine committee members and a limited number of staff. With access limited and members literally sitting elbow to elbow, the meeting took on, at times, an usually informal and frank character.

Chairman Whitten opened the meeting by introducing new members to the committee and approving the committee rules.[9] The cardinals then introduced their subcommittees' contributions to the nonmilitary Desert Storm supplemental. Each chair's introduction was then followed by a statement from the ranking minority member of the subcommittee, which signaled not only bipartisan support but also the likely acquiescence of the administration. The nonmilitary supplemental was divided into two titles. Title I of the bill would be emergency funding in terms of the 1990 budget agreement and therefore exempt from the spending caps. Title II contained a grab bag of provisions that were not considered emergencies and thus were to count against other items for the purpose of sequestration.

When the meeting finally turned to Obey, he rose and gave a grudging endorsement to what had now become the administration's request for emergency funding for Israel. Obey's obvious dilemma points out the price of seeking a leadership position in Congress, which may on occasion necessitate supporting disagreeable policy items—disagreeable both personally and to the district. The voters in Obey's Wisconsin district, who are generally opposed to higher levels of aid to Israel, would likely not understand his obligation as chair of the Foreign

Operations subcommittee to adjust his overall committee jurisdiction to the needs of U.S. foreign policy and the desires of the Democratic party.[10] Mickey Edwards (R-Okla.), the ranking minority member, followed Obey and also rose in support of the money for Israel. Edwards's support indicated the administration's approval. With Obey's support, the additional aid to Israel was quickly approved by the full committee. In accordance with the president's request, the money was added to Title I, or the emergency portion of the bill.

There were several attempts in the course of the afternoon to add other spending provisions to the supplemental. Most significantly, however, virtually none of the additional funds approved was added to the emergency portion of the bill. For example, Robert Mrazek (D-N.Y.) fought to restore funding for the Navy's F-14 Tomcat fighter, which is built in his Long Island district (the Navy has been trying to phase out the F-14 for several years). Although Mrazek succeeded in restoring some of the funds, the additional money was added to the Title II, or nonemergency portion of the bill, and thus was subject to being scored against the spending caps in the 1991 defense account.

Ultimately, the "Christmas tree" attracted only a very few ornaments for a total expenditure of $4.1 billion, or $1.3 billion above the president's request. In the appropriations process success is relative. While a $1.3 billion increment may seem to be quite a bit of an increase, representing a failure of the budget agreement to maintain its discipline, a closer look at the figures supports an entirely different conclusion. Roughly half of the increase that occurred in committee was accommodating the administration's request for additional support for Israel. Of the remaining $650 million, only about $14 million was designated emergency spending and thus exempt from the spending caps. The vast majority of the rest of the spending was in the defense account and was subject to all of the Budget Enforcement Act (Title XIII of OBRA) spending controls.[11] Even in a potential "Christmas tree" bill, the budget agreement had held its own.

In addition to the spending increases, the committee also added language to the legislation that would create policy changes. Although it is not strictly permitted for an appropriations bill to contain provisions that are "legislative," it is increasingly common for the Appropriations Committee to add provisions to its bills to direct (earmark) or restrict (limit) the expenditure of funds for a specific purpose. The reasoning behind these nonbudgetary measures is that virtually no government activity is without financial costs. The Appropriations Committee, then, is supposedly within its rights to control funding by ordering earmarks or limitations. However, this is an area of jurisdictional dispute, as some members believe that this kind of provision violates the jurisdiction of authorization committees. For example, in the case of the domestic dire-emergency supplemental, the committee included language that forbade the payment of witness fees to persons serving jail terms. As one member of the committee quipped, "If we aren't allowed to accept speaking fees, I'll be damned if we're going to let the government pay for them to talk."

Budgeting for the Military Desert Storm

By late afternoon of the same day the committee passed the nonmilitary supplemental ($4.1 billion) and took up the much larger military supplemental appropriation ($42.5 billion). The expenditure of these funds involved a relatively complex process. Because allies in the coalition against Iraq had pledged upward of $50 billion to compensate the United States for the costs of Operation Desert Shield/Storm, the $42.5 billion appropriated would serve as a bridge loan until funds were received from the allies, which would replace U.S. funds already expended.

The administration and the House leadership had agreed in advance that no amendments would be permitted on this legislation. Consequently, whereas the committee had spent some five hours discussing the domestic dire-emergency supplemental, the Desert Shield military supplemental was discussed and approved in about fifteen minutes.

Floor action in the House followed very much the same pattern as committee consideration. The domestic dire-emergency supplemental was much more controversial than the military expense bill. The highlight of floor consideration was the debate and vote on an amendment proposed by Rep. Tim Valentine (D-N.C.) to delete all of the $650 million contained in the bill for Israel. The amendment was easily defeated and was followed by a series of amendments offered by Rep. James Traficant (D-Ohio) to reduce the funding for Israel by $250 million, then $50 million, and finally $13 million. Each proposal was quickly defeated in turn by voice vote. Traficant's intention, particularly the last amendment offered, was to embarrass the membership and symbolize the inviolability of aid provisions to Israel. Funding measures are often subject to these types of amendments, which are part of the show rather than the substance of the legislative process. After final passage of the dire-emergency supplemental, the military supplemental was quickly passed.

Senate Action

Meanwhile, on the Senate side, several changes in the supplementals were being made. Most significant was the addition by Sen. Robert Byrd, chair of the Senate Appropriations Committee, of an extra $200 million in assistance for Turkey.

Besides shifting some of the spending priorities in the bill, the main controversy in the Senate involving the nonmilitary emergency supplemental came from an unexpected source. Sen. Patrick Leahy (D-Vt.) managed to attach to the emergency portion of the bill a measure to increase dairy price supports and allocations for food assistance programs. In other words, Leahy's amendment, if passed, would be exempt from the spending caps and the pay-as-you-go principles governing entitlement programs (of which farm price supports are a part).

This was a moment of truth for the 1990 budget agreement. If Leahy were allowed to circumvent the spending restrictions by use of the emergency provisions of the Budget Enforcement Act, it was likely that other provisions would be introduced through that method. The floodgates would open in violation of budget restraint. The specter of an appropriations feeding frenzy hung over the process even as the Leahy amendment was adopted by the full Senate.

Congress was flooded with messages from consumer lobbies who were particularly concerned about the impact of increased dairy price supports on the price of milk. For his part, the president, through Budget Director Darman, made it clear that he would do one of two things to derail Leahy's amendment. First, the president had the option of vetoing the entire bill. It is important to remember that the president had already received the direct military costs of Operation Desert Shield/Storm in a separate, clean bill. Consequently, he could well afford to veto the domestic dire-emergency supplemental without cutting off the troops in the field.

Alternately, Budget Director Darman raised the possibility that the administration could simply adjudge the Leahy amendment as nonemergency, which would result in a sequester, with the amount of the dairy price support increase being applied to the rest of the entitlement account. This would lead to a corresponding cut in the Medicare, veterans, and other farm benefits programs. In addition, the administration darkly predicted that in raising dairy prices, the cost to the government of child nutrition programs would threaten to eliminate as many as 135,000 eligible participants from the WIC program.[12]

But the final nail in the coffin of the Leahy amendment came when Senator Byrd and Representative Whitten, the two Appropriations Committee chairs, registered their opposition. Their resistance to the amendment highlighted the internal policy conflict that confronts members of the budget and appropriations committees. On the one hand, there is an incentive for members of the committees to use their positions to deliver goods to their constituencies. Clearly, they do take advantage of their positions for that purpose. However, being on one of the budget committees also confers a fiscal responsibility to the nation. The cost of being on one of the appropriations committees is having to say "no" on occasion. In this instance, Whitten and Byrd were fully aware of the potential for harm caused by the Leahy amendment, and they simply refused to accede to the proposal in the conference committee.

CONFERENCE

Conference committees on appropriations bills are generally biased toward overall spending control. Nevertheless, the narrow interests of the cardinals are represented because the leaders of the appropriations subcommittees are generally appointed to negotiate in conference. When the conference committee met on the dire-emergency supplemental, Whitten presided and Byrd represented the Senate. Leahy and Obey (a Wisconsin supporter of the dairy price bill) were there as well, but they were outnumbered by the other Appropriations subcommittee chairs, few of whom had special subsidies in the emergency portion of the bill and most of whom were motivated by the fiscal responsibility incentive. Predictably, the committee voted to delete the dairy price support amendment from the final report, with only Obey and Leahy voting in favor.

The 1990 Budget Enforcement Act had survived its first brush with the supplemental appropriations process with its spending rules and spending caps intact. In the end, the military cost supplemental literally sailed through the process with little controversy over the amount of the appropriation (rather than how the money was to be spent). The domestic, nonmilitary dire-emergency supplemental was more controversial (but not unusually so) and was increased by roughly $1 billion over the president's $3.7 billion request, with virtually all of that increase occurring in the nonemergency, nonexempt (from sequester) portion of the bill. Probably the most expensive additional measures, including aid to Israel and Turkey and the Leahy amendment, were either accepted as necessary by most parties involved or rejected. The budget agreement had been challenged and had withstood the pressure.

CONCLUSION

Perhaps what is most remarkable about the budget process in April 1991 is what did not happen. The Desert Shield supplemental appropriations bill had the potential of a budgetary feeding frenzy, but the budget agreement, at least in its first test, held. The formal requirement that both the president and Congress agree on what constitutes an emergency controlled the baser instincts of members who might have taken advantage of the opportunity provided by the war for special interest funding immune from sequester requirements. Extra funding had been approved, to be sure, mainly in the form of foreign aid to Israel and Turkey, but the outcome in the budgetary sense could have been worse. There was certainly no reason to expect from this experience that the emergency exception in the budget agreement would become a budgetary bonanza.

At the same time, the press of the fiscal year continued to drive the regular budget process. Behind the scenes, with the submission of the president's budget, appropriations subcommittee chairs began to prepare their marks. On the floor, both houses began to tackle authorization measures, which are the first formal steps in the appropriations process.

By the end of April the legislative pace begins to quicken. It is perhaps the first hot and humid days that remind the members that the fall and the September 30 deadline will soon follow. A quicker legislative pace means later evening sessions, more votes in a shorter space of time, and fewer four-day weekends during which members visit their districts. Also, as the deadline approaches, tough choices must be made, tempers flare, and members make their last attempts to include in appropriations bills those special projects that are better known as pork.

NOTES

1. The House Foreign Operations subcommittee of the full Appropriations Committee takes the House foreign assistance authorization as an advisory guideline, especially if the full House has passed the bill prior to consideration of the foreign aid appropriation.
2. Between 1982 and 1990, the Economic Recovery Act of 1981 (the formal name for the 1981 Tax Reform Act) was estimated by the OMB to have cost the U.S. government $1.76 *trillion* in lost revenues. Adjustments (tax increases and budget cuts) to that law adopted in 1982, 1983, and 1984 reduced the total cost to the U.S. Treasury of the 1981 Tax Reform Act to a little over $1 trillion. See the Office of Management and Budget, *Budget of the U.S. Government*, 1982-1990 (Washington, D.C.: U.S. Government Printing Office, 1982-1990).
3. Sec. 251D 1990, Omnibus Budget Reconciliation Act.
4. Letter to the Honorable Willis D. Gradison from Richard Darman, February 14, 1991.
5. Of course there are huge disagreements as to what constitutes pork-barrel spending. One of the best descriptions I have heard is "any spending that has a zip code."
6. The president's threat had managed to reduce substantially the overall appropriation for the original veterans' benefits package.
7. Murtha would also be sacrificing part of his jurisdiction to include Israeli

aid. If Israeli aid were to be scored against the Defense Subcommittee's spending caps, Murtha would lose $1 billion in maneuverability under the caps—money that could be spent on other defense-related programs.

8. The administration was anticipating an Israeli request for $10 billion in loan guarantees for the building of housing for a flood of immigrants that came to Israel from the Soviet Union. There was going to be a significant amount of controversy over the use of those funds to build housing on the West Bank.
9. Under the rules of the House every standing committee must adopt and publish its rules.
10. Obey well knows that there are plenty of votes not only in the committee but on the floor that would support increased aid to Israel with or without the chair's endorsement.
11. Eventually a minor sequestration was ordered by OMB as a result. The resulting .0013 percent "mini-sequester" meant that for every $1 million in spending on domestic programs, $13 was to be withheld. For example, by virtue of that sequester, the OMB itself lost $565. See George Hager, "Tiny Sequester Hits," *Congressional Quarterly Weekly Report,* April 27, 1991, 1042.
12. See George Hager, "Conferees Bow to Administration on 'Dire Emergency' Measure," *Congressional Quarterly Weekly Report,* March 23, 1991, 728-731.

CHAPTER 8

May and June 1991: Appropriating in the Sausage Factory

"Anyone who likes sausage or the law," so the saying goes, "should never see either made." The budget and appropriations process have a very real effect on the lives of people, but the point in the budget process at which the most fateful decisions are made is not always obvious. More often than not in Congress, what divides the realm of theater from that of decision making is what happens on the floor as compared with what happens behind closed doors. Floor happenings are choreographed, designed to produce the image of profound policy differences and deep partisan divisions. Behind the scenes there is a much more cooperative environment, reflecting on one level a basic American consensus and on another level a complex weave of social interaction better known as logrolling.

The quintessential theatrical production in Congress occurred in May 1991 when Senate Republicans attempted to amend the congressional budget resolution for no other reason than to embarrass the Democrats. The sponsors of the amendment knew they would lose, but winning or losing wasn't the point. The objective was to force the Democrats into the position of having to vote for new taxes. The Democratic response, as we shall see, was designed solely to provide political cover for Democratic senators who wanted to avoid the "tax and spend" label. That controversy occurred very much in the public eye. What occurred out of the public eye was the preparation of the chairman's mark, which would certainly have a much more direct effect on the size of the deficit and, more importantly, the distribution of $500 billion in federal largesse.

It is in late spring and early summer that most of the "pork" is handed out in Congress. In the competitive scramble to protect their constituencies, members lose sight of spending or deficit targets. This is a given. The role of the budget and appropriations committees at this stage of the process is to act as traffic cops—to say "no" to the more egregious examples of pork-barrel spending. More than that, it is the role of the institution to make final and irrevocable decisions about how goods are to be distributed. Ultimately the chairs of the various appropriations subcommittees make the decisions that will largely determine what discretionary funding individual members will get for their constituents. What results is a kind of rough justice, reflecting the general hierarchy of power in Congress.

Spring, therefore, is for most members the make-or-break stage of the budget process. This is also the case in terms of the amount of pressure that will develop for expansion of the deficit. At this point the appropriating committees are responsible for winnowing the requests of members, a process that reflects the degree to which there is real budgetary leadership in Congress. If appropriations committees can make substantial cuts in the requests of members, then it truly can be said that there is still enough power and hierarchy in the institution to control overall levels of spending—to make tough decisions to the detriment of individual members, but for the good of the whole. If these committees fail to discriminate between special requests, then the system operates without sufficient constraint and no set of rules will ever be sufficient to protect the overall budget from excess.

In the spring of 1991 the caps imposed by the OBRA budget agreement generally prevailed. This was a victory of sorts in terms of process, but it would be a mistake to read from this success the victory of process over politics. In fact, it is more likely that spending discipline prevailed because of a sort of collective fatigue that spurred the leadership and most of the members in both chambers to reject attempts to subvert the October budget agreement. At a number of points the agreement could have been subverted had there been the will, but there was very little enthusiasm for reopening the budget deal that had been so difficult to negotiate.

On a practical level, the budget agreement did not require that much constraint. Entitlement programs were indexed to inflation; there was less pressure on the defense and international aid budgets because of the collapse of the Warsaw Pact; and the domestic discretionary budget had been given a modest increase by the budget negotiators. In the future, however, as the tensions and inequities produced by the agreement erode, the caps, if not the process, will certainly be challenged if not overturned. Nevertheless, the process worked to a remarkable degree in the spring and summer of 1991. The budget and appropriations committees marched in lockstep through the budget process, generally meeting deadlines and staying under the spending caps. That fact alone made the 1991 legislative year exceptional.

THE BUDGET RESOLUTION AND THE THEATER OF POLITICS

As discussed in Chapter 2, the Budget Reform Act of 1974 imposed an entirely new layer on the budget process. New budget committees were established in both houses that were to be responsible for reporting an annual budget resolution, which was to be a statement of Congress's budgetary intent as distinct from the recommendations of the president. In addition, the budget committees were empowered to reconcile differences between congressional appropriations and the budget resolution.

Unfortunately, the term "congressional intent" works much better as an abstract concept than it does for determining something as contentious as the budget. Consequently, the reformed budget process rarely worked as it was designed in the years after 1974. Budget resolutions were passed late, if at all, and deficit control was rarely the result. In 1991, by contrast, the budget resolution was passed on time and had a relatively important effect on spending decisions. The difference was in the changed emphasis in the budget process.

Gramm-Rudman-Hollings deficit reduction targets dominated the budget process prior to 1991. This emphasis on the bottom line focused the attention of the budget committees on the end of the fiscal year, when the all-important reconciliation bill would force the appropriators to control spending and meet deficit reduction targets. The budget resolution was relatively unimportant because it was largely advisory. By contrast, in 1991 the emphasis in the budget process was on hitting *spending* (as opposed to deficit) targets, which could be incorporated into the budget resolution early in the process. Those spending targets, under the new budget rules, were not dependent on deficit projections. The 1991 budget resolution therefore represented adherence to the spending targets arrived at in the previous October.

Because overall spending targets had been set by the October budget agreement, there was very little the budget committees could do to change aggregate levels of spending. But within those levels the committees, through the vehicle of the budget resolution, had a significant effect on appropriations decisions. In policy terms, the most important change made in both committees was a shift in funding to benefit educational programs. Pursuant to the spending constraints imposed by the budget agreement, this new funding was to be taken out of existing programs in other discretionary accounts. This decision on funding priorities reflected a congressional slant on the budget process—precisely the sort of decision the budget committees were supposed to make when they were created in 1974.

THE BUDGET RESOLUTION AND THEATRICAL POLITICS

The budget resolution also occasioned a reconsideration of the rules of the budget process itself (Budget Enforcement Act—Title XIII). In what became one of the most hotly debated issues in the spring, Senate Republicans attempted to use the budget resolution to amend the Budget Enforcement Act. The Brown amendment was a clear example of the possibilities for policy and politics in the work of the Budget Committee.

Under the budget agreement, changes in entitlement programs have to be funded pursuant to a pay-as-you-go requirement, which means that any mandated increase in entitlement spending has to be offset by a corresponding cut in benefits or a commensurate increase in taxes. During floor consideration of the budget resolution, Sen. Hank Brown (R-Colo.) proposed an amendment that would require any new entitlement program or increase in eligibility in any existing program to be funded only by cuts in other entitlement programs. Tax hikes to fund increases in entitlement spending would be forbidden. Pursuant to Brown's amendment, only cuts in benefits could be used to fund new entitlements.

The politics were more important than the substance of the Brown amendment. Although Senator Brown did not have the votes to get his amendment passed, he could use it to embarrass his Democratic colleagues. To oppose the amendment would be to appear to favor the possibility of raising taxes. During floor debate, speaker after speaker on the Republican side chided Democrats for opposing the Brown amendment and its moratorium on taxation. The Democratic leaders saw to it that their members, especially those who needed political cover, had an opportunity to vote both for and against the amendment.

The Brown amendment arrived on the floor through a circuitous route. In the Budget Committee it had been approved by a narrow margin. Much to the chagrin of Democratic leaders, this could only have happened with Democratic support. On the floor, the amendment was approved as part of the Senate's budget resolution sent to the conference with the House. This was allowed by the Democratic leadership in the expectation that the amendment would be deleted in conference. Because the House had included no such provision in its budget resolution and a majority of the Senate delegation to the conference committee did not really support the amendment, it was deleted as expected. Indeed, the assumption that the amendment would be deleted in conference allowed many Democrats to vote for the measure confident that it would never become part of the final legislation.

The issue, however, did not die in conference. While the Brown amendment was deleted in the conference report, it was resurrected on the Senate floor in a debate over a motion to recommit the budget resolution to the Senate Budget Committee (presumably to restore the amendment). The Democrats were forced to gather the necessary votes to defeat the motion to recommit. In the debate on this motion, Democrats argued that the Brown amendment was simply bad policy. To adopt it would be to cover any deficit in one area of entitlements by cutting other entitlement benefits—and this could take place during a recession when other parts of the entitlement structure were under pressure. Furthermore, Democratic opponents pointed out, there was no actual tax provision on the table; the only thing the amendment would accomplish would be to restrict the ability of Congress to act should a crisis in an entitlement occur.[1]

The Republicans, in generating a public debate, had won a victory of sorts by making the Democrats appear to defend a policy of higher taxes. For the Democrats, then, the issue was lost in the "theater" of politics. The rest of the process for them was damage control. Political cover was made available to Democrats in the opportunity to vote both *for* the amendment before it was sent to conference and *against* the amendment when it was excluded from the conference report.

For their part, the Democrats played hard-ball politics with the budget resolution on the House side, using their majority to impose a policy design on the Republicans. Budget Committee Chair Leon Panetta, on behalf of the majority, wrote a partisan budget resolution that, in turn, was given a beneficial rule by the Democratic-controlled Rules Committee. The resolution was then forced through the legislative process on the floor over the protests of the largely powerless Republican minority. While Republicans complained on the floor that they had been denied access to the budget process when the truly important decisions were being made, they had neither procedural nor actual voting numbers to impose their will.

By contrast, in the Senate, Budget Committee Chair Jim Sasser (D-Tenn.) reported a largely bipartisan budget resolution to the floor. Had he attempted to duplicate the partisan strategy in the House, Senate rules protecting the minority would have bogged down the budget resolution from the start. With a much narrower Democratic majority on the Senate side and the difference in the rules, the majority cannot ride roughshod over the minority. Such is the difference between the two houses of Congress.

BEHIND CLOSED DOORS—THE BUDGET RESOLUTION AND 602(b) ALLOCATIONS

There is a ritual statement in the introduction of almost all appropriations legislation. The bill's floor manager (generally the subcommittee cardinal) makes it clear that, if nothing else, the bill being considered falls below its 602(b) allocation. This statement alone provides a measure of political cover for members desiring to vote for the bill but afraid of being painted by future political opponents as big spenders. By falling below its 602(b) allocation, the bill at least assures members that it has been approved under some kind of unified budget scheme.

The budget resolution plays a role in setting mandatory spending allocations for the appropriations subcommittees. These are known as the 602(b) allocations (referring to Section 602(b) of the 1974 Budget Reform Act as amended).[2] In discretionary spending accounts, the budget resolution sets overall spending limits by governmental function. The appropriations committees then use these guidelines to set overall spending by agency account. These committee guidelines are the 602(b) allocations. Under the rules of the Senate and the House, each of the annual appropriations bills must fall within their 602(b) allocations or be subject to a point of order. It is the responsibility of the full appropriations committees to make 602(b) allocations to their subcommittees.

Passage of the budget resolution allows the cardinals, on both sides of the Hill, to hash out among themselves from a limited pool of money their subcommittees' spending totals. This is a particularly tense time in the process. Subcommittee chairs who fail to make a sufficient case for their own jurisdiction will probably not be able to recover funding later on. When the final 602(b) allocations are made, the chairs of the appropriations subcommittees have tied their own hands—and these allocations are rather rigorously adhered to. In 1991 the 602(b) requirement was particularly important. Inasmuch as the budget committees had completed their work on time, these allocations had the official imprimatur of the budget committees.[3]

The 602(b) allocation dictates to subcommittee chairs exactly where their maximum cutoff line is in preparing the chairman's mark. As noted earlier, the mark is basically a detailed outline of each appropriations bill. While it is possible to change the mark in full committee or on the floor, these changes are rare and their impact on pork-barrel spending is generally minor. Getting into the chairman's mark, therefore, is an important goal of most members of Congress during this part of the congressional session.

As soon as the chair and the subcommittee staff receive their 602(b) allocation, they begin to winnow requests for special favors—and there are many. For example, the Senate Labor, Health and Human Services appropriations subcommittee in 1991 received more than 1,200 special requests from almost every other senator. The chair has the obligation to rank those requests because there is simply not enough money to go around. The chair's way of making those decisions illuminates how the institution of Congress is structured and how members who must compete for a piece of the pie undertake their quest.

PORK

"One man's waste of the public's funds is another man's vital project for his home district." This oft-repeated phrase is regularly intoned, sometimes in more colorful variants, by defenders of various special projects. May and June, if the budget process follows its regular course, are the months of pork on the Hill. Pork-barrel spending, for lack of a better term, refers to projects funded by the government that in one way or another fit the definition of a private good. A private good is a benefit that can be enjoyed by a specific person, group, or constituency to the exclusion of others (or spending with a zip code attached). One of the government's roles is to redistribute funds collected through taxation and the competition over this bounty occupies much time in congressional offices. For the next few pages we will examine the tactics used by congressional offices in competing for the benefits of pork.

PORK IN THE LAW

The likelihood that a special project will be funded is based on two factors: the specificity of the language establishing congressional intent and the quality of the legislative vehicle containing that language. First, there is a rough, direct relationship between the specificity of a bill or report language and the chances that money will be spent for the purpose that was intended. Second, there are a number of legislative vehicles for the expression of congressional intent.

The legislative process produces several types of records. Legislation, of course, is the most unambiguous statement of policy. It is very difficult for an implementing agency to ignore or misinterpret a specific provision of law. In the best of all worlds a member would prefer to see his or her request in the text of the bill itself. Failing that, the next best vehicle for pork-barrel spending is report language.

Most major legislation emerging from a committee is accompanied by a "report." The committee report explains the legislation section by section and occasionally includes minority reports that register disagreements. Strictly speaking, report language is *not* law, and the administration is not bound by it. However, over the years a tradition has developed that the executive branch should consider report language the intent of Congress.

Initially, the Bush administration announced that it was not legally obligated to implement report language, which set off a rather predictable response on the Hill. Committee chairs simply included in the language of the bill specific provisions that would normally have been contained in the committee's report. No one was better off. Appropriations bills became longer, and the administration was disadvantaged by its own decision.

Report language has a great advantage for both the executive and the legislative branches. The language of a bill that has been passed and signed is not subject to interpretation, whereas report language, not being law, allows the administration some flexibility in enforcement. The fact is that the appropriations committees will never be completely able to plan in advance for all contingencies. It is particularly difficult to do so in terms of exact dollar figures. Recommendations in report language give the administration a very clear and sometimes an enormously detailed idea of what Congress wants done while at the same time allowing for flexibility in executing the law if the administration should discover faulty planning in the appropriations bill. Subcommittee chairs will never complain about legitimate noncompliance with report language if there is close consultation between the subcommittee and administration officials.

But report language can vary in its specificity. Language that is very specific is difficult to ignore. For example, in its committee report on the Desert Shield nonmilitary supplemental, the Senate Appropriations Committee included the following language in reference to a delayed Department of Energy cleanup of a uranium mining site in Rifle, Colorado:

> The Committee directs the Department [of Energy] to reallocate such funds, not to exceed $5,500,000, as may be required from within the cleanup program so the required work can proceed during the current fiscal year.[4]

Everything from the location and time period to the amount to be spent is specified, so that it behooved the Department of Energy to carry out this direction.

On the other hand, report language can be relatively vague. The same report referred to an upcoming evaluation by the National Marine Fisheries Service of the applicability of the Endangered Species Act to salmon migrating up certain rivers in the Northwest:

> It is not the intent of the committee to prejudge the outcome of the scientific review process which will attempt to answer questions never before formally considered in a public policy arena. Nevertheless, if a listing decision is warranted by scientific findings, implications could be severe for both regional and national interests.[5]

In fact, it *was* the intent of the committee to prejudge the findings and the implementation of the findings of the upcoming scientific study.

The committee had stated its preference (Sen. Mark Hatfield of Oregon being ranking minority member and former Senate Appropriations Committee chair), and it was then up to the discretion of the Commerce Department, of which the Marine Fisheries Service is a part, to implement the study. The Commerce Department was served notice that it could face retaliation, unless there were some very good reasons to declare Pacific salmon "endangered species" in the Columbia and Snake rivers.

Besides the fact that report language can earmark or specify the use of funds, it can also limit or forbid the use of funds for a particular purpose. Strictly speaking, legislation on an appropriations bill, or policy making is forbidden under House rules in the appropriations process. Consequently, policy recommendations often appear in reports rather than in legislation because report language is not subject to a point of order under the rules of the House (but still expresses the preferences of appropriators).

The record of floor debates, committee hearings, and other discussions on the record can also influence the distribution of funds. For example, floor debate on an appropriations bill is often interrupted by the stilted choreography of a colloquy—an exchange between members on the floor of the House or Senate that establishes committee intent. For instance, in 1991, in considering appropriations for the Environmental Protection Agency, Rep. Lewis F. Payne (D-Va.) engaged Appropriations Subcommittee Chair Robert Traxler (D-Mich.) in a colloquy. Payne was concerned that certain environmental studies related to his district might not be carried out by the EPA because they were not specifically funded in the legislation. In an attempt to guide the EPA, Payne engaged the chair of the subcommittee in the following colloquy:

> Mr. Payne: Mr. Chairman, I wish to clarify whether it is the Committee's intent that the Administrator of the EPA take up this subject. . . .
>
> Mr. Traxler: . . . I would like to thank the gentleman from Virginia for his question. Yes, that is the intent of the Committee.[6]

There are literally hundreds of similar colloquies in the *Congressional Record*. In this case, the Environmental Protection Agency may or may not have taken direction from this colloquy, but would be well advised to do so even though there is no bill or report language to that effect.

Planning for Pork—The Recipients

The member who wants earmarked funding on an appropriations bill would prefer a very specifically worded provision included in the text of the bill itself. Inclusion as bill language virtually assures that the money will be spent for the purpose it was intended. This kind of special treatment is in high demand and thus is relatively difficult to obtain. Members can use any number of tactics to achieve this goal, but before planning a strategy for securing funding for a district project, they must overcome several hurdles. It may be hard to believe, but one of the most difficult problems is generating appropriate, feasible requests from the district.

Breeding Pork

Congressional offices are virtually deluged with requests from constituents for special treatment, but the problem is harvesting the right kind of requests. Members of Congress are anxious to find ways to help constituents, especially in ways that are conducive to good publicity and claiming credit. However, constituents often do not understand that no matter how much money the federal government delivers every year, it will not fund every request. Sometimes even the most meritorious use for public funding may not be authorized under law, which basically doubles the number of legislative obstacles the member must negotiate. Authorization language in a separate bill must be passed in advance of an appropriations earmark.[7]

Fortunately the authorization requirement is not as formidable as obtaining the funding itself. Authorization legislation can be tremendously flexible, and there are very few good public policy ideas that go unauthorized. In other words, in most cases there is an authorization honey pot somewhere in the law for most meritorious requests.

If a constituent request meets the authorization standard, the request can be funded under current law but may not meet the ethics, or "smell" test. There is a rough inverse relationship between the number of people who benefit from an earmarked appropriation and the likelihood that the project will become a political embarrassment. Any special project that disproportionately stands to benefit a single individual, a single corporation, or a small group of people should set off an alarm in a congressional office. Even if no impropriety is involved, the appearance of impropriety is almost certain to emerge from such a narrow project.[8] It is much better for the member to work with local governments, universities, and established charitable organizations in generating requests. Presumably any project requested by city, county, or state governments will easily meet both the ethics and authorization litmus tests.

Most governments, universities, and charitable organizations have some kind of governmental liaison structure that arranges for federal funding. Any congressional office with a good constituency service operation will have frequent, if not daily, contacts with area universities and local governments. Furthermore, congressional staff should have a good personal relationship with their counterparts in those organizations. For example, the staffer who deals primarily with the Army Corps of Engineers would be well advised to have a close relationship with the city planning divisions of the major municipalities in the district. These relationships tend to work both ways. Although city governments and university government affairs offices cannot make contributions to political candidates, as private citizens, government workers and their friends and families tend to be active participants in the political process. A good relationship between a congressional office and local governments cannot help but generate strong political support back in the district.

Assuming that a request meets the ethical litmus test and is authorized as well, the member can then begin to plan a strategy. It is important to field requests for funding early enough in the fiscal year to get in the chairman's mark. Any request submitted later than the middle of April is probably too late to be included for the next fiscal year.

Final adoption and funding for a special request is partially a function of the member's political leverage. Obviously the chair of the Appropriations Committee or the Speaker of the House has a much better chance of funding a special project than a freshman member of the minority party. But within that range, there are degrees of skill and influence in the process that are not necessarily a function of the member's position in the institutional structure.

In either house, a member of the majority on the Appropriations Committee will generally be accommodated for at least part of any reasonable request. Moreover, if a member is on the relevant appropriations subcommittee, he or she will almost certainly receive full funding for a district project. An annual spring ritual in most congressional offices (particularly those that can reasonably expect funding) is the writing of a letter to each of the subcommittee cardinals, in which the member spells out in detail each special funding request that falls within the jurisdiction of that subcommittee. Subcommittees are literally deluged with requests.

As a rule, a member can expect that at least a portion of his or her request will be deleted by the subcommittee chair. This being the case, the member, without being too ham-fisted, will often make requests for more money or projects than are actually needed. Even the best connected committee members cannot get everything they want. At some point the subcommittee chairs will be constrained by their 602(b) allocations. The member should be prepared to sacrifice some of the request, which could be in the form of funding cuts. The subcommittee staff also has the option of including the member's request in the legislation or in the committee report. The specificity of that report or bill language then becomes a bargaining chip.

For junior members who are not on the appropriations committees, getting an earmark for the district requires some tactical skill. First of all, the member has to take stock of his or her own leverage. The chairs of strategically placed authorization committees and subcommittees, members of the leadership, members of the Rules and the Ways and Means committees in the House all have a certain amount of leverage that can be used for appropriations favors. Good personal relationships and previous chits for favors done can also be traded for special consideration from the Appropriations Committee.[9] Ultimately, if the member has no appreciable leverage, this being particularly true of relatively junior members, alliances can be formed with more senior members who do have resources.

It is rarely true that the benefits of a good appropriations project accrue exclusively to one congressional district. At the very least, for every pork-barrel project, there should be two senators who have an interest. Members from adjoining or similar districts or states can be recruited for their special lobbying talents, contacts, and leverage. Of course, there is a price to pay in forming these alliances. Concessions must be made in terms of diluting the funding for the project, adjustments in planning, and, most importantly, sharing credit for obtaining the funds. Claiming credit is one of the primary benefits to be gained by serving constituency requests. If a relatively junior member brings powerful allies into the process, he or she stands to be upstaged by more senior, prominent colleagues.

For nonappropriations Republicans, particularly in the House, getting special projects approved by the Appropriations Committee is extraordinarily difficult. By contrast, in the Senate, members from the minority party have quite a bit more leverage because the rules of the Senate allow a small number of members to tie the legislative process into knots. In addition, Senate Democrats are more accommodating to the Republicans because of the realistic prospect that the Republicans will some day be in the majority (as they were from 1980 to 1986). It is also true that the Democratic majority is much narrower in the Senate than in the House. Consequently, accommodating the Republicans is for the majority the better part of discretion in the Senate.

There are a number of options at the Republicans' disposal for getting access to pork, most of which revolve around the formation of alliances. It is not uncommon for Democrats and Republicans to form alliances both on a long- and short-term basis. For example, many, if not all, ranking minority members on appropriations subcommittees have managed to forge a very close relationship with their respective cardinals and have been relatively successful in getting pork for their districts. These close alliances sometimes attract the ire of junior Republicans, who intimate that their seniors are in too cozy a relationship with their Democratic committee colleagues. For the junior Republican seeking funding, the first task is to forge a relationship with interested Democrats and influential Republicans. The cost for junior House Republicans, at the very least, is almost certain to be the loss of most of the credit for the money they do receive. This contributes to the frustration Republican members feel in their minority status in the House.

Getting a program into the chairman's mark is not the only way to have an influence on the spending process. Indeed, on broad policy issues that are covered under appropriations bills, such as abortion rights, an individual member can have an impact on the floor (somewhat beyond the chair's control). But on pork, the chairman's mark is the central goal in the process. There is always a chance that a member will succeed in getting a request included in the chairman's mark in the other body. Because the budget process is supposed to operate sequentially, with the House acting first, the Senate serves as a kind of court of appeals for House members who have failed in their own institution. However, getting a request in the chairman's mark in specifically worded bill language is the best assurance of success.

At this point, a word or two should be included about the role of the staff in this process. Most pork-barrel politics is handled at the staff level, particularly in the Senate. As a last resort, a staffer may request the personal intervention of the member to lobby colleagues for a spending request, but staffers try to insulate their bosses from the demeaning task of having to plead for money. As one staffer put it, "The senator has more important things to do than request $500,000 for project X. After all, he is a U.S. senator. He has more important things to worry about. At most, we only call upon the senator's personal intervention three or four times a year."[10]

Asking for the member's intervention is, for the staffer, a tacit admission of failure—failure of the staff to make its case and failure of the member to gain the kind of influence that gets things done without question. Nevertheless, there are times or projects that require the personal intervention of the member.

Getting a project included in the chairman's mark does not necessarily guarantee that the item will survive the legislative process. Sometimes a chair will accept a project out of courtesy but leave it vulnerable to deletion either on the floor or in conference. For example, junior members are perhaps at their most powerless during the conference committee stage. Generally only the cardinals (and ranking minority members) and members of the subcommittee with jurisdiction are appointed to conference committees. If the committee chair is not committed to a particular project, he or she may be willing to sacrifice that project in conference in order to trade for something else or simply in the interest of appearing fiscally conservative.

The general inviolability of the chairman's mark was no more vividly demonstrated than in the case of the AuCoin amendment to the defense appropriations bill for fiscal year 1992. Congressman Les AuCoin (D-Ore.) attempted to amend the defense appropriations bill to allow federal dollars to fund abortions for American servicewomen in U.S. military hospitals overseas. Under existing law, women serving in the military overseas have to go to local civilian hospitals for abortion services. Rep. John Murtha (D-Pa.), chair of the Defense Subcommittee and a staunch opponent of legalized abortion (much less its federal funding), blocked inclusion of the AuCoin amendment in his mark. Nevertheless, AuCoin, in a relatively rare move, managed to get the full Appropriations Committee not only to consider but actually to attach this amendment to Murtha's mark.

It should be noted that AuCoin, who was a member of Murtha's subcommittee, had already announced his intention to run for the Senate against Senator Hatfield. The abortion issue is an important one in Oregon, especially for members who support freedom of choice in this relatively liberal state. AuCoin was therefore a lame duck in the House, with little to fear from Murtha's retaliation, but he had much to gain in political benefits even though he had virtually no chance of getting the amendment adopted.

It is the responsibility of the subcommittee chair to request a rule from the Rules Committee. On appropriations bills the Rules Committee commonly waives House restrictions forbidding the inclusion of legislative language (policy making) in appropriations bills. The AuCoin amendment clearly fit the description of legislation and would therefore be subject to a point of order (deletion) on the floor unless the rule under which the amendment was considered contained a waiver. Murtha simply did not ask the Rules Committee for a waiver, so that when the defense appropriations bill came to the floor, the AuCoin amendment was subject to a point of order from the anti-abortion forces on the Republican side and was deleted. AuCoin could do nothing to save the amendment but took the opportunity to score political points at home in Oregon.

Special projects for members' districts have unique life cycles. As a rule, it is much easier to fund an existing program than an entirely new project. Part of the strategy of funding a special project revolves around the current status of the program. If the request is an entirely new endeavor, the member would be well advised to propose a study or pilot project. Once the study or pilot project is completed, there exists a fairly strong case for funding the results of the study or for expanding an ongoing project. Fortunately for the member, once a program is begun, it quickly develops a constituency that will soon become a resource the member can use to keep the funding flowing.

Another important consideration for the member in pursuit of federal funding is the nature, atmosphere, and ethos of each individual subcommittee. By the nature of their jurisdictions, some subcommittees are less conducive than others to earmarking. For example, it is relatively difficult to attach district-specific earmarks to the Labor, Health and Human Services bill. For one thing the LHHS appropriation deals with rather broad-based social programs. By contrast, the Energy and Water appropriations bill is literally a collection of earmarks.

Accessibility to earmarking in appropriations bills also reflects the disposition of the committee chair. Rep. Tom Bevill (D-Ala.) and Sen. Bennett Johnston (D-La.), the respective chairs of the House and Senate Energy and Water appropriations subcommittees, are generally amenable and have fashioned their committee procedures to accommodate member requests. For example, Bevill presides over a series of hearings in the late winter and early spring that review the requests of members from different areas of the country. One of these hearings, informally known as Florida Day, is the chance for members of that state's delegation to line up before the chairman and ask for earmarks. Other states are similarly invited into the process. By contrast, William Natcher (D-Ky.), chairman of the House Labor, Health and Human Services subcommittee, does not, on principle, accept most earmarks.

Pork as Fiscal and Public Policy

Pork-barrel spending is a pejorative term that connotes waste in government. However, there are several things to remember about it. First, pork is cheap. If every member of Congress were to receive a $20 million project for his or her state or district, the total cost would be something in excess of $10 billion. That is a lot of money, but within the context of a $1.45 *trillion* budget and a $300 billion deficit, $10 billion is not going to bust the budget. Although every session of Congress produces egregious examples of pork-barrel spending, in the worst sense of the term, a legitimate case can be made for almost every project. It is only from outside the district that pork-barrel spending seems wasteful.

Second, as surprising as it may seem to the outsider, even in the $500 billion-dollar discretionary budget over which the Appropriations Committee maintains control, there is a surprising degree of oversight for each dollar spent. Egregious or ethically questionable requests are generally deleted by the subcommittee before they become an embarrassment.

Especially at times when funding is scarce, the subcommittee chair will look for and find a good excuse to cull some of the many requests.

To the extent that there is inequity in the system, it exists as a reflection of the hierarchy in the institution. For example, there are some very good public policy reasons for spending federal dollars in West Virginia. However, the fact that West Virginia is the home state of Senate Appropriations Committee Chair Robert Byrd explains the crucial difference in the amount of funding West Virginia receives as compared with other states. In just one fiscal year, 1991, Byrd engineered some rather significant transfers of federal jobs from the District of Columbia and its suburbs to his home state. More to the point, for that year he managed to earmark as much as $500 million in special projects for West Virginia.[11] While Senator Byrd is in some ways exceptional—no other member has his skill or success in the politics of pork—he is also one of the most senior members of the Senate and represents one of the poorest states. There may be some justice in the fact that he is so successful at pork-barrel politics. There are also some very good reasons for keeping those jobs in Washington, D.C. In the end, however, the issue was determined by Byrd's power as opposed to that of the D.C. delegate and representatives of the D.C. suburbs of Maryland and Virginia. In any system of distribution of scarce resources, there will be certain inequities. More to the point, there will be winners and losers. A form of rough justice exists in Congress. The process that allows a skillful senior member of the Senate to commandeer for the few years that he happens to be committee chair a disproportionate share of federal largesse for West Virginia is in some ways fair.

The rough justice that exists in Congress reflects in many ways what is good and bad in the character of our society. There is a certain class bias in the distribution of goods. The middle class receives a disproportionate share of government largesse, particularly in entitlement benefits. The decision-making process in our society as well as in Congress rewards entrepreneurs and individuals who are smart and creative. The institution also disproportionately rewards whites, males, and the relatively wealthy. In that sense, too, the institution represents some of what is not the best in our society. But the institution is representative. It will change as our society changes. Would we want the goods that a representative institution has to offer distributed in any other way?

APPROPRIATIONS IN THE HOUSE, AUTHORIZATION IN THE SENATE

As previously noted, a constitutional requirement calls for the House to be the first to act on revenue and (by tradition) appropriations provisions. Thus in the late spring of 1991, while House floor action was dominated by appropriations legislation, the Senate floor was dominated by authorization activity. In that year Congress faced a more or less typical authorization schedule. In the course of one session, Congress was slated to consider two new thrift bailouts, a major new anticrime package, an energy bill, a five-year reauthorization of highway legislation, and all of the regular authorization legislation. If the Senate was to be able to finish its business by the scheduled adjournment date and to pass appropriations bills before the end of the fiscal year, it would have to dispose of much of its authorization legislation during this time, before the regularly scheduled appropriations bills came to the floor. The Senate leadership tried to do just that. However, befitting the character of Senate rules that allow much more protracted debate, the Senate in June became mired in a debate over the new highway bill.[12]

The interstate highway system is funded through a special Highway Trust Fund that receives revenues from specially designated gasoline and highway-use taxes. Those revenues go directly into the trust fund, which is dispersed according to a formula authorized by Congress in its Surface Transportation Act (the highway bill). That formula determines how Highway Trust money will be spent, what percentage of costs states will have to pay, and for what kind of projects. Roughly 80 percent of the maintenance and construction of interstate highways is covered by the Highway Trust Fund. There has always been considerable controversy over the establishment of a formula for dispersing these funds. Much of this controversy reflects the various constituencies represented by members of Congress. In 1991 changing priorities added another dimension to the debate. For the first time, the proposed Highway Trust disbursement formula was to be manipulated to encourage the building of mass transit and to help states accommodate the provisions of the previously adopted Clean Air Act. In other words, the formula would be more generous to mass transit and less to highways. This provision alone contributed its own subtext to the debate. But the heart of the matter revolved around the traditional regional rivalries and competition for funds.

No matter how the money is distributed through the Highway Trust Fund formula, certain states will feel unfairly treated. The fact is that the ratio of interstate highway miles to population varies greatly from state to state. That reality contributes to an imbalance in a state's need for highway funds relative to the contribution that same state will make to the Highway Trust Fund. Wyoming, for example, has a very small population but a fairly extensive interstate highway system. By contrast, the state of Maryland has a relatively high population density and a relatively small land area. The result is a disparity in the distribution of highway funds, with Maryland paying relatively more per capita into the trust fund than does Wyoming. In fact, Maryland pays more into the trust fund than it receives back in revenues.

This developed into a classic political debate reflecting the special character of the Senate. From a Maryland senator's perspective, a highway funding formula based only on highway miles is grossly unfair, whereas, from a Wyoming senator's perspective, a formula based on population is grossly unfair. The fact is that any formula adopted would leave someone, in some state, feeling slighted. In the end, the outcome reflected the hierarchy and structure of the institution. The new formula, as reported by the Senate Environment and Public Works Committee, did reflect the interests of recipient over donor states (the Senate, after all, has a Western and rural bias). In response, senators from a number of donor states set out to delay passage of the bill. After ten days of debate, Senator Byrd worked out a compromise that awarded half of an $8.2 billion surplus in the trust fund to the thirty-three states that have the highest gasoline taxes. The number thirty-three is significant in the Senate in that the votes of senators from thirty-three states plus one other will override a presidential veto and thus constitute an unbeatable majority. The Senate ultimately adopted the Byrd compromise.

CONCLUSION

By the end of June the House passed twelve of its thirteen regular appropriations bills.[13] Its appropriations work was more or less finished on schedule. There reigned a sense that the spending caps were inviolable, at least for fiscal year 1992. As long as there was general agreement that appropriations bills should fall within their 602(b) allocations (and the budget resolution establishing those allocations was in place before that), the entire system fell into place. But cracks were beginning to show in the budget consensus. By early summer the recession had begun to deepen. At the same time, presidential and congressional politics began to stir. Democrats were already discussing tax measures, child care reform, and other social and domestic programs that would set them apart from the Republicans and potentially deviate from the October 1990 budget agreement.

It was business as usual, however, with regard to pork-barrel politics despite the budget agreement and the tightened spending limits. The bonds on the operations of the appropriations subcommittees were a little tighter, to be sure, but in the main the new budget agreement had little impact on the informal system for targeting federal funds to the districts of individual members.

The authorization process on the Senate side coincided with the appropriations process in the House. The Senate battled during the same months over the symbolism and public policy contained in authorizing legislation. The final fiscal determinations would come later. Behind the scenes in the Senate, senators and their staffs scrambled to get their states' projects included in the appropriations subcommittee chairmen's marks. The outcome of the process was different, yet also the same. What was different was the way the process worked smoothly for most of the year. What was the same was the time-honored, behind-the-scenes competition for pork. Nothing, it seems, no reform, could defeat the desire of members to serve their constituencies.

NOTES

1. There were, in fact, serious shortages in unemployment compensation funds at the state level at the time.
2. Section 602(b) of the Budget Enforcement Act reads: "As soon as practicable after a budget resolution is agreed to, the Committee on Appropriations of each House (after consulting with the Committee on Appropriations of the other House) shall suballocate each amount allocated to it for the budget year."
3. In previous years, if the budget committees did not complete their work on time, the appropriations committees simply based their 602(b) allocation on the budget resolution as it stood at that stage of the process.
4. U.S. Senate, Committee on Appropriations, *Report to Accompany H.R. 1281: Dire Emergency Supplemental Appropriations for the Consequences of Operation Desert Storm/Shield, Food Stamps, Unemployment Compensation Administration, Veterans Compensation and Pensions, and Other Urgent Needs for the Fiscal Year Ending September 30, 1991, and for Other Purposes* (Washington D.C.: U.S. Government Printing Office, 1991), 36.
5. Ibid., 33.
6. *Congressional Record,* June 6, 1991, H4048.
7. As a consequence, pork-barreling for a special interest often becomes a multiyear quest. In the beginning the goal is to get an authorization. Only after authorization language is obtained can a lobbyist (and a member) ask for funding.
8. Members have to be very careful in sifting through the numerous requests of organizations. Sometimes those that appear to represent a wide constituency can be exposed as a front for an individual or a small group.
9. Many members raise money for their own political action committees, which in turn make contributions to the campaigns of other members. In that way, a member can trade fund-raising skill for legislative alliances.
10. Personal interview, March 25, 1991.
11. See Mike Mills, "Byrd's Eye View," *Congressional Quarterly Weekly Report,* September 21, 1991, 2682.
12. S. 1204, "Surface Transportation Efficiency Act of 1991," 102nd Congress, 1st session.
13. A transportation appropriations bill was the only one delayed in the House. Subcommittee Chair William Lehman (D-Fla.) was still recovering at the time from a stroke suffered earlier in the year.

CHAPTER 9

July and August 1991: The Available Work Expands

Within the fiscal year Congress has several mini-sessions. Before each recess, there is a rush to complete legislation that, if not completed before the target date set by the leadership, would surely push back other matters when Congress reconvenes.

The August recess marks the end of one mini-session. In 1991, as in the past, the end of the summer mini-session was marked by a rush of legislation and a series of late night sessions, primarily in the Senate. But because Senate rules allow for substantial delay, by the end of August the body was nowhere near completing work on its appropriations bills. In the end, while the House completed its appropriations work, delays in the Senate put the process on hold. By the August recess the Senate had passed only three of thirteen appropriations bills, with one measure (for funding the District of Columbia) certain to be returned because of a presidential veto. It seemed almost certain that at least one and probably several continuing resolutions would be needed to cover the interruption of spending while Congress finished its budget work at the end of the fiscal year.

This delay was not totally unexpected. Even by the beginning of summer, two months before the end of the fiscal year, the House Speaker's projected date for adjournment, October 4, was laughed off with derision. At the beginning of the session a target of early October made a certain amount of sense. With the budget deal in place, there was no reason why Congress could not complete its budget work by September 30 and use a few extra days to tie up loose ends. But this estimate did not take into account the Senate's delays. By the beginning of the summer recess in August it seemed certain that Congress would not finish its work before Thanksgiving.

THE SENATE AND FLEXIBLE DEADLINES

It can easily be said that in Congress the available work expands to fill the time allotted. One of the most important principles of the legislative process is that *deadlines force compromise.* One of the greatest incentives to broker an agreement is not constituent pressure or the spirit of fair play and generosity but collective fatigue and an airline ticket in a senator's pocket. Deadlines dictate that a compromise simply has to be negotiated on must-pass bills such as appropriations measures. This being the case, the leadership in both houses of Congress is constantly trying to construct artificial deadlines before the inevitable crush at the end of the legislative session.

Deadlines are relatively easy to impose for House leaders who can use the Rules Committee and the body's rules that limit debate. Much to the exasperation of the House, however, the Senate operates under no such constraints. Because legislation cannot be completed without the Senate's assent and complete agreement of both houses on the final measure, the Hill marches to the rhythm of the Senate. And the beat is slower on the Senate side. In the first nine months of the first session of the 102nd Congress, the Senate met for 40 percent more hours than the House and required almost twice the number of pages in the *Congressional Record* to document its proceedings.[1]

As a result, Congress looks to the skills of the Senate leadership to broker agreements that will ensure a timely adjournment. Senate leaders, however, have nowhere near the institutional power of their House counterparts. There are few formal institutional restraints on debate, nor are there many firm limits on the number and types of amendments that can be attached to bills on the Senate floor. The Senate leadership must therefore negotiate delicate compromises called unanimous-consent agreements, which set the terms of debate—how long it will continue and what kind and number of amendments will be permitted. As the term implies, these agreements must be accepted by all the senators. Failing such an agreement, the rules of the Senate—recent reforms notwithstanding—favor the prerogatives of the minority, even a minority of one. This is the best and worst institutional feature of the Senate.

Ultimately, this requirement of unanimous consent causes substantial delays in the Senate for any number of reasons. Senators have the right to place a hold, which will result in delaying consideration of a bill. This is generally done for policy reasons, to allow extra time to work out a compromise, but it is not uncommon for a member to place a hold on legislation for scheduling reasons, such as travel plans, campaign stops, or individual appointments. The leadership will exchange scheduling consideration for a member's support on unanimous-consent agreements. The political skills with which Senate leaders of both parties handle these delicate scheduling negotiations in large part determine the speed with which the Senate's work is completed. At the beginning of the session, members are told precisely when they can expect to leave town. The leadership hopes that by setting these dates in advance a compromise will be forced, a speech shortened, or an amendment withheld (if only because travel plans have already been made). And if a compromise cannot be reached, the leadership needs to have the sense to know when to withdraw a bill from the floor.[2]

All this uncertainty in Senate scheduling lends itself to a degree of flexibility and delay in Senate floor action. Senators will know only in a very general sense which bills are scheduled to be considered and when members are supposed to be on the floor. Consequently, it is not uncommon for the Senate to break away in the middle of an ongoing debate, only to take up another matter. Both House and Senate proceedings are now televised. Staffers in the Senate need to keep a constant eye on the floor to make sure that issues important to their bosses are not suddenly and unexpectedly brought to the floor.[3]

FOCUS ON THE SENATE

By July 24 the House finished the last of its appropriations bills, and the measures began to come to the floor of the Senate. Its appropriations subcommittees had been doing their work since the beginning of the session. Nonetheless, respecting the constitutional mandate, the Senate delayed floor consideration of appropriations measures until the bills left the House.

Appropriations legislation is subject to one of the very real congressional deadlines: the beginning of the fiscal year. Must-pass legislation cannot be carried over to a second session (unless continuing funding is authorized). Particularly in the Senate, the looming end of the fiscal year makes it easier in some ways and harder in others to pass vital legislation. Its passage presents legislative opportunities for members of the Senate. Must-pass legislation can become a vehicle for legislative riders, or nonrelated amendments that are piggybacked onto important legislation as it proceeds through the Senate. Prior to the 1990 budget agreement, it would have been not entirely undesirable for senators to delay passage of appropriations legislation, if only to take advantage of the opportunities provided by a continuing resolution.

Continuing resolutions are stopgap funding measures that are, in every sense, law. In the past, members used hurriedly drafted and rapidly considered continuing resolutions as vehicles to attach pork-barrel legislation that never would have survived the regular committee review. The October budget agreement with its pay-as-you-go provisions made it very difficult to use continuing resolutions as legislative vehicles. Any additional funding in the resolution that exceeded the spending caps would result in a sequester of other government functions in that account. Without the prospect of a fertile continuing resolution, quick passage of the regular appropriations should have been more likely.

In the Senate, however, must-pass legislation is always vulnerable to modification by any member who cares to delay the legislative process, for whatever reason. Toward the end of the fiscal year, the process is beset by complex legislative maneuvering precisely because time is running out. If there is obstruction at that point, it is almost certain that the extra time spent on the Senate floor is to the advantage of an individual or small group of senators. There are very real tactical benefits to be gained by adopting an obstructionist strategy. Senate holds and largely unlimited debate hold up Senate action before a deadline precisely because the end of the session or a mini-session approaches.

For senators unwilling or unable to play the insider's game, the fact that the rules allow for the protection of the minority (even a minority of one) encourages the adoption of a strategy of obstruction. In the House, by contrast, where members with fairly radical views can simply be overwhelmed by the majority, an obstructionist strategy has very few policy payoffs. In the Senate, however, it has some very real strategic, policy, and political payoffs. The result is an institution that is beset by delays.

Senator Helms and the Tactics of the Fringe

The master obstructionist in the Senate is Jesse Helms, the senior senator from North Carolina. Helms, a front man for a broad range of conservative causes, often delays consideration of must-pass legislation. Nevertheless, he still manages to deliver federal goods to his state and, at the same time, enjoy a modicum of success in promoting his conservative causes. Helms is not the most popular member in the Senate. Even so, for some members he exemplifies the special nature of the Senate (and American democracy), an institution that goes out of its way to accommodate minority rights. Other members are tolerant of Helms's tactics because they know that at some point in their legislative careers it is likely that they, too, will be a minority of one and dependent on the rules of the Senate.

Senator Helms is an expert at using a number of legislative strategies that are especially well adapted to the Senate's rules. In particular, he is skilled at framing issues in such a way as to garner majority support. Social scientists recognize that most issues cut across several dimensions.[4] For example, the budget has both fiscal and policy dimensions. Sometimes the policy dimension overwhelms budget considerations. For example, during the Persian Gulf War there was little support for budget cutting at the risk of reducing troop resources in the field. Intentionally or not, a primary task for any member of Congress trying to promote a particular piece of legislation is to frame an issue so as to generate a majority coalition.

In the House the leadership controls the Rules Committee and therefore the amendments that are allowed to be considered. For that reason, it is very difficult for the minority party to frame issues through legislation. In the Senate, however, with its generally unrestricted rules on the submission of amendments, members such as Jesse Helms can use amendments to transform the coalition of support for a particular piece of legislation—either to kill or alter the policy intent of a bill.[5] Helms is particularly skilled in the use of this tactic. Often his goal is to offer an amendment so politically difficult to oppose that it cannot lose. For example, he was enormously successful in getting the Senate to adopt an amendment to an appropriations bill that would require all medical personnel, under threat of criminal penalty, to be tested for AIDS.

Helms is a vocal advocate of more extensive testing of medical personnel for AIDS—despite the fact that most medical experts agree that the AIDS virus is very difficult to contract through routine medical procedures. Nevertheless, there is a tremendous amount of public concern about the spread of the disease not always based on fact. Helms saw the opportunity to play on this public fear as a means to promote more extensive testing for AIDS. He saw his chance in 1991 during Senate consideration of the 1991 Omnibus Crime bill.[6] On July 10 during floor consideration of the crime package, he attempted to introduce an amendment to make it a federal crime, punishable by imprisonment for up to ten years, for health care workers to transmit the AIDS virus to a patient. This amendment put other members of the Senate in a difficult position. Opposing the amendment would expose them to the wrath of constituents who want to be protected against the AIDS virus regardless of cost considerations or scientific reasoning to the contrary.

By introducing this amendment, Helms had put himself in a win/win position. If the amendment passed, he would have advanced his policy agenda. If it was voted on and failed, his political opponents would be forced to explain what could become a very embarrassing vote. The only way that Helms could lose would be if the amendment never came to a vote. This was the hope of the leadership on both sides of the aisle, who realized that the consequence of its coming to a vote would be either bad politics or bad policy. But it is a demonstration of the relative powerlessness of the Senate leadership that, despite their united opposition to the Helms amendment, they could not avoid a vote. It came about as the result of the interplay of complex factors that are emblematic of Senate politics.

One way to prevent a direct vote would have been to raise a point of order against the Helms amendment, which, if sustained by the chair, would have killed the proposal. In very few instances in the Senate can a point of order be sustained against an amendment. There is no germaneness requirement in the Senate (as there is in the House), except in one major instance. (The germaneness requirement means that an amendment has to be relevant to the bill being discussed.) Once the Senate votes to invoke cloture, or to limit debate, it is possible to raise a point of order questioning the germaneness of a particular amendment.[7] Theoretically, in order to avoid a vote on the Helms amendment, the leadership could have invoked cloture and then raised a point of order against the proposal.

There were two problems with this strategy. First, the leadership could fail to get the votes to invoke cloture. It takes a so-called super majority of sixty to close debate.[8] It is exceedingly difficult to generate this kind of super majority, especially in the consideration of a controversial issue. Furthermore, even if the leadership managed to invoke cloture, an important obstacle still needed to be overcome. If the leadership managed to invoke cloture and to raise a point of order against the Helms amendment, there would still be a vote to sustain a point of order—a vote they could lose, with consequences well beyond the matter at hand. Members of the Senate jealously protect the prerogatives provided to them under the rules. If Senator Helms's amendment were ruled out of order, the leadership would be victorious, but individual senators would lose some of their maneuverability. In other words, bringing the point of order to a vote would subtly change the issue. Rather than simply voting on the Helms amendment, the Senate would also be voting on the principle of the application of the germaneness rule. If the leadership were to lose that vote, it would set a precedent that would seriously weaken the already limited restrictions under the cloture rule. Faced with such a choice, the leadership decided to compromise and offer Helms an opportunity to introduce his amendment on another piece of legislation later in the session—legislation over which the leadership had better control.

Helms was also not sure he would win, so he agreed to hold the amendment until a few days later when the Senate considered the Treasury-Postal Service appropriations bill. Introduced as part of the appropriations process, the Helms amendment was not only quickly brought to a vote but also passed overwhelmingly (81-18). Even a leadership attempt to present a weaker compromise measure that would provide political cover for those senators wishing to vote against Helms was not enough. The leadership compromise amendment required health workers to follow appropriate safety procedures, but without the threat of criminal penalties. The leadership alternative passed unanimously but was not enough to derail the Helms amendment.

Helms had won, or had he? A number of obstacles still had to be overcome in order for the amendment to be included in the final legislation. The widely held expectation in the Senate was that the provision would be deleted in the House-Senate conference committee on the Treasury-Postal Service appropriations bill. House members would certainly oppose the amendment (which was not part of the House bill), and the Senate delegation, which did not include Helms, would probably concur.[9]

Helms, however, did make his point. Eighty-one senators were on record favoring a prison term for health workers who infect their patients with AIDS. Furthermore, even though the Helms amendment did not survive the conference committee, the leadership compromise (to require health workers to follow more stringent safety precautions) did get into the final law. Helms had not endeared himself to other members, but he had made his point and even some kind of law.

The Tactics of the Mainstream

While Helms is a master of the tactic of shaming his colleagues into voting for his proposals, most of the other members take a more diplomatic route. Rather than building a coalition by creating a piece of legislation members cannot vote against, others try to forge compromises that most members can agree to support. This is the tactic of the mainstream, whereas that of Helms is the tactic of the fringe. Nevertheless, both approaches are accommodated by the Senate rules.

Of course, the tactic of forging an agreeable compromise that accommodates the concerns of as many members as possible raises the problem of the least common denominator. This is reflected in most of the legislative product of the Senate—policies that are inoffensive or that serve the interests of a large enough group of members to garner a super majority. This means that the Senate acts as a constraint on the process of policy development. (Some would prefer to term this constraint a moderating influence.) This is the case despite the fact that in 1986 the Senate amended its institutional rules to make it easier for a majority to dominate the legislative process.

Rule 22.2 of the Senate provides that, by a vote of sixty or more, debate on any "measure, motion, other matter pending before the Senate" can be closed. Upon approval of such a cloture motion, no more than another thirty hours of debate will be permitted. At that point a vote on the legislation will be in order.[10] This remarkably flexible rule is considerably *more* restrictive than the rules governing debate prior to 1986 and, particularly, prior to 1917. Even so, the cloture rule is weak enough to ensure that a majority is generally not enough to rule the day on contentious issues. A super majority is necessary to pass most controversial legislation. This fact of senatorial life was no more vividly demonstrated than in the Senate's consideration of an amendment sponsored by Sen. Christopher Dodd (D-Conn.) in 1991 to cut off military assistance to the government of El Salvador.

Dodd's amendment to the foreign aid authorization bill was strongly opposed by the administration and a significant number of mostly Republican senators.[11] The first real test of the amendment came on July 25 when Minority Leader Robert Dole moved to table (or kill) it. The motion to table failed 43-56. That would seem a resounding victory for Dodd's amendment, but not in the Senate. In fact, there was visible disappointment on the winning side because it was almost certain the amendment would never survive.

As soon as the motion to table was defeated, Sen. John McCain (R-Ariz.) rose to express his disappointment with the results of the vote and issue a threat: "Mr. President, I will do everything in my power to see that this bill does not leave this body." [12] McCain was signaling, in a not so subtle way, that he intended to exercise the time-honored Senate prerogative of a filibuster. In announcing his intentions, McCain set off an increasingly common sequence of events. Rather than allow a filibuster to proceed, the Senate simply short-circuits the process and moves straight to a cloture vote. Should cloture be voted, the losing side generally admits defeat and waives the thirty hours of debate to which it is entitled. After all, the result is inevitable; why hold up the entire process? If cloture is not voted, the losing side (generally the bill sponsor) admits defeat and withdraws from its position.

On the Dodd amendment the cloture motion failed 52-44 (a majority but not a super majority voting in favor of closing debate). Despite majority support, the amendment was doomed. McCain could simply talk the bill to death. Recognizing the hopelessness of his cause, despite the fact that his proposal was supported by a strong majority, Dodd withdrew his amendment.

The Senate's antimajoritarian bent has often been the target of attack by frustrated policy makers. As President Woodrow Wilson said in expressing his frustration over the Senate's inability to approve a bill to arm merchant ships prior to U.S. entry into World War I (an action he later took on his own authority): "The Senate has no rules by which debate can be limited or brought to an end, no rules by which dilatory tactics of any kind can be prevented." [13]

Frustration with delays in the Senate, especially in the period leading up to World War I, provided the impetus for passage of the first cloture rule on March 8, 1917. Ever since that day, the Senate has operated under some kind of rule that provides for the closing of debate. This rule, in whatever form, has nonetheless been carefully crafted to preserve the traditional role of the Senate, as George Washington put it, as the "saucer in which the passions of the public are cooled." This has been a never-ending source of frustration for those in the majority who find that in the modern Senate nothing involving any great controversy can be done that does not have the support of at least sixty senators. But the fact is that the Senate has always been that way and has been even more protective of minority rights in times past.

The public policy effect of this Senate structure (or lack thereof) on the budget process is delay and a bias toward the protection of existing law. The fact that Senate rules do little to limit the number of amendments submitted results in a process in which any and all senators, regardless of their role in the committee consideration of the bill, have a right to put their mark on legislation. Again, because the Senate leadership is so dependent on unanimous consent for the passage of legislation, members can petition and are generally permitted to include almost any amendment for consideration under unanimous-consent agreements. For example, more than forty amendments related to the 1991 defense appropriations bill were considered on the floor. As a practical matter, most of these amendments were dealt with quickly, but some of the more controversial proposals took as many as two legislative days to dispense with. All thirteen appropriations bills go through the same basic obstacle course. The result is substantial delay.

The de facto requirement that a super majority be gathered in order to change existing law (in the case of controversial measures) means that it is easier to block than initiate change. Programs such as military aid to El Salvador in 1991 develop constituencies both outside and inside the Senate. When proposals for changing the direction of an existing program are considered on the floor, there is almost invariably a well-entrenched opposition to that change, usually structured along party lines. As long as the minority party in the Senate has more than forty votes, controversial legislation can almost invariably be blocked in the Senate. The legislation is then changed to fit the demands of the minority or it dies. As a result, the Senate plays a moderating function that will continue as long as the cloture rule is not strengthened further.

This sensitivity to the rights of the minority requires a certain degree of consensus in the Senate. Sometimes, as in the case of Senator Helms's activities, the Senate responds to a part of the national consensus that is neither rational nor compassionate. Nevertheless, the outcome does represent a point of view that is widely held.

Such results contribute to the legitimacy of the Senate as a uniquely American democratic institution. At the same time, its protection of minority rights helps ensure that a majority faction will not run roughshod over a minority. In this way, the legislative process in the Senate, as frustrating as it is, still fairly well mirrors the political philosophy of the Framers of the Constitution.

THE MID-SESSION REVIEW: THE SUMMER SURPRISE

In mid-July the Office of Management and Budget issues its mid-session review of the budget. Because economic conditions change over the course of the year and so many budget estimates made by the OMB and the Congressional Budget Office are dependent on economic conditions, a periodic review of economic forecasts and their effect on the budget are necessary. In the past, before the 1990 reconstruction of the Gramm-Rudman-Hollings deficit reduction law, these mid-session reviews came to be semi-affectionately known on Capitol Hill as the "summer surprise."

The surprise in the mid-session review was almost invariably an unpleasant one—generally an increase in the size of the projected federal deficit—part of the shell game played by budget estimators on the rules of Gramm-Rudman-Hollings. The estimates in the mid-session review almost always reflected the fact that there was a bias in the OMB's original January economic forecasts. As noted in previous chapters, this bias was a function of political motives that allowed for, through manipulation of economic forecasts, deficit reduction that could be achieved without sacrifice. But phony projections cannot produce a rosy reality. Ever since the passage of GRH in 1985, by the middle of the fiscal year the effect of real economic conditions on the federal budget was made painfully obvious; the gap between the real and imagined in budgetary politics continued to widen.

Under the old Gramm-Rudman regime, the summer surprise almost always set off a flurry of activity as Congress scrambled to meet its deficit targets mandated in the law. With little more than two months before the end of the fiscal year, Congress would have to cobble together a last-minute deficit reduction package. More often than not, Congress, in league with the OMB, managed to hit those revised deficit targets, not so much by cutting spending or raising taxes but by relying on unrealistic, overly optimistic economic forecasts. And so the cycle of smoke and mirrors would begin all over again. Congress would again be surprised by another much higher than expected deficit projection at the end of the fiscal year.

The budget process stumbled along in this manner until 1990 when the gap between deficit reduction targets and the real budget deficit became so large that it was no longer plausible or politically possible to piece together a deficit reduction package that could come anywhere near meeting the Gramm-Rudman-Hollings deficit reduction targets for fiscal year 1991. Phony economic forecasts would neither be sufficient nor realistic enough to close the gap. Furthermore, the size of the cuts necessary or the revenues needed to meet the targets would be so great that the economy might well suffer the effects of such a major cutback in public investment.

Those were the seeds of the budget compromise of October 1990. It was no longer possible to fake a solution, so the task of budgeting was changed. Rather than having to meet deficit reduction targets, Congress would now have to stay below certain preordained levels of spending regardless of the deficit. The mid-session review became less of a cause for concern in the legislative sense. No matter what the results, there were no longer hard and fast deficit targets that needed to be met.

Nevertheless, the results of the 1991 mid-session review were clearly shocking. In October 1990 the president and Congress had become attached to the notion that any budget agreement should reduce the deficit by at least $500 billion over five years. There was no specific reason for choosing the figure of $500 billion, but once the president and the congressional negotiating team had made a commitment to that amount, any attempt to back away from it was considered impolitic. Consequently, in October 1990, as part of the budget deal, the OMB (this time in complicity with the Congressional Budget Office) was placed in the familiar position of having to make overly optimistic economic projections in order to arrive at the conclusion that the budget agreement would actually result in a $500 billion saving. Just as in the past, these projections were highly inaccurate.[14]

Specifically, the OMB was wrong about the depth and impact of the 1990-1991 recession. In February 1991, at the time of the president's budget submission, Budget Director Darman had predicted that the recession would be relatively short and shallow. By July, however, there were few signs that the economy might be slowly coming out of its decline. What the OMB failed to predict was the degree to which the recession had a negative effect on the federal budget.

When on July 17 Darman appeared before the Senate Budget Committee to make his mid-session report, there was palpable disappointment in the committee room. Chairman Jim Sasser summed up the committee's feelings when he said in his opening remarks:

> This week the Administration released a mid-session budget review that, in my judgment, looks more like a mid-session *overhaul*. . . . In February, you told this Committee that for each of the years covered by the Budget Agreement, the consolidated deficit estimate promises to be better than the year before. Today we see this is not the case. The

> 1991 deficit estimate has dropped by $36 billion to $238 billion, but then we go considerably in the wrong direction in Fiscal 1992.[15]

Going "in the wrong direction" was something of an understatement. The OMB reported that while the deficit outlook for the current fiscal year was somewhat better than expected, it was much worse for the upcoming five years.

For fiscal year 1992, beginning on October 1, 1991, the OMB projected a deficit $68 billion higher than the deficit forecast made six months before. The increased deficit, in turn, produced its own deficit increases. After all, deficits have to be financed by borrowing. Projecting the costs of that additional shortfall over the next five years meant that only $380 billion would be left of the $500 billion in projected savings that resulted from the October budget deal. According to Darman, most of this loss would occur as the result of a shortfall in federal tax receipts.[16] The results of the April 15 federal income tax collections were central, Darman said, to the making of this revised determination. While he was not entirely sure of the reason for the shortfall in revenues, it was clear that the OMB had initially underestimated the effects of the recession.

There was a political dimension to the OMB's faulty estimates. Chairman Sasser was particularly annoyed that the OMB, by making such a dramatic error in February, had allowed the president to reap a publicity benefit from deficit reduction that now appeared somewhat unjustified. In addition, Sasser complained that mistakes of this size made fiscal planning absolutely impossible.

Although it was not unusual for the OMB to deliver an unpleasant mid-session surprise, the procedures designed to deal with that announcement were very different. Under the newly revised Gramm-Rudman-Hollings Deficit Reduction Act, the OMB's report did not touch off a legislative scramble, as it had in the past. Rather, the fiscal year 1992 deficit reduction targets were "held harmless" from the results of a mid-session review. Only at the beginning of the next fiscal year would deficit targets be shifted upward on the theory that there was no logical mid-session legislative remedy for the shortfall in revenues that resulted from unexpected economic conditions. Presumably, if the economy pulled out of recession, in short order revenues would begin to increase and the deficit shortfall would begin to narrow. More importantly, because under the new law Congress did not have to craft a new deficit reduction plan, there was no need to make more phony economic projections in order to justify another round of illusory deficit reductions (leading to further deficit shocks somewhere in the immediate future).

Because the OMB budget estimates had no legislative implications and, consequently, no reason to lie, the 1991 figures were perhaps the most accurate in recent years. But the news was not good. For fiscal year 1992 the OMB was projecting a $348 billion deficit, the largest in the nation's history. Soon thereafter the projection was adjusted upward to forecast a deficit approaching $400 billion.

THE BUDGET DEAL THREATENS TO UNRAVEL

As it became clear that the budget deal, so dearly fought for, was not going to balance the budget, support for the agreement began to erode. The immediate impetus for such a development was a series of events that conspired to change budget priorities. The year 1991 was a momentous one. A five-year budget agreement that did not take into account changes in the world seemed obsolete in its first year.

With regard to the economy, the October budget agreement effectively blocked the ability of the federal government to use fiscal policy to combat the recession. The agreement made it impossible for the government to use further deficit spending to stimulate the economy. This may have been beneficial in budgetary terms, but the government's inability to act to stimulate the economy under the law had a reverberating effect throughout the nation. States and localities began to suffer as federal spending was controlled, with no further prospect of assistance. Since many state constitutions have a balanced-budget requirement, and because the recession negatively impacted state as well as federal revenues, the only option that governors had in dealing with the recession was to raise taxes or cut spending (and services). Unemployment compensation funds, state-funded education, and social service funds all began to feel the strain of the 1991 recession. Local and municipal governments also began to feel the strain.

By the end of August the negative effect of this budget strain was serious enough to touch off a series of budget crises at the state level. The end of August is significant in many states because September marks the beginning of many a fiscal year. In some regions the federal government's budget problems, along with the recession, dictated adoption of a dramatic increase in taxes at the state level. In Connecticut, for instance, Governor Lowell Weicker was forced to sign, after a rancorous eleventh-hour debate in the legislature, the state's first income tax. In California, Republican governor Pete Wilson had to break with members of his own party to support a massive tax increase. With state and local governments in trouble all over the country, pressure began to be felt in Washington to do something about the economy. The consensus underpinning the October budget deal began to fray at the edges.

Unemployment Compensation

Of particular concern among Democrats in Congress was the plight of the unemployed. Under the law, unemployment compensation is to be paid to individuals for up to twenty-six weeks. Even though the economy seemed to bottom out by the end of July, it had been in recession for at least six months. Consequently, of the over eight million people who were unemployed at the end of July, a large percentage of recipients who had lost their jobs at the beginning of the recession were about to lose their unemployment compensation as well. Members of Congress had already begun to explore ways to get around the budget agreement. The worsening predicament for workers about to lose their unemployment compensation increased that strain. It bears repeating that Congress is an institution that makes its own rules. As airtight as the budget deal seemed to be for the previous few months, the more political pressure there was on members to evade budgetary restrictions, the less likely the budget deal would hold.

By the government's definition, a recession ends when the trends in national economic performance begin to move upward. This means that even though the economy may be at the bottom of its slide and the effects of the recession are at their worst, the government defines the recession as over. This distinction is important because a recession that is over is not an "emergency" according to the definition in the Budget Enforcement Act. As noted above, a presidential-congressional finding of an emergency would exempt new funding from the spending restrictions of the budget agreement. A disagreement between the executive and legislative branches over this emergency designation in one particular piece of legislation was to become one of the major political controversies of the 1991 budget cycle.

During and immediately after the Gulf War, the president, as an emergency measure, had several times suspended the October budget agreement. In the spring Congress had gone along with the president's request for emergency assistance for Kurdish refugees (spending that was exempt from spending controls). At the end of August a number of members of Congress began to pressure the president to declare the unemployment problem within the United States an emergency, according to the definition in the Budget Enforcement Act.

Up to this point, the president had resisted all attempts to declare domestic needs emergencies. But with the 1992 presidential and congressional elections looming on the horizon, Democratic congressional leaders saw the unemployment issue as a chance to provoke a confrontation with Bush that could not help but make him look bad. They would force the president to declare an economic emergency in connection with the extension of unemployment compensation, or he would suffer the consequences of negative political publicity. On August 2 the House and the Senate passed, by a margin well in excess of the two-thirds vote needed to override a presidential veto, a bill (H.R. 3201) to extend unemployment benefits for some unemployed workers by as much as an additional twenty weeks. Congress's own estimates showed that the payment of such benefits could cost as much as $5.3 billion in new spending. Because this increased spending constituted an expansion of entitlements (in the meaning of the Budget Enforcement Act), some kind of provision had to be made to prevent the pay-as-you-go requirements of the budget law should the increase in unemployment benefits be authorized. Otherwise, under pay-as-you-go requirements, an increase in one entitlement program would result in a reduction in others. This would occur unless the budget law was waived. The only way to waive budget restrictions and clear the way for new unemployment benefits would be to designate the bill emergency legislation, which is precisely what Congress did.

There were undoubtedly enough votes in both houses of Congress to overcome a threatened presidential veto of the unemployment extension (Republicans had deserted the president in droves on this issue). House Democrats, in particular, would have forced the president at least to suffer the political embarrassment of vetoing the bill, if not for a threat by Sen. Phil Gramm (R-Texas) to filibuster the bill in the Senate (and just before the August recess). Rather than risk halting the entire legislative process or losing the unemployment extension altogether, House Democrats agreed to a compromise that would allow the president to withhold funding for the new benefits regardless of whether or not he signed the bill. The Gramm-forced compromise allowed that

> none of the preceding sections of this Act shall take effect unless, not later than the date of the enactment of this Act, the President submits to Congress a written designation of all direct spending amounts provided by this Act (for all fiscal years) as emergency requirements within the meaning of part C of the Balanced Budget and Emergency Deficit Control Act of 1985.[17]

Under this provision, the president could sign the bill and still save the money. The actual expenditure of funds would be dependent on the president's declaration of an economic emergency, which, in turn, would waive the restrictions of the budget agreement.

On both sides of the aisle there was bald cynicism in this largely political maneuver. Senate Republicans forced this compromise because a presidential veto of the bill would not only have been embarrassing to the president but also to congressional Republicans. They would have had to vote to override the president's veto. If they had done so, the president would have been embarrassed and the Republicans would have appeared to be budget busters. Alternately, if they had voted to sustain, they would have appeared to be insensitive to unemployment. It was a no-win situation for Republicans, except for the compromise negotiated as the result of Senator Gramm's threat.

The choice for the Democrats was either to embarrass the president or accept a much scaled down compromise that the president would be willing to sign (the president's proposal would have extended unemployment benefits to only about 5 percent of those covered under the Democratic plan). The Democrats chose to embarrass the president. The real extension of benefits would come later, and maybe the Democrats could negotiate a better deal. The president did eventually sign the bill and refuse to fund it (by failing to declare an emergency). The Democrats, who were by then in recess, vowed to take the fight back to the president in September.

SMOKE, MIRRORS, AND FORWARD FUNDING

Besides the emergency route, members devised several other creative ways to get around the spending restrictions of the budget agreement. For example, in the Labor, Health and Human Services appropriation, the appropriations subcommittee on the Senate side managed to exceed its spending caps without touching off a sequester. The subcommittee's 602(b) allocations severely restricted the funding options available to the chair, and the fire walls in the budget law made it impossible to transfer savings from defense to the domestic budget. The subcommittee chair, Sen. Tom Harkin (D-Iowa), was forced to make a series of Faustian choices—to choose cuts in education in favor of health, and so on.

In one particular instance, Harkin was forced to cut (below the baseline) funding for the Low Income Home Energy Assistance Program (LIHEAP), which helps the poor to pay their heating bills. Under pressure from other key members of the committee, a decision was made to fund the program fully and to make $445 million of the total $1.3 billion appropriated for LIHEAP unavailable until after September 30, 1992—in effect, the beginning of fiscal year 1993.[18] Of course, the $445 million would be counted against the spending caps for 1993, further reducing the subcommittee's maneuverability for that year. But that was in the future. Senator Harkin was under pressure *now* for having reduced LIHEAP's budget from the previous year (from $1.6 billion). Presumably in 1993 the issue or problems arising from the handling of it could be finessed in another way.[19] This *forward funding* mechanism, as it came to be known, was eventually to become a controversial issue, particularly in the House.

The Budget and The Soviet Coup

The budget process is not immune from fast-changing events, even in remote parts of the world. In early August the abortive coup in the Soviet Union against Mikhail Gorbachev resulted in an accelerated decline in the country's economy and military strength. As the Soviet Union began to break up, its military capacity as well as its ability to feed its people deteriorated. Most of the newly independent republics were not self-sufficient, nor did they have the hard currency reserves to buy food on the international market. A significant amount of pressure was exerted on the administration and Congress to find some way to deliver assistance to the Soviet Union before the onset of winter, if only to show America's resolve to support emerging democracies. But the money for such an aid program was not there. With deficit projections ballooning, recession at home, and experts advising the president and Congress that much of the food aid delivered to the Soviet Union would be wasted or diverted, there seemed little chance that the president would declare an emergency to clear funding for food assistance. Furthermore, the fire walls set up in the budget agreement between defense, discretionary, and international assistance accounts made it procedurally difficult to find money for food assistance within the existing foreign aid budget.

Nevertheless, on August 28 during the August recess, House Armed Services Committee Chair Les Aspin (D-Wis.) proposed that his committee reauthorize as much as $1 billion out of the defense budget and earmark the money for food aid to the Soviet Union. Because OBRA made it difficult to transfer funds from defense to foreign aid without overcoming significant political and procedural barriers, Aspin made a unique suggestion. Why not simply purchase emergency food assistance for the Soviet Union out of the defense budget? To do this, he proposed the creation of a Defense Humanitarian Aid and Stabilization Fund, which, he argued, was justifiably part of the defense budget:

> This is defense by different means, but defense nonetheless, so it should come out of the Pentagon budget. During the Cold War, the threat was a deliberate Soviet attack. Now, the bigger threat seems to be chaos in a nation with 30,000 nuclear weapons. If we can reduce that threat by spending less than one half of one percent of our defense budget on humanitarian aid, we're defending ourselves and democracy, too.[20]

CONCLUSION

The Aspin plan to aid the Soviet Union was but one of the stratagems floated by members who wished to circumvent the October budget agreement. It is important to note that neither Harkin's action nor Aspin's plan exceeded the spending caps. The stalled unemployment compensation extension did exceed the spending caps, but it did not survive. Consequently, even as the budget deal began to show signs of falling apart, Congress stayed within the spending limits agreed on the previous fall.

It was a source of great disappointment on the Hill that even as the fiscal year was drawing to a close, the deficit continued to expand despite Congress's adherence to the spending caps. Either the spending caps were too high or the idea that spending control was possible without massive budget cutting or tax increases was profoundly flawed. If the increasingly dismal deficit figures signaled nothing else, they made it even more difficult for members to deny that in the future some increasingly difficult decisions would have to be made.

There was always a certain amount of dissatisfaction with the October agreement, which many members felt went too far or not far enough. The OMB's mid-session review may not have been the nail in the coffin, but it could have been the beginning of the end. By the August recess, very few members expected the budget agreement to hold up for its full five-year term. Attempts to bypass the agreement earlier in the year, which had been rejected out of hand, were now receiving serious consideration. It was only a matter of time before the deal began to hemorrhage.

On the bright side, the budget process had proceeded in 1991 at a fairly accelerated pace. Even though, by the August recess, only two of thirteen appropriations measures were finished and signed into law, there was no reason to believe that the process would stall in September. Nevertheless, before the break, the House Appropriations Committee began to prepare a continuing resolution that would cover any gaps in funding between the end of the fiscal year and the completion of the budget process. It seemed obvious at this point that Congress would again fail to get its work done on time.

But the Senate works at its own pace. No mere change in the budget process is going to alter the operation and delays that are endemic to the Senate's rules. The available work will always expand to fit (and exceed) the time allotted. It is both the strength and the weakness of the Senate that such a great deal of consideration is given to minority rights. The delays that such procedures generate are frustrating, particularly to members of the House who must stay in session and proceed at the pace of the Senate. But it is also one of the strengths of the Senate that it protects minorities in society—not just ethnic minorities but those with a different point of view. To that extent, the Senate is a uniquely American institution.

NOTES

1. During the same period the Senate received more than 40,000 nominations, of which more than 31,000 were confirmed. *Congressional Record,* "Resumé of Congressional Activity," October 1, 1991, D1189.
2. For example, foreign aid authorization legislation is so controversial that in the recent past the leadership has simply withdrawn it from the floor rather than waste the Senate's time on a losing cause. The leadership can do this with an authorization measure, but with a must-pass measure it is often impossible to do anything more than delay legislation.
3. In order to prevent senators from being totally surprised by floor proceedings, the leadership operates a paging system. Nevertheless, warnings on impending legislative action can be delivered on short notice.
4. There is expansive literature on the spatial dimensions of political issues, including Donald Mathews and James Stimson, *Yeas and Nays: Normal Decisionmaking in the United States House of Representatives* (New York: John Wiley and Sons, 1974); Anatol Rapoport, *Mathematical Models in the Social and Behavioral Sciences* (New York: John Wiley and Sons, 1983); and Herve Moulin, *Axioms of Cooperative Decisionmaking* (London and New York: Cambridge University Press, 1988), among many others.
5. In the same way that members can insist on Senate holds, they have a great deal of freedom to offer amendments to be introduced pursuant to unanimous consent. Again, the implicit threat is that a senator who is not allowed to offer an amendment will object to a unanimous-consent request.
6. S. 1241, 102nd Congress, 1st session.
7. The intent of the germaneness provision in the cloture rule is to protect against use of the amending process as a dilatory tactic after cloture has been invoked.
8. Rule 22.2, *Standing Rules, Orders, Laws and Resolutions Affecting the Business of the Senate* (Sen. Doc. 101-1), 101st Congress, 1st session.
9. Pursuant to the rules governing the conduct of conference committees, agreeing with or dissenting from dissimilar provisions adopted by the other house is done by unit rule. It is sufficient for the majority of a delegation to act in the name of the House or the Senate. With regard to the Helms amendment, it was fairly clear that the House would vote to reject and that the Senate delegation to the conference (which, after all, was appointed by the leadership) would accede to the House's preference. For the rules of conferences, see United States Senate, *Cleaves' Manual of the Law and Practice in Regard to Conferences and Conference Reports,* 57th Congress, 1st session, rule 143.4.
10. *Standing Rules of the Senate.*
11. S. 1435, 1st session, 102nd Congress.
12. *Congressional Record,* July 25, 1991, S10899.
13. James D. Richardson, *Compilation of the Messages and Papers of the Presidents,* quoted in Robert Byrd, *The Senate 1789-1989: Addresses on the History of the U.S. Senate,* vol. II (Washington, D.C.: U.S. Government Printing Office, 1988), 122.
14. One staffer for the Joint Economic Committee told this author that the OMB probably knew full well that its economic projections were completely unrealistic and, as a consequence, that the deficit reduction resulting from the October budget deal would be far short of $500 billion.
15. U.S. Senate, Committee on the Budget, "Statement by Chairman Jim Sasser,

Hearing on OMB Mid-Session Review of the Budget," July 17, 1991, 1-2.

16. In future years, according to the OMB, revenue losses would continue, as would losses accrued as the result of increased interest payments on a larger than expected deficit. See Executive Office of the President, Office of Management and Budget, *Mid-Session Review of the Budget*, July 15, 1991, 1.
17. S. 1554, Section 10(b), 102nd Congress, 1st session.
18. H.R. 2707, S. Rept. 102-104, 102nd Congress, 1st session.
19. It should be noted that some of the most vociferous objections to the committee's initial decision to limit LIHEAP came from Sen. Warren Rudman (R-N.H.). Rudman, as a member of the subcommittee, was almost certain to get his way. But even more important, it just so happens that New Hampshire holds one of the earliest and most important presidential primaries. Senator Harkin, who at this point was exploring the possibility of a run for the Democrats' presidential nomination, may have seen New Hampshire as a critical state for his campaign.
20. House of Representatives, House Armed Services Committee, "Aspin: Humanitarian Aid from Pentagon to Ease Soviet Chaos," Armed Services Committee press release, August 28, 1991, 1.

CHAPTER 10

The End Game: September, October, and Beyond

After every opportunity to compromise on the really tough issues has been put off until the very last second in the hope that the other side would blink, the final month of the congressional session is an occasion for the forced settlement of disputes. The forum for the negotiation of most of these compromises is the conference committee. But these committees are merely the surface veneer of a complex bargaining process that has been in progress since the beginning of the year. The easy compromises have long been made. But in the end, often under a veto threat from the president, direct negotiations must be entered and concessions granted. The incentive to come to terms at this stage of the process is a simple one. The alternative to agreement is no legislation at all. For most cases of disagreement, that is a powerful motive, and the conference committee is the method.

Owing to the restraints imposed by the 1990 budget agreement, disagreements over budgeting were even more intractable than usual. In making ends meet when resources are limited, Congress has two choices: leave vital needs unmet or change the rules. In the tradition of an institution that makes its own rules, in the fall of 1991 the coalition in support of the budget agreement began to unravel, less than a year after OBRA was negotiated. For the most part, however, the coalition held, and some tough decisions were made. But the writing was on the wall; the five-year budget agreement was in trouble in its first year. How much longer would it last?

So it is in the modern Congress that the fiscal year does not end so much as it grinds to a halt. The fireworks in October 1990 were the exception rather than the rule. Instead, it is more often the case that when there is no more time in the legislative session, the only choice is to end it there and either compromise or put off disagreements until later. In most cases, the agreements are made and Congress starts the process anew the next January. In this respect the end of fiscal year 1991 was not unusual.

In the waning days of the first session of the 102nd Congress, well after the end of the fiscal year, Congress passed no fewer than three continuing resolutions to cover its delays, but at the same time it completed its work on all but one appropriations bill. The fact that the appropriations process proceeded, delayed but not derailed, made 1991 a year not much different from the others, a year in which the government again managed to muddle through.

CONTINUING RESOLUTIONS

While the budget process proceeded at a relatively normal pace, by the end of September several appropriations measures were still pending. More to the point, on September 1 when Congress came back into session after its summer break, it had completed and the president had signed only two of the requisite thirteen appropriations bills.[1] Despite this meager output, the work on the rest of the appropriations agenda seemed fairly straightforward, and what obstacles there were (mainly political) looked as if they could be overcome given a forceful enough set of incentives. On two specific appropriations bills, however, the Foreign Operations allocation and funding for the departments of Labor and Health and Human Services (LHHS), the disagreements were much more profound. The LHHS appropriation, as we shall see, was mired in the abortion issue and presidential politics. The Foreign Operations measure faced a different problem—the crush of current events.

FOREIGN OPERATIONS

For more than a year after the Soviet Union gave Jews permission to emigrate, Israel had been flooded by refugees. In order to finance new housing for those refugees, Israel asked the federal government for a $10 billion loan guarantee. For several reasons, that request was delayed. First, under the October budget agreement, loan guarantees, even though they do not draw directly on the U.S. Treasury, require an appropriation.[2] Appropriators must set aside a certain percentage (generally between 2 and 5 percent) of every loan guarantee in recognition of the fact that a certain percentage of loans to foreign countries do not perform. For example, when the war in the Persian Gulf broke out, Iraq defaulted on payments for federally guaranteed loans of several billion dollars borrowed for the purchase of agricultural goods. Presumably, at some point, the Iraqis will want to make good on these loans if for no other reason than that they will want more credit.

In the meantime, the U.S. government is responsible for the defaulted payments.

Even though Israel has never defaulted on any loans guaranteed by the federal government, Congress is obligated under the budget law to set aside a placeholder of several hundred million dollars to be counted against the Foreign Operations account.[3] In other words, other foreign aid programs would suffer if the loans to Israel were guaranteed, even if there were no direct and immediate cost to the federal Treasury. Furthermore, the loan guarantees presented a political problem to the president in his attempt to negotiate a permanent peace in the Middle East.

Second, as noted previously, when the war in the Persian Gulf broke out, Congress passed two emergency supplemental appropriations, one of which furnished additional foreign aid assistance to Turkey and Israel. Part of the price that Israel paid in exchange for the extra $650 million (above its annual $3 billion in mostly security assistance) was a promise from the Israelis that they would not return to Congress for more aid until at least the end of September. Consequently, the $10 billion in loan guarantees had not been requested and was not included in the regular appropriations bills. If, at this late date, Israel came to Congress with the loan guarantee request, the appropriations committees would be in a fiscal bind and the president would be in political hot water. For Congress to grant the loan guarantees to Israel at this particular time would hamper the foreign policy of the United States in other foreign aid accounts.

As a result of the war (and the collapse of the Soviet Union), the United States was in a stronger position than ever before to bring the parties to the Arab-Israeli dispute to the bargaining table. It was rumored that the loan guarantees would be used to finance new Jewish settlements for Russian émigrés on the West Bank, thus imposing further barriers to a negotiated settlement. In the early fall when the Israelis balked at meeting with the Palestinian delegation, particularly those members identified with the Palestine Liberation Organization, the Bush administration decided to put pressure on Israel by asking Congress to delay action on foreign aid appropriations in order to avoid the issue of Israeli loan guarantees.

Pending Arab-Israeli negotiations, the administration requested that the appropriations committees hold off on their regular fiscal year 1992 Foreign Operations appropriations bills until March 31, 1992, which the subcommittees agreed to do. The appropriations committees are rarely predisposed to be so amenable to presidential intrusions on their prerogatives, but foreign policy is a special case. Congress is often more willing to go along with a presidential request, especially when the president advises that delicate diplomatic negotiations hang in the balance.

Without a regular appropriation, a continuing resolution would be necessary if for no other reason than that ongoing international assistance programs would need continued funding until at least March 31. On September 26, four days before the deadline, because of the hold on the foreign aid bill and other delays, Congress passed and the president signed a bill (H.J. 332) to extend continuing appropriations until October 29 to all programs not yet funded. During that month Congress cleared another seven appropriations bills, so that by the time there was a need for another continuing resolution (H.J. 360, passed on October 24), only three outstanding bills remained. The Foreign Operations bill was being held, the Defense appropriation was still awaiting its authorization, and the Labor, Health and Human Services appropriation was delayed in conference by policy disagreements and on the floor by a presidential veto.

The need for continuing resolutions at the end of the fiscal year was not unusual. What was different was the relatively nonsubstantive and noncontroversial nature of those measures. In previous years, continuing resolutions were used to fund all manner of special projects. The new budget rules ended all that. Any additional appropriations beyond the spending caps would require a corresponding sequester from other programs in that same account. Continuing resolutions for this year would fund existing programs at the previous year's level or at the level dictated by the House, Senate, or conference report, whichever was lowest.

Continuing resolutions used to be vehicles for programs that received less than the normal degree of scrutiny. The new rules under the Budget Enforcement Act, however, ensured that many constituencies would not be harmed and delicate compromises in existing appropriations measures would not be shattered by well-larded continuing resolutions passed quickly at the end of the fiscal year. Thus, the form of continuing resolutions for fiscal year 1991 was different from that in the years past. In this one small instance, the new PAYGO rules certainly had a beneficial effect on the process, if not the budget itself.

CONFERENCE COMMITTEES

The House and the Senate must pass legislation in exactly the same form before sending the bill on to the president. This requirement makes it necessary for Congress to appoint a conference committee to settle the disagreements in almost every major piece of legislation. Conference committees are sometimes called the third body of Congress because most of Congress's final legislative output is a direct reflection of conference negotiations. Conference committees are not completely independent, nor are they completely bound by the actions of the two houses. Conferees are expected to operate under several general constraints. They are only to negotiate on areas of disagreement within legislation. Theoretically, new provisions in the legislation cannot be included as part of the conference report. (As a practical matter, this is not always possible.) The major constraint, however, is the requirement that agreements be approved by both houses. Maintaining majority support in both houses is the ultimate restraint on any conference.[4]

Because conference committees are a major inconvenience for most of the members involved, as many controversies as possible are solved before a conference committee is authorized. For example, many differences between houses are resolved through amendments on the floor. After a bill is passed by both houses, one or the other chamber may decide to insist on its position or it can recede from its position and concur with the other body's position. Alternately, one or the other body can adopt the other's legislation by amending its own bill, inserting the other bill's language to act as "an amendment in the nature of a substitute." This amending process can go back and forth between the houses, with either house concurring, receding, insisting on, or amending the amendments to part or all of its position. Failing a settlement by amendment, the bill can die or the members of both houses can create a conference committee.

Conference committees are appointed on almost all appropriations bills. The disagreements between the two houses in such matters are generally much too profound and varied to be settled by mere correcting amendments. The fiscal year 1992 Department of the Interior appropriation, for example, had almost 2,000 items in dispute that had to be settled in conference.[5] This is not atypical for an appropriations bill. A conference on almost any other funding bill is likely to be as complex, and even more extensive on some, especially those dealing with the most expensive packages such as defense.

Conferees on the House side are appointed by the Speaker in consultation with the chair and ranking member of the relevant subcommittee. Consequently, most conferees are members of that subcommittee. The Speaker may also appoint members of the subcommittee who are the sponsors or movers behind major provisions of the bill. Formally, Senate conferees can either be appointed by the presiding officer or elected by the entire body. In reality, Senate conferees are appointed in consultation between Senate leaders from both sides of the aisle. In both houses of Congress, the chair and ranking minority member of the full committee with jurisdiction, as well as members of the subcommittee, are almost always appointed to the conference committee.

Within a conference committee, the unit rule prevails.[6] The House and the Senate delegations to a conference vote as a unit. A majority of conferees in both delegations must agree to (and sign) a conference report. Obviously, the unit-rule requirement leads to a number of tie votes, in which case the item is not agreed to and cannot be included in the conference report. In other words, issues are either settled or excluded from the bill. This is a powerful incentive to compromise. Something is better than nothing. Thus the onus of compromise falls on the delegates to a conference who would rather not wait until the next legislative cycle.[7]

Preparing for a Conference

Once a bill is passed by both houses and a conference is agreed to, the respective committee staffs begin to apply a preplanned strategy. Initially, on appropriations bills, the staff will produce a ledger that is a line-by-line accounting of the provisions of agreement and disagreement between the houses. The subcommittee staffs then caucus with their respective chairs to decide what kind of initial offer will be made to the other body. It is at this point that the subcommittee chair will begin to sacrifice preplanned bargaining chips and apply the leverage that has been carefully enhanced to bolster the subcommittee's position.

With a conference almost a certainty for every appropriations bill, subcommittee staffs begin to prepare for it from the beginning of the budget process. Staffs must develop bargaining leverage to strengthen their bosses' hands in making the inevitable compromises that are part of the negotiating process. The House and Senate represent different constituencies, and the different subcommittees reflect the personal predilections and characters of their chairs. Consequently, committee staffs will try to take advantage of foreseeable differences in appropriations bills as they emerge from the House and the Senate. The committee staffs know, in a general sense, what the companion bill (from the other house) will look like—down to the earmarks and special projects. This being the case, the staff and the subcommittee chair have the conference in mind when they make some of their decisions for funding during markup. Staffs shape their funding plans in the preparation of bills for conference in two main ways.

First, the staff may ask for monies and projects on the chairman's mark that are clearly expendable, to be used as bargaining chips. The new rules under the Budget Enforcement Act, however, make over-appropriating for the purpose of bargaining more difficult. Funding that exceeds strict 602(b) allocations can trigger a sequester, which will affect important interests on other subcommittees and even threaten the programs of the chair's allies on the subcommittee. Since bargaining strength in conference is often a function of unity, it is important that the subcommittee chair accommodate as many members of the subcommittee as possible, from both sides of the aisle. Because of this pay-as-you-go requirement under the Budget Enforcement Act, it is much more likely that committee staffs will take a different tack in building political leverage. They can use their own bill to cut the other chamber's funding priorities.

Appropriations legislation is not constructed from whole cloth but is a patchwork of programs, most of which have been in existence for many years. The senior members of appropriations subcommittees have been involved with the process for a number of budget cycles and have a history of support and opposition for various programs. Knowing which earmarks and programs are important to the senior members of the subcommittee from the other House, subcommittee staffs will often cancel or cut back programs that they know are of vital interest to the other side in order to gain a bargaining advantage.

For example, in 1991, in anticipation of a House-Senate conference on the LHHS appropriation, the House subcommittee staff deleted funding in the bill for family planning programs. House LHHS subcommittee chair William Natcher, a stickler for rules, will not fund a program such as family planning that is not authorized. (Family planning authorizations often fall victim to the abortion controversy.) By the same token, he knows that family planning will ultimately be funded and that for Senate subcommittee chair Tom Harkin family planning is a high priority. Nevertheless, he chose to delete family planning funds as a bargaining chip. Harkin chose in one instance to take an earmark important to a Republican member of the subcommittee from the House side and transfer a program intended for the Republican's Michigan district to Harkin's home state of Iowa. This, too, would become a bargaining chip in conference.

Health or Education: The Lesser of Two Equals

What both Natcher and Harkin were preparing for was an anticipated dispute over funding for education versus health programs. As noted in previous chapters, the fire walls in the October budget agreement force negotiators into making unpalatable choices. Since money cannot be transferred from the defense or international assistance account to domestic discretionary funding, appropriators are forced to make decisions about trade-offs within their own budgets. On the LHHS appropriation, for example, the subcommittee had already been forced to sacrifice low-income heating assistance in favor of health spending. The House LHHS appropriations subcommittee adopted a different set of priorities than did the Senate. The House bill put a much greater emphasis on education over health spending than did the Senate bill.

Within the conference something had to go. The politics of budgeting favored education spending. The fact is that education programs tend to be politically easier to fund than most health programs for an important reason related to the budget process. Different programs have different spend-out rates. This means that regardless of the amount of money allocated for a program, some programs spend out or outlay funds faster than others. For example, education programs such as Head Start tend to spend out more slowly than health programs such as the National Institutes of Health (NIH).[8] This means that a budget authority for education programs will result in a smaller outlay than if the same amount of money were authorized for health expenditures. Since deficit calculations are based on money spent or outlays, it is possible to grant bigger authorities for education than for health without adversely affecting the deficit (at least in the short term). This is precisely why programs such as child immunization may be more difficult to fund under the budget agreement than, for example, job training.

The House side at the conference, with Chairman Natcher in the lead, was adamant on its position, as was Chairman Harkin for the Senate. With both goals meritorious, there was no right decision to be made on this issue. The LHHS conference struggled for several days, until well after the end of the fiscal year.[9] Finally, the conference committee decided to do in part what the Senate subcommittee had done during its markup when it decided to forward fund the Low Income Home Energy Assistance Program (LIHEAP). The conference decided to cut only part ($360 million) of the education funding favored by the House and at the same time to put off until the beginning of fiscal year 1993 some additional funding ($175 million) for the National Institutes of Health. The deal was almost unanimously agreed to. However, according to at least one member who objected to the deal, Rep. John Porter (R-Ill.), the conference agreement was "an attempt to get around the discipline of the 1990 budget agreement."[10]

Bargaining

As with most unscripted events on Capitol Hill, conference committees conduct their business behind closed doors as long as possible. Formally, most conferences are open to the public, but in reality the meetings are held in such small rooms that the audience is limited. Those who do show up, mainly lobbyists, line up outside the committee room with little hope of getting in, resigned to the prospect of following the deliberations secondhand. Like expectant fathers, lobbyists await the final delivery of their special projects nurtured over the course of the nine-month legislative session.

Inside the committee room, lined up along tables facing one another, are conferees from the two houses. Crossing the aisle has a different meaning in the conference committee room, where the principle of the separation of powers rules supreme. It is the House against the Senate, and the institutional distance between the two chambers is more evident here than in any other stage in the legislative process. Lined up behind the chair of their respective chamber's delegation is the committee staff, which for months has been immersed in the minutiae of the legislation being considered.

Most disputes have already been settled. One delegation chair or the other (the chairmanship of the conference committee alternates annually) reads off the agreements made by number. Without objection most disputes are agreed to by voice votes. Negotiations concerning intractable disputes are soon to follow. During the negotiations that follow, proposals and counterproposals are made. The staff scurries from one side of the room to the other in order to consult with their counterparts. This is just the latest stage of what is likely to have been months of negotiation.

After the most expendable bargaining chips are traded away, the committee staffs begin to reevaluate programs or earmarks that accrue to individual members. These programs are evaluated according to several criteria. Clearly there is a public policy concern, but beyond that the most important variable is the strategic placement in the congressional hierarchy of the member or members involved. Earmarks for members off the subcommittee that have survived to that point may be the first to go. The Senate may have an advantage at this stage because individual senators are so much more powerful within their institution than are members of the House.[11] The exception to this rule is in the event of a confrontation between a senator and a particularly well-placed member of the House.

For example, during a conference on the agriculture appropriation a dispute arose between Wisconsin Republican Sen. Bob Kasten and Wisconsin Democratic Rep. David Obey. Obey is a cardinal, a member of the majority, and a likely successor to full committee chair Jamie Whitten. In a dispute over a program that would distribute funds either statewide or to projects in Obey's district, the House prevailed.

In order to counter their weaknesses, nonmembers of the conference will try to recruit those on the committee. The conference session is often interrupted by members presenting amendments in behalf of a colleague not present. Sometimes these presentations are pro forma, simply done as a favor, but at other times members of the conference will go to great lengths in support of a particular position. Of course such support has a price. Members of conference committees expect in-return favors to be delivered elsewhere.

Deleting or failing to include a program is a difficult decision. The conference committee must explain its decisions to colleagues when the conference report is brought to the floor. However, just as in preparing the chairman's mark, conference committees have several options, short of granting a request, that can ameliorate the sting of rejection. Even though there may be no money to fund a program, the committee can include in report language instructions that provide everything from earmarks to vague statements of support (in principle) for a member's program. Again, as with preparing the chairman's mark, the specificity of report language significantly determines whether a program will be carried out, according to congressional intent, by the bureaucracy.

Administrative Versus Programmatic Spending

It is easier to compromise on certain types of appropriations than others. There is a clear distinction in bargaining between administrative and programmatic costs. The administrative costs of an agency are fairly well predetermined. Salaries for civil service workers are dictated on a government-wide basis. The number of employees—the primary administrative expense in most agencies—is fairly constant from one year to the next. Thus legislative differences in administrative appropriations are not large, nor are they subject to spirited disagreement. The gaps between the House and Senate in this regard are largely settled by splitting the difference. For example, in the FY92 Department of the Interior appropriation, the office of the secretary received approximately $66 million from the House, $58 million from the Senate, and the conference report allocated $64 million.

A major sticking point in most conferences is programmatic and policy differences. These are disagreements in emphasis or on the manner in which money is spent. For example, it is almost impossible to split the difference on emotional and moral issues such as abortion. Even in the appropriations process, most of the heated debates generated in conference concern political and philosophical issues. As we shall see, the two major controversies in the Department of the Interior appropriation were the fees charged for cattle grazing on public lands and the funding of obscene art by the National Endowment for the Arts.

Instructions

Some provisions are easier to protect in conference than others. In preparing a conference report for the floor, the chairs of both delegations must be conscious of the need to develop a broad consensus for the purpose of final adoption, particularly in the Senate, where minority rights are well protected. It is generally more difficult in conference to insist on a provision that was supported by a relatively weak majority. One house or the other (generally both) can also express its will by instructing its conferees. Either House can enhance its bargaining position by displaying a high degree of unanimity on a particular bill or portion of a bill. For example, in the case of the Helms amendment discussed above (criminal penalties for transmission of AIDS), the House insisted not only that it be dropped but also that a Senate leadership compromise amendment be dropped as well. In deference to the expressed will of the Senate, because both the Helms amendment and the leadership amendment passed the Senate by overwhelming margins, the Senate leadership amendment was retained.

Corn for Porn

Conference committees are sometimes held up by completely intractable disputes. In 1991 such a dispute developed in the Department of the Interior appropriation bill conference. The Interior and Related Agencies appropriation funds everything from the Bureau of Land Management to the National Endowment for the Arts. In the course of consideration on the House side, an amendment was attached to the legislation that would have raised the fees charged by the federal government to cattle ranchers who graze their livestock on public lands.[12] Under current law, cattle ranchers pay much less than the prevailing commercial rate for public grazing rights.[13] House sponsors of this amendment argued that in times of huge federal deficit it is difficult to justify this indirect government subsidy to cattle ranchers.

True to its urban and eastern bias, the House voted for these increases, while, true to its rural and western bias, the Senate voted against the increases. The House insisted on its position in conference, and so did the Senate. The Senate position was stronger, as sixty senators voted against the increase—not only enough votes to win the issue but also well in excess of the forty votes needed to block cloture in the event that a conference report was not to their liking.

On the same bill the Senate attached an amendment that would have prohibited the National Endowment for the Arts from funding "patently offensive" art.[14] Jesse Helms sponsored this amendment, crafted to give senators what, in essence, was the choice of voting for or against pornography. Helms offered the amendment in response to a controversial NEA-funded exhibit of photography by Robert Mapplethorpe depicting, among other things, homosexual acts. The Helms amendment was adopted 68-28 (a super majority).

The Senate seemed to hold all the cards. However, the House Interior appropriations subcommittee chair, Sidney Yates (D-Ill.), would not budge. Yates, an urbane, sophisticated congressman from suburban

Chicago who has always been a strong supporter of the arts, objected vehemently to the Helms amendment. He held firm despite the fact that the House had approved, by wide margins (286-135 and 287-133 respectively), two nonbinding resolutions sponsored by Rep. William Dannemeyer (R-Calif.), prohibiting the NEA from funding theater groups whose performances depicted homosexual acts. Up to this point, because House rules allow the subcommittee chair to dominate the markup of the bill, and the House leadership dominates the rules of the debate, Yates had succeeded in keeping Dannemeyer's funding restrictions off his NEA appropriation bill at every stage of the process.[15]

For two days the conference committee met without agreement. Finally on October 16 the impasse was broken when House conferee Les AuCoin (D-Ore.) proposed that the House drop its insistence on the grazing fee increase in exchange for deletion of the Helms amendment. The deal was consummated and both delegations approved. National ranchers' associations were delighted. Dannemeyer was outraged. He termed the deal "arrogance of the worst order."[16] This unusual deal, popularly dubbed "corn for porn," cleared the way for the settlement of the rest of the outstanding disputes on the bill. The conference report was then sent to the floor.

Conference Reports on the Floor

Conference reports, once written and signed, are brought back to the chambers. On the House side, the reports cannot be considered until three days after they are filed. (This rule, which is often waived, gives members time to review the final conference agreement.) At that time, conference reports are privileged (they can be brought to the floor at any time) and are considered under a standing rule that allots one hour for debate. In the Senate, conference reports can be brought up at any time. The reports are not amendable in either chamber and are subject to an up or down vote. In most cases the legislative process ends here, and the bill is sent on to the president after it clears the other body. Most appropriations bills, however, are accompanied by amendments that are to be taken up by the chambers in order to settle intractable disputes or to ratify agreements made outside the authority of the conferees. (Conferees must sometimes exceed their authority in order to reach an agreement.)

The floor manager (probably the head of the chamber's conference delegation) has three options in bringing disputed amendments to the floor. He or she can move that the House insist on its disagreement to the Senate amendment, move that the House recede and concur in the Senate amendment, or move that the House recede from its disagreement with the Senate and concur with a further amendment.

The floor manager's position is generally predetermined by settlements made in conference. For the chamber to deviate from any of the motions made by the floor manager and conference committee is to threaten the entire structure of compromise embodied in a conference agreement. Disputed amendments, therefore, rarely generate much debate.

Two exceptions to this rule occurred in 1991 toward the end of the budget process. On October 9 Republican gadflies Robert Walker (Pa.), Dan Burton (Ind.), and Harris Fawell (Ill.) decided to raise objections to a conference amendment on the transportation appropriations bill (H.R. 2942) in order to make a point. The entire bill, they believed, had been laced with too much pork-barrel spending. First, they opposed an amendment providing $249 million for eighty-nine highway "demonstration" projects, the archetypal form of pork. The amendment, they argued, bypassed the authorization process (the highway authorization bill had not yet been adopted). They lost. Then they focused on a particular project that would provide $162 million for a highway in West Virginia, the home state of Senate Appropriations Committee Chair Robert Byrd. "He doesn't want to bring home the bacon," Burton said of Byrd, "he wants to bring home the whole pig." [17] They lost again. But there was no way they could win. Had the money for West Virginia or the other projects been deleted, the whole conference report and literally hundreds of transportation projects for many members from both parties would have fallen through. As Transportation Subcommittee Chair William Lehman commented, "It takes votes in both chambers to pass an appropriations bill. We have to deal with the Senate in good faith." [18]

Burton and his cohorts tried again on November 6 when the Labor, Health and Human Services conference report was brought to the floor. The report was accompanied by sixteen controversial amendments, most of which dealt with the roughly $4.3 billion in forward funding that was either part of the original Senate bill or the result of compromises made in conference. To reiterate, forward funding is the technique used by the Senate LHHS subcommittee to bypass the budget agreement's spending caps by authorizing spending in one fiscal year and obligating part of the funds in the next. Burton rose to object to this practice, arguing that forward funding violated the spirit if not the letter of the budget agreement.[19] (Even so, there was general agreement that forward funding was technically in compliance with the law.) Burton lost. Whether or not the other members agreed with his position, here again the conference agreement was much too delicate, the conference committee had met for too long, and final adjournment was too close for members to vote to topple the deal. (It is interesting to note that many members of the Budget Committee, including Chair Leon Panetta, voted with Burton.)

The Presidential Veto

There is a key actor behind the scenes who is not in attendance at the conference. The president exercises substantial influence at the end of the budget process, primarily through the presidential veto. In fact, the veto may make the president as powerful at the end of the appropriations process as at the beginning. In February the president set the budget agenda. In November he used the veto and the threat of the veto to amend the final outcome.

The presidential veto is as important as a threat as it is in actual use. Several factors contribute to the president's influence through the veto. The veto threat must be credible. The president cannot make idle threats. The veto, when applied, must be successful. If Congress is able to override the president's veto with some frequency, the president's influence is diminished. As a consequence, the president must be careful to pick his spots in selecting bills to veto. Selecting the proper target requires a skillful reading of the president's support in Congress. For a president to suffer a high percentage of veto overrides or to lose on an extremely important piece of legislation is to suffer a loss of influence. For example, President Carter suffered a setback in 1977-1978 when he attempted to veto a public works bill because he objected to several of the projects therein. Carter should have known that public works legislation, in particular, is built on a foundation of extensive support in Congress, with projects widely distributed. To attack part of this kind of deal is to attack all of it, a fact that Carter learned to his regret.

President Bush was 100 percent successful in his use of the veto in 1991 for several reasons. He was unambiguous and true to most of his veto threats. On one issue in particular the president was adamant. No one doubted his willingness to veto legislation expanding abortion rights. (It helped that the president held a veto-proof minority in the House on this issue.) During the course of the appropriations process in 1991, President Bush used his veto power three times to get his way on abortion. In September the president vetoed the District of Columbia appropriations bill in order to delete language that would have permitted the public funding of abortions. An override attempt failed, and the bill was resubmitted and passed without the offending language. The president was also successful in his attempt to influence the language of the defense and LHHS appropriations.

On the defense appropriations bill, a provision was deleted in conference that would have permitted U.S. servicewomen and the dependents of servicemen stationed overseas to obtain abortions in U.S. military hospitals. The provision was dropped, not only because the chair of the House Defense subcommittee, John Murtha, is opposed to abortion but also because the president threatened to veto the entire defense bill over this one small provision. In light of the fact that the president had vetoed the District of Columbia appropriation for much the same reason and inasmuch as the defense appropriation was running very late, the conferees decided not to risk the delay associated with fighting the president on this item. There was, however, an abortion issue on which some members chose to stand and fight.

THE GAG RULE

Through the regulatory process, the Bush administration had ordered a ban on abortion counseling at federally funded family planning clinics. The administration's regulation was brought before the Supreme Court and upheld in the case of *Rust v. Sullivan.*[20] The Court, in a narrow 5-4 decision, ruled that the regulation prohibiting abortion counseling was a proper interpretation of the law and within the power of the executive. Nevertheless, it was entirely within the power of Congress to overturn the Court's decision by rewriting the statute. This Senator Harkin did in his Labor, Health and Human Services appropriations bill.

Family planning clinics are funded under Title X of the Public Health Service Act, which is part of the Department of Health and Human Services account. Senator Harkin included language in the appropriations bill that would reverse the original regulation, widely known as the gag rule. (While this is technically legislation on an appropriations bill, the Senate is much more tolerant of such provisions than the House.) When the president issued a veto threat, Harkin decided to challenge him.

Harkin was running for president and would benefit from the confrontation with President Bush. In general, congressional Democrats recognized that, win or lose, this issue would be an embarrassment for the president. A majority of Americans support freedom of choice and found the gag rule particularly repugnant. Were the president's veto overturned, he would suffer a significant setback—the first of his vetoes to be overridden. Even if the president's veto was sustained, there was significant publicity to be gained by forcing the Republicans' hand on this unpopular cause. (To be fair, there was also significant Republican support for overturning the gag rule.)

In order to give the bill the best chance to overcome the president's veto, opponents took two steps to reframe the issue to their best advantage. First, conferees decided to drop controversial language that would have required parental notification when abortions were to be performed on women under the age of consent. Such language would confuse the issue and potentially divide opponents of the gag rule. Opponents of the president's position wanted to guarantee that the anticipated override vote would be a referendum on the gag rule and the gag rule alone. Second, opponents of the gag rule tried to reframe the issue by arguing that this was not a question of abortion rights but of freedom of speech under the First Amendment and the privacy of the doctor-patient relationship. In fact, opponents argued, the gag rule had implications for all federally funded programs. Presumably, if the gag rule were allowed, speech could be limited in the context of any federally funded program.

The LHHS appropriation, as we have seen, was beset by controversial policy disagreements. Consequently, it was not a complete surprise that the conference report was approved in the Senate by a margin well in excess of the count needed to override a presidential veto, whereas the House failed to pass the measure by a two-thirds margin. However, there was still hope. Once the funding questions had been settled and agreed to, they could not be changed. The only issue the members would be voting on when they voted to override the expected veto would be the gag rule.

As predicted, the president vetoed the bill. On November 19 the House voted to override the veto and failed by a dozen votes (276-156). A companion measure (H.R. 3839), identical in every respect to the conference report with the gag rule (Sec. 514) language deleted, was prepared and quickly introduced. On November 22 the House, by a large margin, and then the Senate, by voice vote, adopted the measure.

With that act, the process for the adoption of the fiscal year 1992 budget came to an end. But there was still one more loose end for Congress to tie up before adjournment, a supplemental appropriation left over from the previous fiscal year. With the passage of that bill, on November 27, Thanksgiving eve, the session and the appropriations process came to an end.

CONCLUSION

As befits the end of the fiscal year and the congressional session, Capitol Hill during the months of September, October, and November was a blizzard of activity. Much of what was happening, however, was off the floor. Conference committees and committee staffs doggedly searched for compromise as the end of the session approached. The agreements reached were then quickly debated and passed on the floor. Much of the result was unpalatable to many members, but, for most, something is better than nothing. The rush of the upcoming holiday season ultimately produces the incentive to accept what had heretofore been unacceptable. In a flurry of activity the session comes to an end—until it is slated to start all over again the following January. Staffs are already beginning to prepare for the next year's budget even as the session draws to a close.

The rush at the end of the 1st session of the 102nd Congress was completely normal. Regardless of the procedural changes under the budget agreement, to say that the available work fits the time allotted still aptly applies to the deliberations of Congress. Most appropriations legislation was completed well after the end of the fiscal year. That the overall budget totals were less controversial than in previous years was undeniable, despite the fact that by the end of the year the budget deficit was slated to become, for 1992, the largest in history.

In the past, under the old Gramm-Rudman-Hollings regime, Congress in September and October was consumed by the need to meet mandated deficit reduction targets. Under the 1990 budget agreement, however, deficit restraint was removed from the process. While the appropriations subcommittees certainly did strain under the bonds of the spending caps and fire walls, much of the controversy at the end of the session was related to policy disputes such as the gag rule, abortion, and aid to the Soviet Union. Whether this outcome is to the betterment of the budget process is largely debatable.

The inevitable continuing appropriations bills that come at the end of the session were heavily influenced by the Budget Enforcement Act. Because of its pay-as-you-go provisions, there was simply no advantage to members to lard continuing resolutions with special interest funding. Under the BEA any extra spending in a continuing resolution would result in offsets, forced or otherwise, somewhere else in the appropriate account. This transformation was clearly a consequence of the BEA, a development that made the budget process more orderly and rational.

The work of the appropriations committees, hammering out agreements in conference, was in some ways different but in most ways the same. There was still plenty of money for pork-barrel spending. After all, within the context of the entire budget, pork is rather cheap. But there were also harbingers of trouble. External conditions such as the collapse of the Soviet Union and the contributions of our allies to Operation Desert Shield temporarily took some of the pressure off the defense and international assistance budgets. The only problems with those accounts was what to do with the extra money and whether the fire walls and spending caps set up a year before were appropriate to changing international conditions. Real pressure, however, began to build in the domestic discretionary account. These are the programs that take care of people and finance the government. Forward funding and cuts in other areas of domestic expenditures could only mean that the pressure for additional discretionary spending at home would increase and strain against the spending caps in the next session.

The end of the 1st session of any Congress marks the beginning of the political cycle. As Congress adjourned for the year, members began to position themselves for reelection. In normal years this involves claiming credit for bills sponsored, pork delivered, and constituent services performed. But in November 1991 the electoral outlook was different. Redistricting had destabilized a number of congressional districts, the economy was in dire straits, and the president was up for reelection. In order to compensate for political weakness and to attack or defend a weakening presidency, Congress in the last days of the session began to explore grand strategies of economic revival that strained against the budget process. Conservatives as well as liberals began to object to the constraints of the budget agreement. Would it survive another year? Was it worth the effort?

NOTES

1. The District of Columbia appropriation had been passed by both houses and gone through Congress, but the president vetoed the bill over the issue of public funding for abortions.
2. 1990 Budget Enforcement Act, Title XIII, Subtitle B, Section 13201 (credit accounting).
3. A placeholder is a monetary set-aside, a kind of insurance account, held against the possibility that a loan will not perform. The amount of the placeholder is a small percentage of the loan guarantee, the amount determined by the estimated creditworthiness of the loan recipient. Because Israel is a relatively trustworthy aid recipient, the placeholder required for loan guarantees is a relatively small percentage of the total.
4. Much of the background for this section is drawn from Stanley Bach, "Resolving Legislative Differences in Congress: Conference Committees and Amendments Between Houses," *CRS Report for Congress,* July 8, 1991 (revised), Congressional Research Service Report #91-538.
5. *Congressional Record,* October 24, 1991, H3486-H3490.
6. Conference committees are run under virtually no formal rules, being neither the province of the House or the Senate. The rules discussed in the following section (with the exception of the unit-rule requirement) are all a part of tradition or the result of a decision made by the conference itself. See Bach, "Resolving Legislative Differences," 28-29.
7. Conference committees have the option of issuing a partial conference report that covers all areas of agreement, leaving outstanding issues to be settled by the amending procedures of the respective chambers. If, for example, the House agrees to a partial conference report and adopts amendments in disagreement (insisting on its position), which, in turn, are agreed to by the Senate, the bill is completed and sent to the president.
8. The NIH primarily issues grants or, in essence, subcontracts for services. Thus NIH money is spent well in advance of the service (medical research) being performed; hence the higher outlay rate.
9. See Julie Rovner, "Conferees Unable to Choose Between Education, Health," in *Congressional Quarterly Weekly Report,* October 19, 1991, 3036-3037.
10. Quoted in Julie Rovner, "Labor-HHS Conferees Haggling Over Dollars, Not Issues," *Congressional Quarterly Weekly Report,* October 26, 1991, 3134.
11. While neither chamber allows the amendment of conference reports, on the Senate side the report is subject to extended debate unless cloture is invoked.

Thus, as a practical matter, at least a super majority is needed to approve a conference report.

12. User fees are not considered taxes and therefore are properly the province of the appropriations committees rather than the revenue committees.
13. The House bill (H.R. 2686) would have raised the fee from $1.97 per animal unit month (the amount of forage a cow can eat in a month) to $8.70 by 1995. Private grazing fees average about $9.66. See Phillip A. Davis, "Westerners Win Showdown over Higher Grazing Fees," *Congressional Quarterly Weekly Report*, September 21, 1991, 2684.
14. Specifically, the amendment barred the NEA from using funds "to promote, disseminate, or produce materials that depict or describe, in a patently offensive way, sexual or excretory activities or organs." See Phillip A. Davis, "Interior Conference Makes a Deal: 'Corn for Porn,' " *Congressional Quarterly Weekly Report*, October 19, 1991, 3020.
15. It should be noted that Yates's position was probably not in the minority among the general membership of the House (and even the Senate). Had a large majority of the House really wanted to amend the Interior appropriation, it would have succeeded. Instead, the way this delicate matter was handled provided political cover for most members involved. For those members who simply could not appear to support government funding of pornography, there were the Dannemeyer resolutions. For those who supported freedom of expression in the arts, there was Chairman Yates. In the Senate, too, members were well aware of Yates's strategic position and unflinching position in support of the arts.
16. Davis, "Westerners Win Showdown."
17. Quoted in Mike Mills, "House Turns Away Attempts to Cut Highway 'Pork,' " *Congressional Quarterly Weekly Report*, October 12, 1991, 2941.
18. Quoted in Mills.
19. *Congressional Record*, November 6, 1991, 9450.
20. 111 S. Ct. 1759.

PART III

Assessments and Reforms

CHAPTER 11

The Budget Agreement: More than a Failure, Less than a Success

The more things change, the more they stay the same. If this proverb was not coined to describe the work of government, it should have been. While the fiscal year may end, the problems of public policy continue to fester. The year 1991 was an eventful one. The Soviet Union died at age seventy-four; the United States entered and won a major war; and Congress operated under another new budget process. By year's end, however, the demise of the Soviet Union had not ended U.S. concern about the status of Russian weaponry or stability across the entire region. The victory in the Persian Gulf had not brought peace to the Middle East, nor did the new spending process bring the budget into balance. It is hard to know if the actions taken by government had a positive effect in dealing with these policy realms. After all, government is always trying to hit a moving target, relying on policies drawn from the lessons of the past. Anticipating the future is quite another matter. But it is fairly clear that the collapse of the communist bloc and the destruction of the Iraqi military made the world a safer place, if not as safe as we hoped or had been promised.

So it was with the reform of the budget process. There were marked improvements in the fiscal responsibility of the system, if not in the size of the deficit itself. But here again we must evaluate the success of reform against a moving background. In 1991, the year in which the 1990 budget agreement was fully implemented for the first time, the economy was in a full recession. Would the deficit have been even worse than its record-breaking $400 billion had the process remained the same? Probably so. Although no sea change took place in the fiscal health of the federal government as a result of the budget reforms, there were positive changes along the margins. There were problems with the budget reforms as well, irrationalities and diminution of democratic control. Almost certainly, however, significant advances were made in the procedural control of deficit spending, as well as a positive effect on the size of the deficit.

What remains to be determined is where the government should go to improve the system further. What changes in the process should be made? And, more importantly, what spending can be cut and what taxes raised so that the budget can be brought further into balance without threatening our economic and social system? In that respect, the October budget accord was a major disappointment. The cuts it mandated or made possible and the taxes it raised did little but reduce the increase in the deficit along the margins without attacking, head on, the regulatory failures, revenue shortfalls, and exploding entitlement budgets that are the core of the nation's deficit. As tough as it was to arrive at the October accord, the next step in budget reform is likely to be more difficult. From where will the leadership come for such a reform, and will the public be willing to follow? Is another adjustment in the process going to be enough, or is it going to take an even more dramatic change in the way that we as a society look at government policy?

THE 1992 DEFICIT—HOW BAD CAN A $400 BILLION SHORTFALL BE?

There might seem to be no way to soften the blow. For fiscal year 1992, the OMB was predicting a record $399.7 billion deficit. The previous high was a $268 billion deficit in fiscal year 1991. As serious as this situation may seem, these figures are misleading for several reasons. First, budgetary figures have no meaning unless compared with one another on the same scale, either controlled for inflation or standardized as a percentage of the gross national product. According to the OMB in February 1992, the deficit for 1992 would be 5.8 percent of GNP. In comparison, the deficit for 1983 was 6.3 percent of GNP (the previous post-Korean War high).[1] Averaged over five years, the deficit for fiscal years 1991-1995 would be about 3.4 percent of the gross national product, or well below the 1985-1990 average of 3.8 percent. (See Table 11-1.) Viewed in that context, the deficit figures for 1992 (about 6 percent of GNP), as alarming as they may seem, are more or less normal for the previous decade. According to mainstream economists such as John H. Makin, "Deficits averaging 3 percent of GNP have not proved debilitating either for the United States economy or other advanced industrial economies over the past ten years."[2]

Second, as dire as these numbers may seem, there is reason to believe that the deficit problem may actually be improving. Indeed, by some measures, the budget deficit is actually shrinking, or at least not getting worse. This measure is known as the primary deficit—the net

TABLE 11-1 Actual and Adjusted Deficits as a Percentage of Gross National Product

	1985	*1989*	*1990*	*1991*	*1992*	*1993*
Actual deficit	5.4	3.0	4.1	5.4	5.8	4.3
Business cycle effect	−1.0	0.3	−0.3	−1.3	−1.0	−0.6
Deposit insurance	0.1	−0.4	−1.1	−1.4	−1.9	−0.9
Interest payments	−3.3	−3.3	−3.4	−3.5	−3.5	−3.6
Adjusted deficit	1.2	−0.4	−0.7	−0.8	−0.6	−0.8

Source: Congressional Budget Office projections; and Rudolph G. Penner, "The Political Economics of the 1990 Budget Agreement" (Paper delivered at the American Enterprise Institute Annual Policy Conference, Washington, D.C., December 3, 1991).

deficit in interest payments on the debt. After all, interest payments are the only component of government spending that are pure transfer payments without economic effects. In fact, about the only effect of an increase in interest payments on the debt is to transfer resources from taxpayers to government bondholders, most of whom are U.S. citizens.[3] Otherwise it is difficult to calculate the true deficit effects of most of the rest of the budget. Defense spending, for example, may generate enough revenues to cover the cost of the original expenditure. Certainly, money spent on capital improvements such as roads, bridges, highways, sewers, and public transportation have economic (and revenue) benefits that may well exceed their costs. Because interest payments on the debt slowed in 1992 from an annual growth rate of 18 percent in the 1980s to about 5 percent, the primary deficit problem seems to be improving. In fact, when controlled for inflation, the growth of the primary deficit in 1992 was basically flat.

Finally, if we are to recognize the distinction between a structural deficit (one that is endemic to the system) and a cyclical deficit (one that is caused by a temporary downturn in the economy), there is some reason to be optimistic about the size and direction of the deficit, even as traditionally measured. The economy was in recession for all of 1991 and all of 1992. Consequently, some of the deficit, and probably a large part of the shortfall in revenues forecast by Budget Director Darman in his mid-session review, was a cyclical deficit. This cyclical deficit seems likely to disappear when the economy recovers.

Nevertheless, there are still some troubling signs that the federal government has yet to turn the corner completely in the permanent reduction and control of the structural deficit. Many unfunded commitments to provide governmental services have yet to be factored into the budgetary equation. For example, the federal government charters and oversees an entire range of credit guarantee programs known as GSEs (government-sponsored enterprises). These GSEs represent risks and public subsidies in the sense that they defy the market by providing investment credits for regions of the nation or sectors of the economy that are not served by the private market. Ginnie Mae (Government National Mortgage Association), Freddie Mac (Federal Home Loan Mortgage Association), Fannie Mae (Federal National Mortgage Association), the Farm Credit Administration, and the Student Loan Marketing Association all represent potential liabilities for the federal government. In fact, these five GSEs alone are carrying about $980 billion in outstanding obligations. While most GSEs are profitable and well capitalized, they are ultimately backed by the federal government.[4]

As previously noted, the Budget Enforcement Act made significant advances in instituting new accounting procedures that would factor into the budget the true costs of federal loan guarantees. For example, in the case of Israeli housing loan guarantees, the BEA requires that Congress set aside from the spending side of the budget a small percentage of the value of the loans to cover the costs of nonperforming loans. Nevertheless, there are many existing government liabilities that have yet to be adequately addressed in existing law. The failure to properly regulate the savings and loan industry has cost the federal government and the public billions of dollars. The cost of the bailout in 1992 was approximately $115 billion. This is the kind of unexpected expense that can be incurred as the result of federal guarantees. The government also provides deposit insurance for banks and pension funds and guarantees the survival of government corporations (such as the Postal Service) and loan assistance programs. All these guarantees represent a massive potential commitment some time in the future if banks and pension funds should begin to slip into insolvency. While it may be true that the savings and loan bailout is a one-time-only obligation, not enough was done in the Budget Enforcement Act to protect against similar occurrences in the future. Permanent banking legislation has hopefully put the savings and loan problem behind us. Nevertheless, there is still no way to account for the budgetary impact of costly regulatory (or deregulatory) policies.

EVALUATING THE OCTOBER BUDGET ACCORD

Even if the budget accord produces a modest improvement in deficit projections, it is not certain which parts of the agreement, if any, will or should survive. Which elements of the new process are of lasting value, and which components are neither politically expedient, fiscally responsible, nor democratically responsive?

Procedural Reform

Without question, the introduction of the pay-as-you-go (PAYGO) imperative is both a popular and a necessary improvement in the federal budget process. In 1991 PAYGO requirements forced appropriators to make some very tough decisions about priorities in federal funding. This sort of spending constraint on members of appropriations subcommittees has been effectively imposed all too rarely. Indeed, while there are still some ways to get around the PAYGO requirement (forward funding and emergency spending), the successful use of these exemptions was relatively rare and, in dollar terms, a very small percentage of the overall budget. The exceptions to the rule—funding for Desert Storm and for farmers savaged by a year-long drought—would certainly qualify as worthy exemptions to the PAYGO requirements.

Besides the regular appropriations bills, the PAYGO requirement also had a significant impact on other forms of budgetary legislation. Continuing resolutions, once the province of some of the most egregious and questionable pork-barrel spending, flowed through the legislative process, emerging in an unprecedented pristine form. PAYGO requirements removed the incentives and made it politically impossible to add most pork-barrel spending. The requirement that any new spending above the caps will trigger automatic sequesters in other accounts virtually guarantees broad-based opposition to the addition of discretionary spending to continuing resolutions.

Supplemental appropriations, too, were restrained by the PAYGO requirements. The fact that both the president and Congress have to agree that the spending is an emergency (to exempt it from sequestration rules) makes it exceedingly difficult to design supplemental appropriations that are catchall spending measures intended to make up for highly publicized cuts or the intentional underfunding that occurs during the regular appropriations process.

Tax bills, too, were affected by the PAYGO requirement. It is no longer as easy for members to bypass the appropriations process and use tax cuts to reward their constituents. Tax cuts must be revenue neutral or impose corresponding tax increases somewhere else. This requirement virtually guarantees there will be entrenched opposition to any changes in the tax code.

As noted above, the Budget Enforcement Act also introduced improved accounting procedures that went part of the way (albeit not far enough) to rationalize how the federal government scores the budgetary impact of its credit policies. It makes sense that the budget should account for these credit policies up front, before the inevitable costs of nonperforming loans are incurred. If anything, this philosophy in accounting for federal credit guarantees should be extended to other areas of regulatory policy.

FIRE WALLS

Although there seems to be a consensus in support of the PAYGO principle, some serious disagreements arose over whether prearranged spending caps and fire walls force decision makers into formulating inappropriate or irrational choices. While changing conditions had rendered the budget allocations under the spending caps somewhat irrelevant, with the exception of some modest changes, the caps did hold for another cycle in 1992.

The defense spending caps were probably too high and the domestic discretionary caps were probably too low. This is understandable, as it is difficult, if not impossible, to predict well in advance the needs of the government—precisely what the spending caps were intended to do. Economics is not an exact enough science to predict the performance of the economy, nor were political analysts capable of predicting as dramatic a change in international affairs as the collapse of the Soviet Union. In that respect, the spending caps and fire walls, which made it impossible for Congress to tailor its priorities to changing conditions, were about as useless as the old Gramm-Rudman-Hollings deficit reduction targets.

Before the 1990 budget accord, Congress was supposed to hit deficit reduction targets that had little relation to current policy. As a result, in order to meet its short-term responsibilities for deficit reduction under GRH, Congress was often forced to sacrifice programs that may have had a long-term, positive budgetary impact (such as capital improvement programs). Furthermore, Congress and the president were forced to create phony economic predictions to ensure that they met, as required by law, a shifting target over which they had only partial control. So it was with the spending caps and particularly the fire walls, which were an essential part of the 1990 budget accord. Fire walls prevented the transfer of needed monies from one account to another, and spending caps were quickly rendered obsolete by changing conditions.

There was no reason, in the midst of the collapse of the Soviet Union, accelerated by the August 1991 coup, why levels of defense spending allowed under the budget accord should have been set so high. Yet Congress could not transfer funds from the defense account to the domestic discretionary account because of the policy-making distortions imposed by the budget agreement. Of course, Congress is an institution that makes its own rules and could have breached the agreement (and it was tried several times). However, the fire walls in the budget agreement reinforced the position of supporters of higher levels of defense spending who intimated that any breach of the fire walls would result in the collapse of the entire accord.

In addition, the agreement created a distortion in the budgetary process. Under the new rules, any attempt to breach the spending caps or fire walls in the Senate was subject to a point of order that could only be overridden by a super majority (sixty votes) on the floor. This procedural requirement further reinforced the spending caps regardless of their relevance to current events.

Another distortion created by the spending caps and fire walls was the tendency of the appropriations committees to treat the caps as *floors* rather than *ceilings* on spending.[5] As originally envisioned, the caps were intended to be maximum levels of spending. Theoretically, any savings achieved in the spending accounts would be applied to deficit reduction (prevented by the fire walls from transferring the savings to other accounts). In practice, however, there were no savings to be applied to deficit reduction. The budget accord neglects one of the most basic principles of government budgeting: *appropriators tend to spend every cent they can get.* Money is power. To sacrifice programs for no good purpose other than to reduce the overall deficit—an exercise that will generate few, if any, political benefits—is not likely to happen. Instead, because there is no shortage of programs that deserve to be funded in every account, almost every penny available under the spending caps has been obligated. Only if the fire walls are breached will there at least be an incentive to change priorities in response to changing conditions.

Deficit Reduction

Former Comptroller General Rudolph Penner suggests that when adjusted for the business cycle (the recession), the savings and loan bailout, and interest on the debt (all spending that Congress can do little about), the deficit has been steadily declining since 1986.[6]

Much of this reduction, Penner argues, can be attributed to one-time-only cuts in defense and other discretionary accounts (the unpopular foreign aid account was particularly heavily impacted during this period). Penner predicts that this decline in the adjusted deficit will continue, despite the fact that savings in defense are not likely to be applied to deficit reduction (but rather are to be transferred to domestic programs) and that nothing has really been done to decrease the budgetary demands of entitlement programs. If Penner's (and the CBO's) projections hold, we can only conclude that procedural changes will continue to hold down that part of the deficit for which Congress is responsible. In fact, when controlling for the effects of the recession and subtracting what the deficit might have been had the existing law not been changed by the October budget agreement, current deficit projections yield a modest structural deficit reduction. According to John Makin, the budget accord resulted in a net $93 billion reduction in deficit spending across the five-year life span of the budget deal.[7]

Democratic Accountability

For years fiscal conservatives have been demanding that some kind of limit be imposed on the (profligate) spending powers of Congress. Among the most prominent suggestions are constitutional amendments that either require a balanced budget or allow for a presidential line-item veto. Of the two proposals in whatever form, the balanced-budget amendment is the more egregious diminution of democratic control. Requiring a balanced budget regardless of public demands or of public policy is not only undemocratic but also negates one of the most important functions of modern government. Government often serves to mitigate the negative effects of an economic downturn on its citizens. Furthermore, a balanced-budget requirement does not make economic sense. Forcing the government to cut spending just when the economy slips into recession is the height of folly. That is why most proposed balanced-budget amendments contain some kind of escape clause. In time of emergency the balanced-budget requirement could be waived.

The spending caps and the fire walls in the budget agreement are also undemocratic (and do not make much economic sense either). The caps are arbitrary, negotiated in advance as the result of a process that could have done little to account for the anticipated policy needs of the nation. As with the balanced-budget requirement, there are escape clauses that allow the requirements of the spending caps to be waived. But requiring a sixty-vote majority in the Senate to waive the act is an arbitrary, undemocratic condition.

By contrast, the line-item veto, while clearly a boon to presidential power, is certainly not undemocratic. The president, after all, is elected and (at least during a first term) subject to recall. In exercising a line-item veto, the president would face all the political consequences of making controversial budgetary decisions. In addition, because this veto represents a net gain in presidential power, the federal budget would reflect more of a presidential or national constituency than a congressional one.

The provision under the budget agreement that requires the president and Congress to agree on what constitutes an emergency exempt from the spending limits has come to resemble a limited line-item veto (limited in the sense that only appropriations beyond the spending caps are subject to the emergency waiver provisions). Consequently, these provisions should be judged differently according to a democratic standard. When Congress goes beyond the caps, particularly in voting supplemental appropriations, that marginal increase is subject to what, in effect, has become a presidential line-item veto. Should the president refuse to designate a particular budget item an emergency, for all intents and purposes that item will not survive.

President Bush's refusal to declare the Democratic unemployment compensation extension package an emergency is illustrative. The president's refusal presented congressional leaders with the choice of getting nothing, imposing a corresponding sequester on other entitlement accounts, or agreeing to some form of the president's proposal. The Democrats chose the last option. Is this exercise of presidential power undemocratic? Absolutely not. Whether the president was correct and whether it is better to have more of a presidential vision imposed on budgeting are other questions. Certainly a case can be made for the proposition that in a modern integrated economy the president's national perspective should be more strongly represented.

A final and crucial procedural adjustment to the spending caps results from changes in economic projections. The spending caps are subject to adjustment according to economic conditions. Projections of economic performance are the province of professional economists, mainly in the OMB. While this provision certainly confers a great deal of authority on professional economists, it also makes a great deal of sense. Adjusting the spending caps to the economy, while subject to the whims of anonymous economists, is a more democratic process than the fixed deficit reduction targets under GRH. To separate federal spending from the economy in either its discretionary or its mandatory forms, as was the case under Gramm-Rudman-Hollings, is to divorce the work of government from reality. It is senseless *and* undemocratic. There has been some concern that the OMB would abuse its forecasting power, but these fears have yet to be realized. Furthermore, both the public and Congress can check the abuse of the OMB's forecasting power in several ways. (After all, the OMB is directly responsible to the president.)

In terms of democratic control, therefore, the October budget accord is a mixed bag. Fortunately (albeit regrettably to some), the most blatantly undemocratic provisions of the agreement, the spending caps and fire walls, are only going to survive until fiscal year 1993. At the same time, the emergency designation exemptions and the process by which the caps are adjusted to economic conditions withstood controversies and uncertainties to be institutionalized as an accepted and valuable component of the revised budget process.

Winners and Losers

The appropriations committees, particularly the subcommittee and full committee chairs, are the big winners within the framework of the new budget process. The authority of the Appropriations Committee chair to make 602(b) allocations to the subcommittees was especially important in 1991 when the overall spending caps were already set by the October 1990 negotiations. In previous years the Appropriations Committee chairs had been dependent on the all too slow budget committees to produce the general outlines of the budget. With spending caps already entered into law, the appropriations chairs knew exactly how much money they could spread around to their subcommittees.

The appropriators played an especially active role in establishing the spending guidelines under which they would have to work. Senator Byrd, Appropriations Committee chair, was a key actor in the original negotiations establishing the budget accord. As a result, the cardinals in both the House and Senate, particularly Senator Byrd (who kept the 602(b) allocation process very centralized), were the primary beneficiaries. While the overall amount of discretionary spending may have been limited by the budget agreement, what money there was more closely followed the hierarchy of the appropriations process.[8]

The budget committees were, by contrast, the big losers. In 1991 they were relatively powerless because their primary function, setting budget priorities, had been supplanted (at least for three years, 1991-1993) by the budget accord. The budget committees were largely relegated to an investigatory role—to oversee the costs of Operation Desert Storm or to explore ways to reform the process even further.

The president also gained certain advantages through the new budget rules. The fact that the OMB is responsible for making the most important cost estimates of legislation for the purposes of calculating the PAYGO implications of any particular bill is a very important advantage to the White House. The emergency provisions in the budget agreement also give the president substantial independent authority in dealing with new entitlement spending or beyond the spending caps along the lines of a line-item veto.

In policy terms, probably the biggest winners were existing as opposed to new programs. PAYGO requirements made it politically difficult to adjust existing entitlements, create new entitlements, and tinker with the tax code. Under the new regime, every tax cut or entitlement adjustment generates entrenched opposition from constituencies who are made to suffer the cuts generated by PAYGO sequesters. Because it is so much easier to block rather than initiate policy through the legislative process, the PAYGO principle tends to lock in the existing tax code and entitlements. It is not clear that it is rational (or fair) to place further barriers against changing the tax code and the Social Security payroll tax, both of which were changed to the benefit of the wealthy in the 1980s. Nor should the government's array of entitlement programs that mainly benefit the middle class be held

TABLE 11-2 Spending Allocations by Appropriations Subcommittees, Fiscal Year 1992 (in billions of dollars)

Subcommittee	*Amount*	*Percentage change*
Commerce, Justice, State, and Judiciary	$ 21.9	12.5
Defense	269.9	−4.8
District of Columbia	.7	27.3
Energy and Water Development	21.8	4.9
Foreign Operations, Export Financing, and Related Programs	14.3	−13.1[a]
Interior	12.3	4.8
Labor, Health and Human Services, and Education	204.9	11.9[b]
Legislative	2.3	4.1
Military Construction	8.6	2.4
Rural Development, Agriculture, and Related Agencies	52.5	−2.9
Transportation	14.3	10.0
Treasury, Postal Service, and General Government	19.9	−4.9
Veterans Affairs, Housing and Urban Development, and Independent Agencies	80.9	2.5

Source: House Appropriations Committee.

[a] Does not include emergency Desert Storm assistance to Israel and Turkey.

[b] About 70 percent of the LHHS account is entitlement spending.

immune from budget cutting. By the same token, as noted above, the spending caps that have become de facto floors to spending and the fire walls that make it procedurally difficult to change priorities lock in existing discretionary priorities.

The original agreement, however, did mandate some important shifts in priorities (even as it established a process that tended to lock in the status quo). Table 11-2 traces changing priorities in budgeting, as reflected in the Appropriations Committee's fiscal year 1992 budget. Notwithstanding the problems with the budget *process,* this budget represents some important changes in response to shifting international and domestic priorities. Presumably, if the spending caps are further adjusted (renegotiated) for future budgets, the new priorities established will be more responsive still. It should be noted that the inflation rate for calendar year 1991 was about 3.1 percent. Any increase above that percentage rate represents a net gain for that particular function. Any increase (or decrease) below that rate represents a net cut.

At least in areas of spending controlled by the appropriations committees, the budget agreement allows for changing priorities. Nevertheless, only a little more than half of all federal spending is funneled through these committees. Almost all nonhealth, entitlements ($504.1 billion for fiscal year 1992), and interest on the debt ($206.3 billion for fiscal year 1992) are beyond the control of the regular appropriations process.

FOR THE FUTURE

By the above standards, the new budget process seems a modest improvement over existing law, particularly Gramm-Rudman-Hollings. As a result of the implementation of the agreement, some limited deficit reduction occurred and some important changes in the process were initiated. As with most budgetary politics, however, despite these changes our problems are far from solved. What direction should Congress take for future reform? There is much that still needs to be done.

The only way to know where to go is to examine where we have been. The following is a discussion of budgeting trends for the period 1981-1991, with a separate analysis of fiscal year 1992—the first year the new budget process was fully in place. Unlike Table 11-2, no distinction will be made here between controllable and uncontrollable funding, the assumption being that what is now uncontrollable in the budget can be made controllable through future reform. It is also important in considering the future of the budget process that we examine both trends and scale. After all, to eliminate all of the recently adopted Senate pay raise would be to eliminate only about $2 million in government spending, an insignificant figure within the context of a $1.45 trillion federal budget. Although the Senate pay raise has important symbolic political significance, in order to control the deficit much more fundamental issues have to be addressed. For example, raising federal income tax collections by as little as 10 percent would generate $29 billion in new revenues.

Overall, from 1981 to 1991, federal spending (when not controlled for inflation) increased more than 95 percent. At the same time, revenues increased only 76 percent. This means that either a 20 percent reduction in spending or a 20 percent increase in revenues (or some combination thereof) will bring the budget into balance. It is within that range that decisions must be made if true deficit reduction is to be achieved.[9]

RECEIPTS

Table 11-3 is a broad accounting of receipts collected over the course of 1981-1991. (Note that all figures for this period are expressed in average annual rates of change.) There are basically four sources of federal

TABLE 11-3 Federal Revenues, Fiscal Years 1981-1991 and 1992 (average annual rate of change)

Fiscal year	*Income tax*	*Corporate tax*	*Payroll taxes*	*Other*	*Total*
1981-1991	6.4%	6.1%	11.7%	3.3%	7.6%
1992	10.8	.6	7.9	9.9	8.7

Source: Joint Economic Committee, *Economic Indicators: November 1991* (Washington, D.C.: U.S. Government Printing Office, 1991). It should be noted that all estimates for fiscal year 1992 factor in the results of the OMB's 1991 mid-session review.

revenues: income taxes, corporate taxes, payroll taxes (mainly Social Security), and an assortment of other revenues including excise taxes, tariffs, estate taxes, and the collection of fees. Overall, revenues increased at an annual rate of 7.6 percent between 1981 and 1991. During the same period, expenditures increased at an annual rate of 9.5 percent. For fiscal year 1992, revenues were projected to increase 8.7 percent, or at a faster rate than in previous years (but still less than expenditures). It should be noted that the exact figures in the following section are subject to change, albeit in percentage terms by very little. By expressing these figures in percentage terms, I have preserved the general accuracy of my analysis; these figures in percentage terms are and will be accurate relative to one another as well as to the budget as a whole.

INDIVIDUAL INCOME TAXES—From 1981 to 1991 revenues from income taxes increased at an annual rate of 6.4 percent, or significantly slower than other revenues (not to mention spending). In fiscal year 1992 income tax collections were accelerated by, among other things, a decision in the budget agreement to correct for anomalies in the tax code that applied to those in the upper tax bracket (the so-called bubble). Income tax collections were projected to increase 10.8 percent in 1992. Income tax receipts represent about 45 percent of government revenues.

CORPORATE TAXES—Corporate taxes increased at an average annual rate of 6.1 percent during the 1980s. This, again, was at a rate slower than other revenues (and expenditures). For fiscal year 1992, reflecting the ravages of the recession, business profits were down, as were revenues from corporate taxes. In addition, the 1990 budget accord extended a number of tax breaks (net revenue losers) to business that were set to expire in 1991. Consequently, corporate tax collections in

1992 were to increase less than 1 percent. Corporate taxes, however, account for only about 9 percent of government revenues.

PAYROLL TAXES—In the 1980s Social Security taxes took a spectacular jump. At an average annual rate of 11.7 percent, Social Security contributions increased at a much faster rate than other government revenues as well as the expenditure rate. Hence, the federal government has been borrowing against the resulting Social Security surplus to help cover the deficit. For fiscal year 1992, payroll tax collections were to increase at a rate of 7.9 percent, much slower than in the past ten years. This occurred despite the fact that there was a substantial widening of the wage base (from $51,000 to $125,000) subject to the Medicare payroll tax. Nevertheless, payroll tax revenues are down because Social Security reforms agreed to in the early 1980s to shore up the actuarial strength of the program have already been implemented. Also the economy in 1992 was weak so that salaries and payroll tax collections were down. Payroll taxes represent about 40 percent of government revenues.

OTHER REVENUES—From 1981 to 1991, federal receipts from excise and other taxes increased at an annual rate of only 3.3 percent. For fiscal year 1992, these collections were projected to increase at a rate of 9.9 percent. This substantial increase largely reflects a 5 cent per gallon increase in the federal excise tax on gasoline agreed to during the October 1990 budget negotiations. Collections in this category represent only about 8 percent of government revenues.

This brief review of the federal tax structure suggests two important trends. First, the federal tax burden in the 1980s became significantly less fairly distributed. In other words, the 1980s were the decade of Robin Hood in reverse. The two largest sources of federal collections, payroll and income taxes, reflect this trend. As previously noted, income taxes (which grew at a slower rate) tend to be less class biased than payroll taxes (which increased). The 1990 budget accord went part of the way toward redressing this disparity. Not only were income taxes increased for the rich and cut for the very poor; the payroll tax system was made fairer by an extension of wages subject to the Medicare surcharge. Unfortunately, much of this improvement in the fairness of the tax structure was offset in 1990 by a substantial increase in federal excise taxes for gasoline, telephone service, and alcohol. Excise taxes are generally regressive.[10]

Second, it is clear that collections lagged, and continue to lag, behind expenditures. A fairly strong case can be made for the proposition that much of the shortfall in federal income taxes in the early 1980s was the unintended consequence of the Federal Reserve Board's successful attempt to control inflation in 1981 and 1982. The dramatic drop in the inflation rate had a dramatic *negative* effect on the deficit. When the inflation rate drops, so do tax collections. A lower inflation rate means that fewer individuals are pushed into a higher tax bracket. At the same time that revenues were falling in the early 1980s, the economy slipped into a severe recession that put further upward pressure on the expenditure side of the budget. Finally, even though the inflation rate declined, the federal government was still committed to paying a relatively high rate of return on Treasury bonds issued in the early 1980s. Interest rates, at the time, were relatively high (relative to the rate of inflation), which resulted in a substantial real increase in interest on the debt. Of course, there was also the effect of the Reagan administration's decision to cut taxes while at the same time increasing defense spending.[11]

Contrary to popular belief, taken as a whole, the Reagan tax policy was not a massive net revenue loser. Rather, the combination of the 1981 tax cut and the increase in the payroll tax had the effect of *reordering* the tax burden on a national scale. The poor and the middle class paid more and the rich paid less. Nevertheless, had the 1981 Tax Reform Act never been enacted, there is some reason to believe that the deficit would have been quite a bit smaller. In fact, Robert McIntyre, director of Citizens for Tax Justice, estimates that for 1992 alone the effect of the tax reforms that occurred starting in 1977 was a total loss of $164 billion.[12] McIntyre's estimates suggest that one major step toward deficit reduction would be to return to the tax code of earlier times (with much higher income taxes for the very wealthy).

For fiscal year 1992, federal revenues were expected to fall even farther behind federal spending. There is general agreement that much of this latest shortfall could be attributed to the effects of the recession. Much of this larger shortfall would occur because of increases on the spending side of the budget. Thus expenditures would increase in 1992 at a rate much faster than in the previous ten years. We will examine below the spending side of the federal budget.

EXPENDITURES

Table 11-4 is an examination of the expenditure side of the budget. It is important to note that in this table mandatory and discretionary spending are combined—this is *all* federal spending. It is also important to remember that the percentages below are average annual rates of change. Overall, between 1981 and 1991, spending increased at an annual rate of 9.5 percent. In 1992, despite adherence to the spending limits imposed under the 1990 budget agreement, spending was projected to increase at an annual rate of 12.9 percent. (Remember, during the same periods, revenues increased only 7.6 and 8.7 percent respectively.)

TABLE 11-4 Federal Expenditures, Fiscal Years 1981-1991 and 1992 (average annual rate of change)

Fiscal year	*Defense*	*International affairs*	*Health*	*Medicare*	*Income security*	*Net interest*	*Other*	*Total*
1981-1991	7.3%	2.4%	16.5%	16.7%	7.2%	18.4%	6.7%	9.5%
1992	14.3	10.5	22.1	9.4	8.6	5.4	27.7	12.9

Source: Joint Economic Committee, *Economic Indicators: November 1991* (Washington, D.C.: U.S. Government Printing Office, 1991).

DEFENSE—During the 1980s, defense expenditures increased at an average annual rate of 7.3 percent, much slower than the general rate of spending. In 1992 defense spending increased dramatically, reflecting the one-time-only costs of Operation Desert Storm. These defense figures are somewhat misleading, however, inasmuch as defense expenditures, more than any other discretionary account, tend to fluctuate dramatically over time. Large increases in defense expenditures in the years 1982-1986 have been offset to some degree by decreases (and smaller increases) of late. It may be appropriate to cut the defense budget at an even faster rate in future years. However, defense spending does not seem to be a major factor in the dramatic increase in deficit spending over the last few years. The defense budget comprises about 21 percent of total spending.

INTERNATIONAL AFFAIRS—Between 1981 and 1991, the international affairs budget increased at an annual rate of 2.4 percent, well below the general rate of spending and even below the rate of inflation. In 1992, foreign assistance was to increase at a rate of 10.5 percent reflecting the costs of the crisis in the Middle East. The international affairs account comprises only 1.5 percent of the overall budget and therefore is not a major contributor to budget deficits.

HEALTH—The federal government sponsors a number of programs that deliver health services and engage in health care research. About three quarters of the expenses in this account are incurred by the Medicaid program, which delivers health services to the poor. Between 1981 and 1991, the government's health costs increased at an annual rate of 16.5 percent, almost twice the rate of other expenditures. In 1992 that rate of increase was projected to rise even further to 22.1 percent. As with any other health care purchasers in the United States, the federal government would benefit from cost containment. However, direct health costs comprise only about 6 percent of total spending.

MEDICARE—Medicare is an entitlement program that provides health care mainly for the elderly. These expenditures have increased between 1981 and 1991 at an annual rate of 16.7 percent, almost twice the rate of other spending programs. In 1992, reflecting reforms adopted in the 1990 budget agreement, Medicare costs were slated to increase only 9.4 percent. The budget agreement mandates a substantial reduction in payments to health care providers, which will certainly save money but may make it more difficult for Medicare recipients to find doctors willing to accept the lower fees. Medicare payments comprise about 8 percent of total federal spending.

INCOME SECURITY—This is the welfare, food stamp, and unemployment compensation account. Between 1981 and 1991, this account increased at an annual rate of 7.2 percent, slower than the increases in some other areas of spending. For 1992, the spending rate in this account was expected to increase 8.6 percent, reflecting the consequences of recession (programs in this account are most sensitive to cyclical trends). Income security programs comprise about 12 percent of total federal spending.

SOCIAL SECURITY—Social Security disbursements increased at an annual rate of 9.3 percent throughout the 1980s—less than the overall rate of increase in expenditures. In 1992 this rate of increase was projected to fall back to 6.5 percent. Among other things, this slower rate of increase reflects a much lower rate of inflation that will affect cost-of-living adjustments for Social Security recipients. Social Security disbursements are not prohibitive, especially inasmuch as the entire system is in surplus (because of concurrent payroll tax increases). Social Security expenditures account for about 20 percent of federal spending.

INTEREST ON THE DEBT—Interest on the debt increased more dramatically than any other spending account in the 1980s, at an average annual rate of 18.4 percent. For fiscal year 1992, the interest on the debt was slated to increase at a rather modest rate of 5.4 percent. This drop in the rate of increase reflects, in part, the dramatic decline in U.S. interest rates in general. Interest on the debt constitutes about 15 percent of total expenditures (in 1981, by comparison, interest on the debt accounted for only about 10 percent of total spending).

OTHER—This is a catchall category of spending that includes transfers to state and local governments as well as the costs of federal banking system insurance funds, including the Federal Savings and Loan Insurance Corporation (now defunct), the Federal Deposit Insurance Corporation, and the Resolution Trust Corporation. These expenditures increased at an annual rate of only 6.7 percent throughout the 1980s, but this figure is misleading. The account was actually in decline prior to 1989, reflecting, in part, cutbacks in federal revenue-sharing programs. In 1989, spending in this account jumped almost 30 percent, reflecting the costs of the savings and loan bailout. In 1992, with the ongoing bailout, these expenditures were expected to increase at a rate of 27.7 percent. This account constitutes about 18 percent of total federal spending.

What these spending figures tell us is that the most dramatic increases in expenditures occurred and are still occurring in health-related accounts, interest on the debt, and costs associated with the savings and loan bailout. Since interest on the debt is truly uncontrollable (government really does not have the option of defaulting on its debts) and is also a function of other factors in the performance of the economy and budget, three priorities seem the most obvious targets for spending control: health care costs, the savings and loan bailout, and further reductions in the military.

The rising cost of health care in the United States is not only a national disgrace (in the sense that it creates a two-tier health delivery system), it is beginning to get in the way of the functioning of government and the competitiveness of American business. American manufacturers are at a distinct disadvantage when pitted against foreign competitors who do not need to compensate as much for this added cost of doing business. Government programs for the delivery of health care to individuals will continue to shortchange the needy either in scope or coverage until the rising cost of health care is brought under control. This is mainly a regulatory problem. Regulatory policy, which has an enormously complex effect on the budget, has yet to be factored into the process. It is true that the OMB does a cost-benefit analysis of all the regulatory policy proposed by administrative agencies, but it is not clear that the OMB is using the right standards. The budget agreement does not have a mechanism for factoring into the budget equation the costs or money saved by timely regulatory policy.

Another example of the negative effect of a failed regulatory policy is the savings and loan debacle. Had the savings and loan industry been better regulated, the cost of the bailout could have been avoided. Eliminating the estimated $115 billion the government was expected to spend in fiscal year 1992 to cover the savings and loan bailout would have gone a long way toward balancing the budget. The savings and loan scandal teaches us several important lessons that we may not be philosophically predisposed to learn. First, *some government regulation is useful,* especially when there is the potential that the public may be left holding the tab for the negative consequences of deregulation. In the case of federally insured deposit insurance, the government has a fiduciary responsibility to see to the health of the nation's federally insured banks and thrifts. The government failed in this responsibility, to the detriment of our fiscal health.

Second, some industries such as airlines and banks provide a public service that acts as a major lubricant for the economy. Certainly, a cost-benefit analysis of the deregulation of the airline industry is not complete until we enter into the equation the cost to society of the small and medium cities that are no longer served by airlines or the costs to society and to individual communities of the unemployment created by the collapse and/or reorganization of Eastern, Continental, Midway, Braniff, or Pan American Airways. Regulation is sometimes preferable. Deregulation, as a rule, is not always good. These are lessons that have yet to sink in and are certainly not addressed by budget reform. The Bush administration was a consistent advocate of the further deregulation of savings and loans, banks, and other industries.

Finally, on the revenue side, the effects of the budget agreement on the deficit are mixed. The short-term decline in revenues that contributed to Darman's gloomy mid-session review is probably less a consequence of the tax code or the budget agreement than it is the likely result of the recessionary economy. The fact that the budget agreement seems to limit the government's ability to stimulate the economy through fiscal or tax policy in times of recession is probably a weakness in the process. After all, the spending caps that restrict discretionary spending and the PAYGO requirements that limit entitlement and, particularly, tax policy do not distinguish between programs that are stimulatory, such as capital investment, and programs that are compensatory, such as unemployment compensation. It might make more sense to distinguish, for scoring purposes, between government spending for capital improvements and other governmental expenditures. Infrastructure maintenance and expansion have a different effect on the budget than do other types of government spending.

Certainly, government has a role to play in economic planning, but under the budget agreement the options of elected officials are so limited that only the Federal Reserve Board has the freedom to counter a recession. As we have seen, in 1982 the unintended consequences of the Fed's effort to stem inflation contributed to a massive deficit. Manipulating the economy through the Federal Reserve System is a tremendously unpredictable and undemocratic way of dealing with this most important function of government—regulating the economy. There must be a better way.

CONCLUSION

Ultimately, the budget agreement seems to have been more than a failure and less than a success. Although every year is different and it is hard to generalize from just one case, the establishment of spending caps as targets, the emphasis on spending as opposed to deficit control, and the imposition of PAYGO restrictions in 1991 seem to have had their intended (largely positive) effects. There are still irrationalities in the system, to be sure, but the budget process as a whole flowed more smoothly and came to a more complete decision in 1991 than it had for several years. The automaticity of the spending caps and the fire walls sometimes forced the government into a policy of the irrational. Nevertheless, the new accounting rules for compensating for the costs of federal credit programs make quite a bit of sense and are a good preliminary step in the right direction.

The reforms still to be made have less to do with the budget process than with our way of thinking. As much as half of the $400 billion fiscal year 1992 deficit could have been saved if the savings and loan system were not insolvent and the American system of health care delivery were rationalized. Avoiding these pitfalls requires a change in our attitude toward regulation. Not all regulatory policy is bad or costly. But changing our way of thinking is much more difficult than changing the budget process along the margins. The budget reforms, on a whole, are a good beginning, but leave a long way to go. There is, however, some reason to be optimistic. There is no structural reason that a more profound change of mind cannot be adopted. After all, Congress is an institution that makes its own rules.

NOTES

1. Office of Management and Budget, *Budget of the United States, Fiscal Year 1993* (Supplement), Part Five, 17-18.
2. See John H. Makin, "Perspective on America's Fiscal Policy: Before and After the 1990 Budget Agreement," (Paper delivered at the American Enterprise Institute Annual Policy Conference, Washington, D.C., December 4, 1991), 4. Makin is the director of fiscal policy studies at the American Enterprise Institute.
3. This also means that, as a collateral effect, high interest payments on the part of the government represent a net transfer of wealth from the poor and middle class to the rich who hold Treasury bonds. This raises certain fairness questions. For a discussion of measurement problems associated with the deficit, see Allan H. Meltzer, "Debt and Deficits: Some Measurement, Economic, and Political Issues," (Paper delivered at the American Enterprise Institute Annual Policy Conference, Washington D.C., December 4, 1991), especially 2.

4. See Congressional Budget Office, *Controlling the Risks of Government-Sponsored Enterprises* (Washington, D.C.: U.S. Government Printing Office, 1991). The report concluded that only one GSE is in a truly precarious financial position, the Farm Credit Administration, which is dependent on the vagaries of the growing cycle. The FCA holds about $63 billion in assets, mainly in the form of performing loans (see pages 82-83).
5. For a more complete rendition of this argument, see the "Statement of Allen Schick before the Task Force on the Budget Process, Reconciliation, and Enforcement," House Committee on the Budget, October 10, 1991, 4-5.
6. Rudolph G. Penner, "The Political Economics of the 1990 Budget Agreement," (Paper delivered at the American Enterprise Institute Annual Policy Conference, Washington, D.C., December 3, 1991), 11. Penner is currently an economist at the Urban Institute.
7. Makin, "Perspective on America's Fiscal Policy," Table 2, 63. While extremely modest, this amount of deficit reduction is probably appropriate given the downturn of the economy in 1991. A massive reduction in federal spending or a large increase in taxes in the midst of a recession could further exacerbate an already bad economic situation.
8. As much as $41 billion in new discretionary spending was gained by congressional appropriators during the October 1990 budget negotiations. Of this amount, there resulted $14.5 billion in outlays. See George Hager, "A One-Year Deal," *Congressional Quarterly Weekly Report*, December 7, 1991, 19.
9. Joint Economic Committee, *Economic Indicators: November 1991* (Washington, D.C.: U.S. Government Printing Office, 1991), 33. It should be noted that all estimates for fiscal year 1992 factor in the results of the OMB's 1991 mid-session review.
10. For a more complete comparison of the economic impact of the tax reforms contained in the 1990 budget agreement, see Pamela Fessler, "This Year's Battle May Be Over, But the War Has Just Begun," *Congressional Quarterly Weekly Report*, November 3, 1990, 3714-3717.
11. For a more complete rendition of this argument, see Robert Heilbroner and Peter Bernstein, *The Debt and the Deficit: False Alarms/Real Possibilities* (New York: Norton, 1989), especially chap. 2.
12. See Robert S. McIntyre, "Borrow 'n Squander," *New Republic*, September 30, 1991, 11-13. McIntyre arrives at this $164 billion figure by adding the direct costs of revenues lost as the result of tax cuts in 1978, 1981, and the Tax Reform Act of 1986 to the interest costs of the lost revenue.

EPILOGUE

When All Else Fails

Since the end of the first session of the 102nd Congress, the budget process has taken some twists and turns that are more or less predictable. Predictably, the fire walls imposed by the 1990 budget accord have been and still are under siege. Estimates of the budget deficit have continued to swell. More dramatic, however, has been the move toward the adoption of a balanced-budget amendment. At times during the session, it seemed possible that Congress would take such an amendment to the brink of the necessary two-thirds majority in both houses of Congress. Ratification by the states would probably then be a formality. Fortunately, the movement for such an amendment died. However, there is no reason to believe that the impetus for this sort of budgetary tomfoolery is permanently behind us.

The most outstanding feature of the second session of Congress was the overriding influence of electoral politics leading up to the 1992 elections. The second session of any Congress has never been a fertile environment for responsible policy making because members are positioning themselves for reelection and are distracted by events at home, especially if they have a credible opponent in their primary or general races. The result is a congressional session characterized more by the politics of theater than the politics of public policy. In most election years in the past, however, the influence of electoral politics has been muted by the power of incumbency, which insulates most members from a significant electoral threat.

But 1992 was an unusual year. Redistricting destabilized many constituencies; the scandals in Congress involving the members' bank and the House post office caused the public's opinion of Congress to plummet to an all-time low. Polls began to show, for the first time, that the majority of citizens were willing to condemn not only Congress but also their own representatives and senators. As a consequence, because members were vulnerable or just plain frustrated with congressional life, retirements in Congress rose to a historic high. A number of well-entrenched members lost in their party primaries. Add to this caldron the tumult of presidential politics and the ravages of a sustained recession, and all the elements were there for another round of politics of the irresponsible.

In 1980, with American hostages being held in Iran and the economy in the grips of stagflation, the American public was in a mood to accept the false and misleading promises of supply-side economics. The result, as we have seen, was one of the largest deficits in history. In 1992, in yet another fit of anomie, Americans seemed ready to embrace the next round of budget demagoguery. The argument that the national budget can be balanced by constitutional amendment is flawed in so many ways that it is hard to know where to start. If such an amendment were to have no effect at all (and it will not on the budget), it would be possible to ignore it and go on from there. However, a constitutional amendment of this type engenders much potential for a serious diminution of democratic control.

ON THE ROAD TO WEIMAR

One of the misfortunes associated with this movement toward a balanced-budget amendment is its poor timing. The tragic opportunity to be missed here is the historic chance to do nothing—or, more accurately, to stay the course. Any problem that took more than a decade to develop will probably take at least as long to resolve. And, in many ways, resolution seems at hand. Even as the deficit has soared to record highs (and higher still according to estimates made in 1992), it would be useful to compare this deficit to the previous post-World War II record in 1983; the numbers are roughly the same (as a percentage of GNP).[1]

In 1982, in the depths of recession, the gross national product *declined* at a rate of 2.5 percent. The 1983 deficit reflected this downturn. In 1991 the GNP again *declined* at a rate of 2.8 percent.[2] In turn, the fiscal year 1992 deficit reflected this decline. If the economy had performed at the same clip in 1992 as it did in 1984 (when the economy was in recovery), the deficit for 1992 would have been about 20 percent lower (and heading downward). As pointed out in the last chapter (Table 11-1), nearly *three-quarters* of the 1992 deficit was a function of the business cycle and increases in interest payments; neither factor is a direct function of the annual budget process. Much of the rest of the deficit was a function of the savings and loan bailout and unusually rapid increases in the costs of Medicare and Medicaid—the solutions for which are unlikely to be produced through the budget process.

We are about to kick the dog because the cat scratched the furniture. The programs that risk being cut as the result of a balanced-budget amendment have little to do with the increase in the deficit. Since we cannot cut payments on the debt or discontinue the savings and loan bailout, and because it is unlikely that we will cut off medical care to the indigent and senior citizens, any budget cutting will probably occur in the discretionary accounts. Besides the fact that discretionary spending has taken the largest budgetary hit in the last few years, it does not make much fiscal sense to cut these accounts across the board.

It bears repeating that *not every dollar spent by the federal government has the exact same effect on the economy*. Not only are the programs most likely to be cut not responsible for the deficit, they represent, in many cases, a long-term profitable use of our nation's resources. In other words, the balanced-budget amendment, as it will probably be enforced, will itself be a budgetary loser. Aid to education, law enforcement and infrastructure repair—large portions of the discretionary account—all have long-term payoffs. A balanced-budget amendment does not distinguish between winners and losers in the budgetary scheme. As serious as that is in the fiscal sense, even more disturbing is the potential of such an amendment for the diminution of democratic legitimacy.

Congress already has all the authority it needs to adopt a balanced budget. Its reason for not doing so has nothing to do with a lack of power. Therefore, the adoption of a balanced-budget amendment alone will not magically create the political will to achieve this goal. We have already seen that this was the case in the 1974 Budget and Impoundment Control Act and, later, the requirements pursuant to Gramm-Rudman-Hollings. The enforcement of a balanced-budget amendment would in all likelihood lead to a reprise on a grander scale of "doctored estimates" and the taking "off budget" of accounts in deficit, as occurred in the enforcement of previous budget-balancing laws.

The failure of a balanced-budget amendment to achieve its purpose would further erode public confidence in the problem-solving capacity of our government. As Louis Fisher, senior specialist at the Congressional Research Service, so aptly describes the potential of a failed balanced-budget amendment:

> Having failed to comply with statutory mandates in Gramm-Rudman and other laws, Congress will now advertise that it has no greater respect for constitutional commands. This result would only deepen public cynicism and disrespect of the national legislature. Large deficits in the annual budget threaten our nation. So do deficits of trust in our governmental institutions.[3]

Supporters of the balanced-budget amendment show an incomplete understanding of constitutionalism. The Constitution is more than a document sitting in the National Archives in Washington. Most nations have written constitutions that guarantee all manner of rights and liberties. What separates constitutional regimes from dictatorships is the degree to which government and society feel bound by the outlines of their constitution. By adding amendments to our Constitution that will ultimately result in deception and evasion, we erode the true foundation of constitutionalism in this country.

Having such an amendment in the Constitution has the potential to open a Pandora's box of new constitutional disputes. While it is not clear what the final balanced-budget amendment might look like, there is no way such a requirement can be constitutionalized without generating all manner of disputes that would eventually end up in the courts. So much of the procedure would be subject to disputed interpretation that federal budgeting would likely be dictated by the courts.[4] Are they any better equipped than Congress to do the job?

Supporters of the balanced-budget amendment argue that most state constitutions (forty-eight) have some kind of a balanced-budget requirement. Those states manage to balance their own budgets, they say, so why can't the federal government do the same? Hardly any argument in this entire debate is more pernicious and deceptive than this one. The fact is that *states operating under balanced-budget requirements do not balance their budgets.* In fact, they may do worse than the federal government.

In 1985 the General Accounting Office (GAO) studied the so-called balanced budgets of states with a constitutional balanced-budget requirement. The study reported that most states achieve balanced budgets simply by taking much of their spending off budget. In other words, when states authorize most capital improvement projects, including roads, schools, sewers, or housing, they fund the project by selling bonds. This is simply another way for government to borrow money. These bond obligations incurred are then excluded from budget accounting.[5] Thus, according to the GAO, states balance only 47 to 66 percent of their total budgets. The rest of the spending is off budget (but the debt is still there).[6] Were the balanced-budget amendment to pass, it seems likely that the federal government would adopt the same tactic. Is this deception a desirable alternative to a real calculation of assets to debts?

A MODEST ALTERNATIVE

I have made no secret of my support for some form of line-item veto as an alternative to the balanced-budget amendment.[7] However, the line item is no more a cure-all for our budgeting problems than is the balanced-budget amendment. This is true because a line-item veto would do little to address the true sources of the deficit: interest on the debt, the rise in the cost of health care, the savings and loan bailout, and the cyclical downturn in the economy, none of which are directly a function of the budget process. Nevertheless, the line-item veto has two great advantages; it is a democratic reform and addresses a very real weakness in the legislative process.

The line-item veto is democratic in the sense that it is wielded by political institutions subject to political control. The president will have to answer to the voters for deleting from the budget items that he believes are unimportant. Members of Congress, in turn, will also have to take the political heat for either voting to sustain or override the presidential veto. The balanced-budget amendment, by contrast, is undemocratic because it requires a budget in balance regardless of what the public wants or needs.[8] An automatic, arbitrary process for controlling budgeting is an authoritarian system of choice.

The line-item veto addresses a very real problem in the legislative budget process—the absence of macroeconomic planning. The U.S. economy in the eighteenth century was fundamentally different from that of the twentieth century, which is now completely integrated. The economic fate of one region is inextricably connected to the fate of the rest of the nation. The constitutional requirement that Congress regulate interstate and foreign commerce is more important now than ever before. And yet it is not clear that Congress is capable of macromanagement of the economy.

A line-item veto of some kind would undoubtedly enhance the power of the president to make budgetary decisions.[9] That is almost certainly the reason why Congress will oppose any form of the line-item veto. More to the point, a partial shift in budgetary focus to the presidency would lend a more powerful national perspective to the budget process. Because federal fiscal policy is such a crucial component of economic planning, it does not make sense for the president to be as removed from the budget process as he is today. A line-item veto would impose a democratically accountable, powerful macroeconomic influence on the budget process.

Nevertheless, there is some reason to be concerned that a line-item veto in the form of a constitutional amendment would subvert the American system of checks and balances and separation of powers. We should be loath to amend the Constitution, not only because of the obvious risks but also because constitutional amendments often have unintended consequences. The line-item veto should not be in the form of a constitutional amendment, nor should it require a two-thirds vote in Congress to override the president's veto. In fact, some of the power the president needs to veto individual items in the federal budget already exists, but may need to be strengthened.

We have already seen that the emergency requirements in the Budget Enforcement Act mimic, in a very limited sense, the characteristics of a line-item veto. The president, by refusing to designate an item as an emergency, can force the imposition of pay-as-you-go requirements (cuts in the budget in the amount over the spending cap). This provision worked well in 1991 when the president and Congress were forced to make some very tough decisions, especially when Congress passed three supplemental catchall appropriations for the Gulf War and emergency farm-drought assistance (and also the extension of unemployment compensation).

Another statute also mimics the line-item veto. Title X of the Budget and Impoundment Control Act authorizes the president to rescind appropriations already approved. These rescissions are then subject to congressional approval. If Congress does not act in forty-five days to approve the rescissions, the funds must then be released. As a practical matter, most rescissions are never acted on by Congress and therefore never approved. Nevertheless, on occasion, when there is a strong consensus in favor of budget cutting, large-scale rescissions have been approved. For example, after the 1980 election, President Reagan managed to get Congress to accept a number of rescissions that molded, in accordance with Reagan's preferences, the budget that he inherited from Jimmy Carter. More recently, in the spring of 1992, Congress approved a package of rescissions recommended by President Bush. The package approved by Congress, $8.2 billion in rescissions, did not resemble *in content* the president's proposals, but it did exceed *the amount* of the president's recommendations.[10]

On the basis of this experience, it is quite possible that the president will continue to use the Impoundment Control Act to require that Congress take a second look at some of its spending decisions. In the past, the president has either been unsuccessful or reluctant to use the Impoundment Control Act in this way precisely because of what happened in May 1992; he got the amount of rescissions he requested but not in the areas he wanted to cut. If we desire more centralized spending control, it might be necessary to strengthen the president's hand in the use of the Impoundment Control Act (which can be done through statute rather than requiring a constitutional amendment).

There are two basic ways to amend the Budget and Impoundment Control Act. First, changes can be made in the way that Congress considers the president's rescission proposals. For example, the bundling of rescission requests could be restricted. Congress should vote on each rescission proposal individually in order to gauge its merits more accurately. However, since Congress is an institution that makes its own rules, it is likely that any internal rules change would be waived at the convenience of the institution. Instead, a more likely target for reform would be in the sequence in which impoundments are considered. As the law now reads, Congress need not act to disapprove presidential rescission requests. It would be possible to amend the law to require Congress to act. Were Congress not to act, the rescission would then stand. While this proposal has some potential practical and legal problems, the result would be a more modern approach to national budgeting.[11]

CONCLUSION—TRIUMPH OF THE WILL

Even this reform is unnecessary if Congress and the president are willing to act together. *There is no shortage of procedural tools that Congress and the president can use to manipulate the budget.* I am reluctant to suggest in the conclusion of this tome on procedure that a procedural solution is not the answer to our deficit problems. However, in good conscience, I am forced to come to that conclusion. A modified line-item veto only improves our ability to better manage the economy. No procedure, no system, no method is going to suffice to cut the budget in the absence of the will to do so. Americans are great believers in structural rather than political solutions to the problems of governing, but they are simply wrong about this. No matter how much we as a people detest politics as a solution to our problems, there is no other way.

In truth, there is no procedural fix in budgeting to ensure that we will make ends meet. We may be able to balance the budget, but the only way to decide who wins and loses in this struggle will be through the rough and tumble of the political process. There is no "equal" way to cut the budget because there is no societal consensus on what constitutes equality. Therefore, the pursuit of equality in budget cutting or any other societal endeavor will always be an ongoing quest. *The best we can hope for in our democracy is that decisions concerning the distribution of goods will be made by responsible individuals and institutions—responsible, that is, to the will of the people.* The only alternative is authoritarianism—the authoritarianism of automaticity (the balanced-budget amendment) or the authoritarianism of decision making beyond political control (bureaucratic decision making).

The lure of demagoguery is the siren song of democracy. By suggesting that we do nothing at this pivotal point in our history, I am suggesting that we lash ourselves to the mast that is our Constitution. To weaken that structure and fall victim to the appeals of those who would tell us that there are easy solutions to difficult problems is to risk dashing our country against the shoals of financial and political ruin.

NOTES

1. *Budget of the United States, Fiscal Year 1993.*
2. Joint Economic Committee, *Economic Indicators, June 1991* (Washington, D.C.: U.S. Government Printing Office, 1991), 3.
3. Statement by Louis Fisher, Congressional Research Service, before the House Budget Committee, May 11, 1992, 6.
4. For a discussion of all the potential problems in interpreting at least one of the most likely models for a balanced-budget amendment, see James V. Saturno, "Memorandum: H.J. Res. 268, a Proposal for a Constitutional Amendment to Require a Balanced Budget: Potential Questions of Interpretation," Congressional Research Service, July 10, 1990.
5. In just one instance, the *Atlanta Journal/Constitution* reports that in 1991 the five counties that compose the metropolitan Atlanta area incurred more than $800 million in debt through the sale of bonds. In comparison, only about half that amount of debt was incurred in the previous year. It should also be noted that almost $600 million of those new obligations in 1991 were undertaken *without voter approval.* See Richard Whitt, "Bond Deals Pinch Taxpayers," *Atlanta Journal/Constitution,* June 21, 1992, A1, A9.
6. General Accounting Office, "Budget Issues: State Balanced Budget Practices," December 1985.
7. See Daniel P. Franklin, "Wishful Thinking and the Budget Deficit," *Public Affairs Quarterly* 3 (October 1989): 1-14.
8. In actuality, the most prominent balanced-budget proposals would allow deficit spending if a super majority were to concur. For example, H.J. Res. 290 (with almost 280 cosponsors), Section Two, requires a three-fifths majority in both houses to increase the debt. This requirement would contribute to a tyranny of the minority, which could block deficit spending.
9. This is not an absolute certainty. In many states where the governor has a line-item veto, the legislature still dominates the budgetary process.
10. In May 1992 the Senate passed an $8.3 billion rescission package (S. 2403), and the House approved $5.8 billion. The president had rescinded $7.9 billion. The final amount, almost $8.2 billion, was negotiated in conference committee.
11. One problem with this proposal is that it might be considered by the courts a "legislative veto," in the meaning of the 1983 *INS v. Chadha* decision (462 U.S. 919) and, therefore, unconstitutional. There is also the potential here for a tremendous increase in the legislative workload. As a practical matter, it is going to be impossible to prevent the bundling of presidential rescission proposals if for no other reason than to save time.

Index